Indien Ethnography

◈ **Cultural Traditions of Native North America** ◈

Dr Jay Miller

Apt images drawn by Owen Shaffer for these ethnographies appear in

North American Indian Arts, Andrew Whiteford, Golden Press   1970

Foreword

Culture is endlessly engaging (whether near or far) because it varies so among humans, often ingeniously. It is, or can be, the same, similar, different and deliberately reversed among neighboring communities. It is like life itself. For the past to be carried into the present, though, cultural experiences become sifted down to relevant and remembered details mixing the most ancient and the most recent, with the midrange often left out. In written traditions, however, basic documents remain behind to fill in nuance and complexities. Oral traditions, especially when reported by outsiders, leave out much in the on-going process of sorting and translating. Complex systems of information build upon profound ideas, derived from everyday and prosaic basics, and enrich them with symbolic meanings that are known to varying degrees throughout a community.

To convey such fragile richness and variety, this book attempts to do many things while concentrating on engendered variations in Native North America. Further, our presently known world is huge, with North America just part of this whole. Events and attitudes now involving natives often developed far away in other places and contexts around the globe. Too often, texts about Native Americans lose sight of the larger anthropological context of all humanity. For that reason, this book includes comparative examples and illustrations from other places and times.

In the preface, ordinary complexity requires many names. While Native Americans in the United States and First Nations in Canada are currently the politically correct terms, we will use ochers, Indiens, and tribal designations interchangeably. Similarly, European, chalk, and settlers will be used for the newcomers, colonists, and misnamed pioneers. People have many names, not just one, depending on different kinds of situations.

After several decades devoted to understanding Native North America, four useful terms help to translate basic Americanist concepts. Each will be considered in turn.

A word already accepted elsewhere resolves major difficulties for cross-cultural comparisons. Adopting the French (also Italian, Danish, etc) spelling of <u>Indien</u> clearly distinguishes natives of the West Indies and Americas from those of far off India (Indians).

The all-pervading concept of power~life force~potency~energy~vitality of the engendered cultures of the Americas will be called *puwha*, blending terms from Algic languages (*powwow*) of the East and Numic ones (*puha*) of the West. Capitalized names indicate immortal species rather than biological mortals. Raven is mythic but raven scavenges on the beach.

Two terms, needed to convey the patterned complexities of these native lifeways, are anagrams of <u>sig(er)</u> from "special interest group (leader)" and of <u>tysic</u> from the first letters of the words "time space center" with vowels pointing down (y) and up (i). Yup'ik Eskimos of Alaska nicely capture this temporal and spatial fusion (time + space as one) in their design ☉ of a circle around a central dot, as their language does with words like <u>ciuliaq</u> = "ancestor, leader" from <u>ciu-</u> meaning "the forepart of a body, front area, or time before"; in contrast to <u>kingu-</u> = meaning "rear end, back area, or time after".[1]

Native elders often complain about the self-centered young. In seeking to have their own way, youngsters often bend to selfish, solipsistic desires. Academia has been in such a mode as critical cultural theories deny the validity of structures, judgments, and basic ("true") understandings. Making it seem mysterious is an old ploy. While most Europeans have seriously failed to grasp the basis for other cultures, each side needs to keep the other guessing. Colonialism is built on doubt.

Any language must have a grammar with units of sound, meaning, expression, and interconnecting logic based in universal ~ pan-human conceptual relationships. These serve to imbed and nest the less expansive notions within broader ones. Such a nested series is a _matrix_ – consisting of specific, generic, and categoric members. A culture, arguably, integrates similar building blocks and interlinking logic with an articulating overall tension. For the Americas, this structuring tension is most often an explicit engendering by Man/Woman as bridged by Mind. Throughout the Americas, however, relations between these genders and matrices vary widely, providing a rich outlet for creativity, regional variety, and local diversity.

Endnotes

1. Ann Fienup-Riordan, <u>Eskimo Essays</u> 1990: 202, 212.

Foreword

TABLE OF CONTENTS

Contents

DEFINITIONS

Special words with agreed upon meaning are important for clarity in the exchange of ideas. They must be mastered in order to grasp the principles and intent of a particular outlook. All fields have such idioms ~ argots, including sports. For example, consider the next two paragraphs.

In 71 words: This guy carrying a fat stick walked up to this rubber square and stood with his knees slightly bent into a crouch. This other guy standing on top of a pile of dirt in the center of the field threw a white ball at the first guy, who hit it. Then he ran around a diamond shape with rubber squares at the corners until he got back to where he started.

In 17 words: The batter stepped to the plate, slammed the pitch, and ran the bases for a home run.

That is why we need definitions, particularly in anthropology where we cross all kinds of boundaries between cultures and disciplines. Pronunciations for most of these words can be found in any English dictionary, but those with foreign origins have been given approximations between "quotation marks". A few are translations into English.

ACADEMIC = Someone who has qualified through a formal course of study, holds a recognized degree, and is employed in a research related career.

AFFINE = Relatives through marriage.

AFFIX = A grammatical particle that must be attached properly to other word forms (units) in order to convey its meaning. Affixes are usually divided into prefixes (as in English re-volve, de-volve), infixes (as in English sit, sat), and suffixes (as in English look-ed, look-ing) .

AGE GRADE = A social group based on the close ages of its members, who are sometimes further divided into age sets that are even nearer in age.

AGNATIC = Relationships traced through the father or males.

AMBILATERAL = Tracing descent through both parents such that one must choose to activate membership in one of a fixed number of descent groups. Some Salish people have options in any of eight descent groups through their great grand parents, only a few of which are activated at any given time.

AMERIND = A contraction formed of American + Indian.

AMITATE = Special relationship between children and someone in the category of paternal aunt, father's sister (FZ).

ARGOT – Specialized words and forms of speech, often associated with an occupation.

AVUNCULOCAL = Residence with a maternal uncle, usually of the groom, in anticipation of matrilineal inheritance from a mother's brother to a sister's son.

BEHAVIORISM = Perspective that holds that the world is understandable in concrete, empirical terms as the result of cause and effect relationships.

BERDACHE "ber-dash" = A man (XY) who adopts the clothing and activities of females, although the role may not involve either homosexual or heterosexual relations. The justification for assuming a berdache position is usually both supernatural vision and personal. A female berdache is a genetic XX who takes on a male identity. Among urban gay natives, "two spirit" is the preferred term.

BILATERAL = tracing descent through both parents equally.

BIOME "bye-ohm" = The largest biological community as recognized by its climax character, including seral stages, such as tundra, desert, deciduous forest, etc.

CACIQUE "ka-seek-ay" = A Jamaican term borrowed by Spanish explorers to refer to the native, often religious, leader of a town, especially a Southwestern Pueblo.

CLAN = A unilineal descent group tracing descent from an ancestor or entity who is often not just human, such as a plant, animal, star, or mythic figure. Clan members share mystic ties and common leaders.

COUP, Counting Coup "koo" = The Plains practice of earning military honors by recklessly touching an enemy, stealing a horse, or otherwise risking one's life for the welfare of the group.

COMPLEX = A convenience term for an assemblage of archaeological features and artifacts from a particular area during a specific time period.

CONFIGURATIONISM = The study of the culture-whole in terms of the key features of its integration.

COUSIN TERMINOLOGIES = The six types of kinship terminologies for categorizing close relatives in the generation of Ego: HAWAIIAN (everyone is brother or sister), ESKIMO (siblings are distinguished from cousins), IROQUOIS (siblings and parallel cousins are combined (lumped together), cross cousins are distinct), SUDANESE (siblings, parallel, and cross cousins are distinct), OMAHA (Patrilineage members are separated out, MB=MBS=MBSS), and CROW (Matrilineage members separated out, FZ=FZD=FZDD).

COUVADE "koo-vaad" = A cultural practice in which the father of a new born simulates the process of giving birth and lying-in to join his wife in following various food, work, or clothing taboos.

CROSS COUSINS = The children of siblings of opposite sexes: FZch and MBch.

CULTURE = The human species-specific adaptation consisting of an integrated conceptual system defining a particular localized society, such as the widening relationship among Echo, Matrix, and Emanations.

CULTURE AREA = A mega-cultural region showing similar patterns of ecological adaptation, social structure, and constituent philosophies, often further divided into provinces on the basis of closer similarities.

CULTURAL RELATIVITY = The basic tenet of anthropology that every society and culture is as good as any other in terms of satisfying the needs and desires of its members.

DIALECTIC = The dynamic process of viewing an entity as simultaneously itself, its opposite, and a synthesis resolving these antagonists.

DIBBLE = a digging stick, used in traditional subsistence activities.

DOUBLE DESCENT = tracing descent from either of both parents such that one parent provides one affiliation and the other parent another membership. Among the Keres, clans are inherited maternally, while religious group (kiva, priesthood) are a paternal inheritance.

EGO "ee-go" = the point of reference for tracing kinship, Latin word for "I."

EMIC "ee-mik" = the attempt to parallel or approximate the viewpoint of a native participant in a community, generally by embedded linguistic terms, conceptual categories, logical relationships, and rationalist arguments.

ENVIRONMENTAL DETERMINISM = The discredited theory that the environment of a people automatically establishes personality (by hot, cold humors) and social patterns. Current ecological opinion recognizes only that the environment will permit or discourage any of a range of possibilities.

ENDOGAMY = Marriage within a specific social group.

ETHNOCENTRISM = The conceit that one culture or society is inherently better than others; usually that one society is your own.

ETHNOGRAPHY = Careful descriptions of human lifeways and expressions.

ETHNOLOGY = Comparative analysis of human lifeways and expressions.

ETIC = the attempt to present an objective, acultural, "scientific", outsider viewpoint on particular phenomena, generally in term of measurable, behavioral, universal, comparative arguments.

EXCLUSIVE/INCLUSIVE = The symbolic cultural opposition between one category defined as bounded, closed, limited, specific, and exclusive; and another opposite category defined as unbounded, open, ambiguous, general, generic, and inclusive.

EXOGAMY = Marriage outside of one's own social group.

GRAMMAR = The structure of all human languages, generally viewed as composed of a sound system (phonology), a meaning system (morphology), and rules for ordering all these elements (syntax).

GUILD = Social grouping or club based on occupation and attendant rituals.

INDIEN = A native whose ancestry is rooted in the Americas, the Indies by extension, following a continental European spelling.

INFLECTIVE = Languages characterized by changes in form that convey grammatical distinctions such as case, gender, number, tense, aspect, voice, etc.

HYPERGAMY = Marriage to someone of higher status.

INTELLECTUAL = A sustained thinker with intuitive ability and probing curiosity.

INTERGLACIAL = A time period of glacial retreat between major glacial advances.

INTERSTADIAL = A time period within a glacial advance represented by minor fluctuations or retreat.

JOKING RELATIONSHIP = Kinspeople, who are often already affines, easing social tensions and likely conflicts by making ribald or obscene insults because they are potential spouses.

KILL SITE = An archaeological site associated with the killing and butchering of large animals.

KINDRED = A kinship grouping (personal, nodal, stem, prestige) based on bilateral descent. In American society, everyone has a "personal kindred" composed of all known relatives. Some Americans also have a "prestige kindred" composed of those relatives who trace a relationship to someone wealthy, famous, or notable.

KINSHIP SYSTEMS = Patterned ways of recognizing descent or relationship with humans and other beings based on marriage and shared substances such as blood, flesh, bone, or spirit.

KIVA "kee-vah" = A semi-subterranean square or round building used for religious and ritual activities by Pueblo peoples, also as a clubhouse by men.

LANGUAGE FAMILY = A collection of languages sharing a common ancestry and considerable internal similarity.

LANGUAGE STOCK = A collection of languages sharing a remote common ancestry and showing considerable internal diversity.

LEXICAL = A linguistic unit of sound and meaning serving as affix, root, stem, or word.

LEVIRATE = Marriage type in which a man married the widow of his 'brother'.

LINEAGE = A unilineal descent group, usually three generations in depth, GF=F= S or GM=M=D.

MANLY-HEARTED WOMAN = Northern Plains women who are noted for their aggressive, outspoken personalities and warrior attributes.

MARKED/UNMARKED = The linguistic opposition between words or concepts that are specific, demarcated, closed, exclusive (marked) and those that are general, ambiguous, open, inclusive (unmarked).

MATRILINEAL = Kinship system in which descent is traced through women, inheritance comes from the mother, and authority passes from someone in the category 'mother's brother' to someone in the category of 'sister's son.'

MATRILOCAL = Residence with the descent group of the bride, who becomes a mother.

MOIETY "moy-et-ee" = A social structure based on the division of the world into halves such as right/left (Kansa), sky/earth (Hochungara), summer/winter (Tewa), light/dark (Sauk), and so forth.

MYSTIC BUNDLE = A container generally of hide in which are kept metonymical aspects of various things, such as feet, claws, birds, stones, plants, etc., which in combination serve to concentrate various cosmic *puwha* at this one place for a given purpose. One Native intellectual once likened a Power Pack to a radio: useless as individual pieces but a powerful means of communication when correctly combined, much as a computer linked to the "web."

NATIVE = an indigenous, deeply rooted inhabitant of Native North America.

NEOLOCAL = Independent residence established by a married couple.

NODAL KINDRED = A bilateral kinship grouping composed of parents, siblings, and spouses clustering around a node of parents, then siblings.

OLACHEN "oo-lik-on" = An anadromous smelt-like fish (<u>Thaleichthys pacificus</u>, Candlefish, eulachon, ulakon, oolachon, hooligan) noted for its very high oil content, and once plentiful in the Nass River during spring runs.

PAIDEUMA "pie-doom-a" (Greek for 'that which is instilled') = The all-pervasive property (echo) of a culture whole, considered, throughout this text, to be dyadic categories in tension.

PALEO-INDIEN = Asiatic ancestors who lived in the Americas 20-7,000 years ago.

PARALLEL COUSIN = The children of siblings of the same sex: FBch and MZch.

PATRILINEAL = Kinship system in which descent is traced through males, inheritance comes from the father, and authority passes from the categories of 'father' to 'son.'

PATRILOCAL = Residence with the descent group of the groom, who becomes a father.

PHRATRY "fray-tree" = A cluster of linked clans.

PIKA = A high altitude lagomorph (<u>Ochotona princeps</u> in the Rockies and <u>O. collaris</u> in the Yukon) related to rabbits and hares, and noted for drying various grasses and twigs in the sun for storage as winter food.

POLYANDRY = Marriage type permitting wife to have more than one husband, generally serving as a means to retain scarce resources among males and children.

POLYGAMY = Many marriages allowed at the same time.

POLYGYNY = Marriage type permitting a husband to have more than one wife, generally correlated with high male status and requirements of hospitality and generosity by his household.

POTLATCH "pot-latch" = A formalized redistribution of crests, privileges, people, and resources before a body of witnesses, who are given food and gifts to validate changes in the fabric of Pacific Northwest societies.

POWER PACK = See Mystic Bundle.

PRECOPERNICAN = A world view which is anthropocentric: pervaded by the human metaphor based on the complementarity of Man and of Woman.

PRONGHORN = An ungulate that is not a true antelope but rather the last surviving member of its class (Antilocapra americana), noted for its swiftness and horns on both sexes.

PTARMIGAN "tar-muh-gan" = A gallinaceous bird (Lagopus spp.) with completely feathered feet, related to grouse, common in arctic conditions.

PUWHA = power ~ life force ~ potency ~ energy ~ vitality of the engendered cultures of the Americas

RATIONALISM = Perspective that holds that the world is understandable in logical terms, which means that nothing is ever only what it seems.

SCHOLAR = Someone who has left a record of his/her thought, experiences, and reflections.

SHAMAN "shah-man" = A part-time specialist able to clarify any ambiguity so that he (rarely she) is adept at mystical journeys, curing, divination, and cosmological mediation.

SIG, SIGER = Special interest group; someone in charge of an activity. Cf tasker

SITE = An archaeological locale (unit, space) associated with human activities, such as a Habitation Site = indicating some type of domestic occupation or a Kill Site = indicating the slaughter, butchering, and processing of larger animals.

SODALITY = A social group that recruits on a voluntary basis, members share only a willingness to have joined and served that organization.

SORORATE = Marriage type in which a woman marries the widower of the deceased 'sister'.

STRUCTURALISM = The study of discrete human productions, often mental constructs, in terms of pervasive relationships, which are frequently found to be dyadic through analysis.

TASKER, Task Leader = A group leader who functions for the duration of a specific activity by virtue of his spiritual puwha, experience, and abilities. Cf Siger

TRADITION = That which holds a community together, generally but not always some belief or practice that is regarded as ancient and venerable.

TRANSHUMANCE = Seasonal movement among a series of fixed camps at resource areas, usually associated with the husbanding of animal herds.

TRANSLATOR = An adept Native intellectual who provides insights and information about the community in which he / she resides as a member, often from birth.

TYEE = Chinook Jargon word for a leader, noble, or member of the elite.

TYSIC = anagram of time space center, a crucial pivot, node, or nexus orienting people to all dimensions.

UNILINEAL = tracing descent through only one parent.

UTERINE = Relatives traced through the mother or females.

WAPITI "wah-pit-ee" (Cervus canadiensis) = Large American mammals, compared to European elk, which are antlered, unspecialized plant feeders.

WEIR = a fence-like barrier set across a stream or river to send fish runs into traps.

The English language allows for certain modifications to any word such as those used here, mostly as a suffix at the end of the word. In this way, -ist means someone interested in something, as a Puebloist is interested in research among the Pueblo Nations of New Mexico and Arizona; -ic refers to language, as Tsimshianic is the language of the Tsimshian; -an makes a noun into a more encompassing adjective, as Puebloan means a wide range of things having to do with the Pueblos.

Similarly, punctuation has been added to extend a meaning of the written text. For directness, the = indicates significant equivalences. Parentheses ( ) after a word presents a more correct, clarifying, or precise way of saying the same thing, such as medicine bundle (power pack). Quotation marks " " mean that the word or phrase should not be taken at face value because irony, distortion, historical bias, or misunderstanding are involved. Words like "primitive" and "beast of burden" are used only because they reflect prejudice of another (European ethnocentric) time. Words for important concepts or spiritual forces appear with a capitol first letter (Spider the trickster, spider the bug) to distinguish them, as noted.

F = father **B** = brother **S** = son **G** = grand, great, **e** = elder, **y** = younger
M = mother **Z** = sister **D** = daughter

For ease of presentation, several icons have been used.

=	the same as, equivalent, translated as
<	derived from
-	connected with, linked in a series
+	closely linked with, overlapping
/	opposed to, in contrast with, intense division between
( )	another way of saying this, substitute word, component parts, means the same as this word in another language
*	listed in the definitions, standing out, distinctive
' '	literal translation in another language
" "	quoted material from another source, ironic usage (not exactly what the words say), sense of a translation

PREFACE
Setting the Tone

A small car drives up to a farm house set well back off the road. An old woman rocks on the porch. The car stops and a young man, an anthropologist (#), gets out to visit with this elder (*) of an unnamed tribe. While thoroughly versed in the language and traditions of her people, she has been, during a long life, an advocate of learning and understanding. She is willing to talk with interested outsiders, including her visitor. She speaks.

* Welcome back, dear. What's on your mind? Didn't you ask all of your questions last time?

No, ma'am, I didn't and I don't think I ever will. There is so much to learn that there are always going to be more questions. I just hope you let me ask you as many as I can.

* Well, that's OK with me. I'm old and not many people come by or seem interested in what I know. I was raised the real old way, you know – I guess you do or you wouldn't keep coming back. Now-a-days they call me an Elder, but I'm really more of a Younger since all that I am and know came to me because of the way I was raised as a child.

I know that, and I really appreciate your willingness to talk to me. I enjoy it, even if it's to end up as a cold record for science and scholarship, you know.

* Well, I don't know about that college stuff. I had a native education, school of hard knocks and advanced disappointments. I went to school some and always did well, but life had more to teach me. All I know is that I can talk to you the way the elders talked to me in the old days – except I wasn't allowed to come right out and ask a lot of straight on questions. It's interesting to me and worthwhile for you, so I guess it's all right. Besides, it gives me company. There are very few people of my own tribe around here who have any interest in these old time things. We all visit and we talk, but we don't remember and ponder the way you and I do. That's what makes your visits so special. At first they were just a novelty, but now I understand more of what you're after and I'd like to encourage more of it. Now I think about Indien stuff a lot more. You've got us all thinking. The other old heads, old timers at elders lunches, are talking a lot more about our memories when we get together, and we like it.

That means a lot to me. I don't want to be just doing something that will be reduced to writing and then collect dust in some library. If I can get people thinking about these things and realizing how significant they are, then maybe some more traditions can be brought back.

* No, it's too late for that. Those times are gone and we need to adapt to new ones, like I keep telling my kids. But we must do so in a way that makes sense in terms of respecting the old ways. We have to conquer the white people, learn what we can that is useful and yet stay faithful to our own ways. That's the hard part.

No, it's not. You're talking about the fallout from colonialism, the European take over of the world, with the victim adopting the arguments of the oppressor. I don't want to get into this, but it is a fact of tribal life that native people never get appreciated on their own terms by most Americans.

* Yeah, I guess so, but we try hard to ignore outside demands. It makes things easier to deal with.

Sure, it's a solution, but it's not a safe one. Always remember that the aim of colonialism is to distort, deny, and broadcast doubt. Only by subverting, belittling, dehumanizing, and denying native people could any European vanguard, using military might or fire power, take over another country. Distortion works its insidious way into all aspects of this encounter. As a strategy, it is also assumed by the colonialized themselves as a way of holding their own. Both sides play off each other, using the distortion.

* And it makes me mad. Our holy places have been insulted and destroyed. Look how they rename them. Sacred stones, peaks, and lakes are now called things like Spook Rock, Demon Mountain, and Devil's Lake. That is wrong. Spirits of this very land lived here long before anyone ever heard of a devil. Only by sticking together can we keep our strength and resolve to persist. The hardest part is that this land, our mother, was taken away from us. We lost our support.

True, land is the source of all things, but only at the end was land alienated. In the Americas, the colonial exchange went through several stages. Initially, the newcomers wanted food, goods, and services. Among these (ironically named) goods were gold and (to Europeans) other valuables, like furs, crops, and minerals – along with novel conveniences like tobacco, hammocks, and canoes. After European settlement, native middlemen arose to bring the goods from the hinterlands to the traders. Tribes and nations such as the Iroquois, Osage, and Chinook arose as tribal powers by trading items into their hinterlands.

* Yeah, but they still took our land. That's for sure.

Getting land of their own was what brought over most English and other people I call "chalks" because their land hunger had been stifled in Europe by a so-called "landed gentry" of nobles. Therefore, the land "exchange" loomed large in the history of the Americas. While conquest by denial played its part in beating natives into submission, along with overwhelming diseases and discouragements, the actual exchange was legalized by treaties, often under force or duress. Most "reserved" to the natives some of their former territory, but usually this was later cut up and taken away by subsequent demands. This is the origin of the reservations of the United States and the reserves in Canada. This was land kept by Indiens themselves, with the rest exchanged for goods, money, gifts, and services promised by representatives of the national government.

* You're talking about our treaty rights, honored when the treaties were made, but more and more maligned as the native population has become a tiny minority. We learned the hard way that numbers count unless you take the long and righteous view.

Unfortunately, that's the way many Chalks see it. With the loss of natural resources, most of the land, and much of their communal wellbeing, natives were left with their labor to exchange, just like any other citizen. In addition, of course, they also had whatever "valuables" were left on their reserves. While these places often appeared barren and desolate in the Far West, hidden reserves of oil, gas, minerals, and gems were sometimes unintentionally included. Thus, occasional tribal wealth (Quapaw zinc, Osage oil, Navaho coal, Laguna uranium) receives disproportionate attention than their population numbers would merit, either to highlight a missed opportunity on the part of American business ("If we had only known, those Indiens would have never been allowed to keep that land") or the divine land-right of Indiens ("The Great Spirit put that oil there to help us poor Indien people"). Even so, the capitalist system thrives on exploiting every potential resource to depletion.

* Things have a way of being ripped apart once outsiders move into an area. The

nicest ones come first to soften us up. Then come those who are more selfish, greedy, and determined.

Adding to the mix of colonial distortions, these very exceptions got more attention then they deserve as ways of attacking natives. For example, the few decades of rivalry potlatching in the Northwest, or, even more so, the few centuries of horsemanship on the Plains became defining characteristics, instead of the recent aberrations they actually were.

Now, wait. Try not to simplify or prejudge. Each culture has its own worth. Never forget that. We need to find ways to understand your culture and appreciate its place in the world. Let's work on that together, teaming my skills as a researcher with yours as an elder-philosopher. We just have to make sure we stay focused on its overall integrity. Your job is to keep me honest, true to the letter and the spirit of the facts from a native perspective. We already know the European slant only too well. Any servant has to know the whims of the master.

That is the most overlooked concern of scholarship. We are taught to take things apart, to dissect and examine all the pieces, but, having done that, we almost never put everything back together. I can see why people get angry with a researcher when they see the final product, a published analysis, derived from what knowledge they have shared, but devoid of any vitality – cold and lifeless. We work more like butchers than like surgeons, hacking off pieces instead of looking at overall health.

With analysis should lead to understanding, a better integration of material with more insight into facts. I can seek and examine, but both of us have to work at these connections to achieve insight and understanding.

* OK, but where do we start? In the sagas of our tribes we always begin to learn about the world when someone starts naming off things. Listing begins to sort out time, space, and culture.

That's exactly right. I've thought about this. You know how everyone uses the term Indiens to refer to the natives of the Americas because of the mistake Columbus made. That name doesn't help at all, and it is confusing for anthropology to have the same name for people on two different continents. Younger people are insisting on the term Native American or just Native, but that is not all that helpful because people seem to think that it means only to be born in a place and to disparage, yet again, that native claims are in any way better than their own to be truly native.

My current idea is to use different spellings for these names like the French. That is the way it's often done in Europe. So, the people who live on the subcontinent of India would have their name spelled with "a" (Indians), while those of the Americas, because Columbus named them in the West Indies would be spelled with "e" (Indiens).

* That's one possibility, but there should be variety. No one ever has only one name, even if they just call themselves "human being." Lord knows, it's a problem we never had until Europeans started arriving and taking over. We always just had a name for ourselves and for close, friendly neighbors that meant "humans, people, fellow beings" and that shaded off into other kinds of people who were less and less like our kind.

I already know what you're thinking. Yes, at base, everything is human or humanlike. All the animals, plants, clouds, and forces in the world have humanlike forms when they are at home. They only dress up when they go outside to do whatever they were created to do. They take on that guise that makes them unique, special, and distinctive as a separate creation or species. As your Shakespeare said, although women can take exception, "The measure of all things is Man." But that isn't because the human is on top of the heap and can do whatever he or she pleases, as most of the modern world seems to believe. It's because humans are the pivot, the focus and nexus, of the whole webbing of the so-called chain of beings. Since we are in contact with everything in the world, communication has to pass through us.

That is profoundly different from the Judeo-Christian notion that humans are the superior species, the apex, except for God and the angels, of the universe. That is, of course, until the Martians land.

* You're right. It is different. We natives believe that all of us are of and from the very land itself. We must learn from and take care of the land because it is our friend, sustainer, and teacher. It is, flat out, our life.

Many tribes call it Mother, believing she is alive, thinking and feeling. She knows what we do to and for her. She also knows when we do harm. She can help, punish, or withhold. These are truly the deeds of a Mother, but there is more than just the land.

There is also Father Sun, the sky, and the layers above and below the earth. All of these have spirits – that's not the best word for them, let's call them immortals – because they have always been, since even before the beginning. They are like transmitters for passing on information, potency, and wellbeing. They are nodes with special intelligence – together with compassion, concern, and justice – that make intercommunication possible and worthwhile in the universe. For many tribes, the universe is structured like a spider's web, composed of pulsating rays and circles moving out from the center and then back from the edges to the nexus. Rippling along these rays and rings is _puwha_ (* energy = life force = power = charged flow) unifying the cosmos. In the moment when memory began, at that instant when some Creator took moral responsibility for sharing existence, Mind originated and permeated the universe to institute time, space, and culture. It is the immortals who channel this _puwha_ and decide to share it with particular novelties, such as objects or humans or families or places. These are the pivots at the intersections of the webbing, nodes providing this internal framework of and for the universe.

You mean guardian spirits and deities, as they are called in the literature. Sometimes, they are considered like angels, or patron saints, or, according to some tribes, the "bosses" of their species.

* Well, that is one way to look at it. They are immortals, each charged with amounts of energy. They have human emotions, harnessed by primordial wisdom. Mind is more important than anything else. As memory, as will, and as intelligence, it is shared by everything, even if they do not seem alive to us. I know of rocks that have _puwha_, some were legendary characters petrified forever and some are just special stones, in and of themselves, and thereby cause for particular human attention.

You know, many Americans believe that God Is Love, but it sounds like you believe that God is Mindful.

* Yes, I do, and now that I have recalled all that, I must explain the source of names. The difficulty with those distorted names that have been given to our tribes by Europeans is that they are taken from the outside. These are false names because they did not grow or come from the place where that language belonged. It is fine to use English names for things in England and German names in Germany. That is where they belong. Because there was no name in use for all the different tribes across the continent, one had to be imposed. But it came from the outside. Repeated use of a name over a

long time does make it hallowed to some extent, but it remains alien. Just because names are old, doesn't mean they are appropriate. Sometimes they need to be changed to emphasize dignity and purpose. Knowing the correct name is the secret of tolerance and courtesy. Using the right name controls a situation.

Yes, I can understand why it is not a good idea to reuse a term like "skraelling" (shrunken, shriveled) taken from the Norse records to indicate the people already here when early Viking colonies were sent to North America. The same applies to "indios" from the Spanish.

* Not quite, because, you see, "indios" has a certain attraction to us since it can be written as "in dios (in God)." This is indeed what all natives tried very hard to be: in tune and in touch with God or some version of the deity: male, female, neither, both, remote, or close. Such deified thought was a Mystery at the focus, if not the apex, of our great chain of beings. In many of our native languages, the word used for the Creator really means the thoughtful because to think is to create.

But how is thought expressed? The immortals seem to use telepathy, but biological life forms certainly have other means of communicating.

* Thought is linked with language. Every place has its own language associated with the local immortals tending it. It had to be spoken so it could be shared. Of course, the immortals also have a language of their own, used among themselves. Telepathy also worked among many living things, but often it gets muddled up with lusts and greeds. It's like it used to be in ancient Europe, thousands of years before things got jumbled up by constant warfare, invading hordes, and refugees fleeing all over the place. Then, every region had its own local language, because communities tended to be isolated and fearful. Important people used Latin to conduct international affairs, so they were able to move freely all over because they could converse with others of the native elite.

We understand because we can think. Our ancients knew that the language used among the immortals was pure thought; they did not need speech to communicate among themselves. Rather, speech only became necessary in order to communicate across species and locales. This spoken word came into existence so neighbors, of all living forms, could talk to each other and develop common cause. Because speech cannot be heard over long distances, many languages had to be developed to cover all of the regions of the world.

Is that because all of the world is related?

* Indeed. Related, but respectful of their many differences as individuals and as communities.

Members of each species already knew and understood each other. Thus, when it came time for names to be spoken, each species and other entities supplied the self-designation it had been using all along. These were true names, they came from within and reflected a particular sense of place and purpose in the universe. This is what all names must be: Direct, descriptive, and rooted in a sense of time, space, and process.

Because of these considerations, only a few terms really satisfy the requirements of true names. The names that have come to me to refer to the two races which confronted each other here in the Americas are derived from their distant lands. I call my own people, the ones who were here, the Ochers, after the red pigment from the land used so much for protection and decoration because it was believed to be symbolic of blood and life. We have recognized this link for eons in the sacred use of pipestone from quarries in Minnesota.

Yes, I can see the advantages of organic instead of descriptive names. For example, some tribes, such as the Pomo of California and the Mesquaki (or Fox) of Iowa, believed that they were created from the local red ocher and so called themselves red earth people. Sauks named themselves after their own yellow earth. Europeans, however, originally used the term Red Man to refer to a group of Beothuks from Newfoundland who had coated their bodies with red ocher as a decoration and a warm weather defense against pesky insects.

* There were many different kinds of Europeans here, but the ones who stayed on and took over were the English, arrogant islanders. We could say that this was ordained because of some advantage they had over the others, an advantage that derived from their relations with the immortal, and, thus, with their sense of place. Of course, it did help that they regarded their rightful place as masters of a world empire. "Whiteman's burden, stiff upper lip, and all that, you know." Their name could also be used to include all of the other European settlers, much as they eventually did by conquest. From what I heard during World War II, the place that meant a lot to the English and all of their allies was the white cliffs of Dover, which they tell me are made of chalk. Therefore, I think that those who came after and have taken control should be called Chalks. It is a comment, too, on colonialism. Sticks of chalk are used in the classroom to change out ways of life.

Ochers and Chalks are what I mean by useful names coming from the land. They're short words, growing out of their sense of place.

Ochers and Chalks. Not bad, when you understand where they come from and what they represent. But it's still best to use self-identifying terms to refer to each of them as individuals and larger groupings.

Of course, in Europe these groupings were much more cohesive because there were so many displacements, migrations, invasions, and military takeovers that survivors had to band closer together to protect and defend themselves. What can't be helped is that people will always make judgments about how they are better than almost everybody else. This is ethnocentrism, a self-superiority in the oldest of human traditions. Of course, if you happen to conquer or run rough shod over people, then you Europeans assume you can tell them what to do. Some will follow directions and organize into work parties; others will balk and develop a system of their own to counteract, quietly or loudly, that of these so-called "masters."

* So, here we are back to colonialism. It's become such a topic of late among our educated Indiens that they've taken to calling it the civ / sav distinction. Somehow, that makes it seem innocuous, but it really wasn't and still isn't, at all. It hurts. It's unfair. It's wrong. We are all the same, even allowing for our many differences.

Yeah, I know. It's bleak, but also ironic. It reminds me of a marvelous quote from Elspeth Huxley,[2] writing about her own girlhood in Kenya – when it was part of the British Empire. I bring it up here because she also mentions woad, the blue earth coloring favored by the ancient Britons, as other nations used ocher. She's along with adult colonists making a visit to the local native leader before they have a picnic. An local Englishman complains that the native men allow the women to do most of the really hard work, and make no effort to excel on their own. Their trouble is that they "have no discipline." His wife replies to blunt this criticism. "I suppose we were all like that once, going about in woad and making human sacrifices, until the Romans came. It seems odd to think that we were civilized by Italians."

The European invasion of the Americas, regrettably, was in this ancient tradition of bringing civilization to the "savages" at the point of a sword, spear, gun, or battalion, as long ago described by Tacitus. The resulting order that comes after the chaos of conquest makes for increasingly more precise levels of organization.

Toward the end of the book, she also gives a nice account of the learning theory favored by societies still in touch with their environments. Observation is the best teacher because firing off a question is like a boom that scares everything under cover. Instead, by being patient and quiet, knowledge will come close to you.

"The best way to find out things, if you come to think of it, is not to ask questions at all. If you fire off a question, it is like firing off a gun; bang it goes, and everything takes flight and runs for shelter. But if you sit quite still and pretend not to be looking, all the little facts will come and peck round your feet, situations will venture forth from thickets and intentions will creep out and sun themselves on a stone; and if you are very patient, you will see and understand a great deal more than a man with a gun."[3]

Clearly, it is best to observe life quietly in its totality, to seek a culture in its overall environment. To do so, however, we must also know the limitations involved. Different families will have valid variant traditions, which must be respected, while also allowing for the possibility of unintended mistakes and sometimes being wrong.

* Right. We are ourselves, engendered of the land, imbued with all-embracing *puwha*, and akin to the universe in word, deed, gesture, and, especially, thought.

2. Elspeth Huxley, <u>Flame Trees of Thika</u> 1959: 114.
3. Elspeth Huxley, <u>Flame Trees of Thika</u> 1959: 264.

INTRODUCTION

Names are significant. While "Native Americans" in the United States and "First Nations" in Canada currently are the politically correct terms, throughout this text, Ochers, Indiens, and distinct tribal designations will also appear. Similarly, European, Chalk, and settler will serve for the newcomers, colonists, and misnamed pioneers (since natives planted themselves long before). No one name can serve in all settings. People, times, places, and purposes vary.

After several centuries devoted to understanding Native North America, we have many clarifications but few definitive conclusions. Indeed, the continued survival of native lifeways relies on keeping everyone guessing. Varieties of distortion have kept do-gooders and others from "getting a clear shot" at cherished beliefs. Four useful terms, nevertheless, have emerged to grasp basic Americanist concepts. These are *puwha*, siger, tysic, and Indien.

A word already accepted in a limited way will be extended because it already solves a difficulty long debated. Adopting the European spelling of <u>Indien</u> clearly distinguishes the natives of the West Indies and Americas from those of the subcontinent of India (East Indies, Indians).

Puwha

Similarly, since natives believed all things shared intelligent life, this all-pervading, animating concept of power + life force + potency + energy + vitality will be called <u>puwha</u>. It translates the native concept and blends terms from Algic languages of the east (<u>puw-</u>, as in Pow Wow, Powhatan) and Numic ones of the west (<u>puha</u>) to indicate its special significance. It infuses the engendered cultures of the Americas, and takes it continued strength from the union of Man and Woman.

Every living thing was involved in constant negotiations. Foods and raw materials sustained some species via the death of others. To assuage any sense of guilt, the remains were thanked with a gift and prayer. Because these exchanges were highly ritualized to give thanks and provide blessings, such regulated transfers of food between humans and other species of peoples (plant, animal, fish, spirit) helped to make America a Holy Land.

Shrines were at nodes in its web-like pattern of concentric rings and rays pulsing with the flow of *puwha*. Any place where people clustered could and would concentrate potency there. Moreover, fixed abodes at landmarks are identified in legend as "holy homes" {* = hollow hills, whirlpools, water falls, dangerous eddies, high mountains, hot springs, and distinctively eroded elevations}. Generally, these locales marked intense motion, such as landslides, rock falls, roiling water, and geysers.

Entrances to these domains were through caves, lakes, springs, or fissures, provided that an individual had ritually prepared by fasting, bathing, and meditating before his or her quest. These holy homes were communal lodges, where holy doctors (shamans) visited in trance to arrange for the exchange of souls – those of local animals in return for those of humans from distant groups to sustain life. Provided the meat was not wasted and the remains ritually treated, these souls were reborn into other bodies.

The divide between immortality and mortality has to be keenly maintained. Among its most common expressions is the need for a woman to seclude herself during each of her menstruations. This life-giving rhythm had to be kept separate from flows of *puwha* and spirits, otherwise something like a short circuit would occur to kill those all-too-mortal and careless.

While *puwha* is diffusely everywhere, it is most effective when sent through a transmitter. It was enshrined in a place or embodied in an ageless being ("immortal") at the symbolic intersection (node) of the rings and rays of the universal *puwha* web. As noted, capitalized names serve to indicate such immortal species rather than biological mortals, so Raven made the world a mythic character but a raven calls from a tree.

Four increasing levels in the intensity providing human access to *puwha* are dreams, visions, bundles, and shrines. Dreams are fleeting connections between a human and an immortal, conveying limited information – often a warning or premonition. Visions establish permanent partnership between mortal and immortal, confirmed by assembling appropriate items into bundles – also called medicine or power packs. At the initial contact, a visionary was told to assemble crystals, animal parts, intriguing stones, and figures emblematic of the intended effects of this partnership – such as hunting success, healing, community wellbeing, or protective magic. After a long life of use, most bundles are buried or dispersed at the death of their compiler. Some become magnified into tribal or national palladia, as among the Pawnee, Crow, and other Plains tribes. Shrines, often the hallowed hollows within peaks and mounds, are fixed on the landscape and regarded as eternal high-intensity transmitters of *puwha*.

Grounding

Proper interlinkages bind a people and a place to a community patron (totem, dodem). This is the local immortal, dispensing *puwha* from its holy home, a primordial, pristine part of the landscape. The locale was both geological and geographical so humans carried its image in their heads and, if needed, could actually visit there to make special pleadings.

The most vital aspect of any partnership was a song (or series of songs), given at the encounter (quest, vision, dream), and thereafter used to set rhythms to activate, signal, and direct *puwha*. The melodic lines are turns and twists in the trail followed by *puwha*.

With this partnership go obligations that include scrupulous respect for the immortal and its manifestations. These are strict taboos on the eating, use, or exposure to related species. Occasional offerings are given in recognition of on-going blessings. These taboos were personal, observed privately, without ever stating them aloud. Thus, a good wife would have to notice that her husband never ate geese, for instance. She then saw that it was never served or offered to him. Similarly, having Spider *puwha* might require avoidance of plucked string music from a fiddle or guitar. These taboos prevent over-identification or merging of *puwha*s, thus maintaining their mutual needs for each other. Failure to keep up these obligations meant that the *puwha* would leave and the person become defenseless.

What distinguished these patrons, of course, were their relative strengths. Sometimes these were obviously correlated with the size, age, and attributes of that species or being – most often respectfully addressed as "grandfather." Therefore, an Ant alone was less strong than a Deer, which was weaker than a mean Grizzly. Habitat also was involved, since those that lived high up, like Eagles, used panoramic vistas looking far in all directions to safeguard and augment their *puwha*. Upriver mountain immortals, nearer the remote source of the flow, were more powerful than those downstream or at the mouth (outflow) tainted by heavy and confusing traffic.

Yet most attributions were not this straight forward. Immortals and *puwha* have protective strategies and camouflages. One Ant may represent a whole colony or all the ants in the world, and thus be invincible. Patrons sometimes had decoys, disguises, or they created distractions, diversions, or deflections for self-protection. Most importantly, more powerful patrons could take much weaker outer forms, though weaker ones could not take stronger shapes. An Ant might really be a Thunderbird, but never the reverse. Therefore, observing the greatest care and respect was the safest way of surviving and benefiting from any such encounter. It was best to take a very cautious (if not paranoic) attitude.

Further, humans were never limited to only one partner. Members of the elite often had several guides and guardians. Shamans frequently had many for their own protection and that of their families and patients.

Community

Two acronyms express basic patterns of order. Throughout America, flux and flow indicated vitality. Leadership was more often informal and fleeting, very much of the moment as it was needed for a task. This aspect of authority is <u>sig(er)</u> from "special interest group (leader)," ranging from a story telling session or type of food processing to complex rituals renewing the universe. The siger was in charge for only as long as he or she was needed to lead the group and accomplish whatever task was at hand.

Throughout, providing focus, is a *tysic* from "<u>t</u>ime <u>s</u>pace <u>c</u>enter" with vowels pointing down (y) and up (i). As noted, Yup'ik Eskimos of Alaska nicely capture this temporal and spatial union in their ubiquitous use of a ⊙ decorative circle with a central dot. Their language has words like <u>ciuliaq</u> = "ancestor, leader" from <u>ciu-</u> meaning "forepart of a body, front area, or time before"; in contrast to <u>kingu-</u> meaning "rear end, back area, or time after".[4]

A native community might include members of four possible social classes, usually known as old, high-born families, as good families, as weak families, or an ahuman underclass of slaves – captured in war, purchased, or born to this lot.

Formal community leaders were drawn from families of the highest rank to become a chief, captain, priest, shaman, and matron. Chief or captain (war chief) led their community during, respectively, times of peace or warfare – serving as head either of civil or of military stances. The matron – often the daughter, wife, and mother of chiefs – supervised the activities of women in a community. Shamans saw to the emotional, medical, and spiritual needs of their own family and then of the wider community. In addition to these positive leaders, there were also others "on the dark side" as witches (if inherently born) or sorcerers (if trained).

While their cultures were god-given at holy places across the Americas, their ancestors came to North America hunting big game animals during the Ice Age. Once in their own homeland, however, communities specialized on local foods and conditions. They became careful tenders of their landscape, and then tillers of planted crops. The earliest of these were indigenous, later ones were imported – such as the famous Mexican trinity of maize (corn), beans, and squash. Plant care and harvests needed and still need all-important rituals to assure success.

Of course, each prior adaptation continued somewhere in the Americas. Hunters of big game thrived on the bison (buffalo) herds of the Plains, or on sea mammals along the Arctic coasts (as Eskimos). Archaic foraging was improved by autumn over-burnings to clear off land, and by selective spring scattering of "wild" seeds to guarantee annual harvests. Such tenders once lived throughout the west and north of North America, where some still do. Farmers or tillers lived in the east and south. Usually women did most of the summer farm work, while men hunted in season. Only the Southwestern Pueblos assign the irrigated field work to men, though women do have kitchen gardens.

Each lifeway adapted itself to regional climates. Moreover, it contributed to the vast trade network that exchanged the meat and furs of hunters for the crops and crafts of farmers. Special local treasures, such as copper ore, turquoise, shells, minerals, and mica served as exotic trade goods, often to indicate the elite ranks of old, high families.

4. Ann Fienup-Riordan, Eskimo Essays 1990: 202, 212.

Alert ~ Aware ~ Watchful (Eternal Vigilance)

All of Native America, since traditional times, was and is alive, aware, and interconnected by thought, senses, and emotions. The comfort, health, and wellbeing of everything depended on the conscious goodwill of everyone else. Closest ties were with own kinspeople, then with fellow members of the band, tribe, and culture. Stress and pressures caused by daily life were deflected toward outsiders, either enemies or unknowns. All of the cultural features of harmony and peace now valued by ecological, cosmic, New Age types applied only to members of your own group. They did not extend to enemies, except during the best of times.

Each day, therefore, involves decisions and negotiations to stay fed, warm, healthy, and content. A good person works hard to hunt, farm, fish, or harvest whatever foods are available – thanking each and every one for their kind gift. But some people are lazy and steal food, or are crippled and have to be fed. Despite careful planning, hard work can end up spoiled or moldy because supplies somehow got wet. Sometimes the crops shrivel up and die before harvest, or fish do not come.

A good person prays for things to improve, learns from mistakes, moves to someplace better, or does all of these and more. Sometimes, neighbors with plenty are visited, coaxed, threatened, or attacked to get food. In all cases, he or she rises above any nasty situation to be a "good person".

But no one in the Americas can get food without access to *puwha*, a gift from an immortal. Therefore, it is even more important to get *puwha* than to get food, since food follows automatically from *puwha* but not the reverse. Where *puwha* is concerned, however, access could be good or bad.

"Good" means of attracting and holding *puwha* involve fasting, praying, enduring pain, and promising to help others. "Bad" ways involve selfishness and theft, siphoning it off from others – like pilfering food, killing those who already have it, or contaminating its source to take advantage of the resulting scarcity.

Native life, therefore, is self-defensive and necessarily suspicious, since attacks could be spiritual, emotional, physical, or all of these. Everything from spoiled food to malevolent influences has to be accounted for and dealt with. Responsibility, therefore, is often oblique, circumspect, and diffuse so as not to attract undue special attention. A good leader gets things accomplished without seeming to do so. He or she sets a high example and puts good works in motion by urging, coaxing, or prodding – but never by direct or outright command that it be done.

Imagine, if possible, living in a house where great but potentially harmful *puwha* could be unleashed unknowingly by a mis-step or wrong action. Or living in a world where fierce and venomous beasts can and do give vent both to their own will and that of someone with ill-intentions. Or surviving in an environment, full of fangs and claws, where flood, drought, earthquake, and enemy attack, by might or by magic, loom large.

Whatever is done affects all others, having long range consequences over time and space. Rituals and thanksgivings involving many participants always contribute to the greater good, while sorcery and theft done in secret evoke the selfish bad. All intelligences – in whatever outer form are nearby just then – become well aware of what is happening. But only their leaders have enough *puwha* to sit in judgment, knowing that the more severe their punishment on one person (of whatever species or quality), the more pain will then ripple out to inflict the rest of the world.

Therefore, people go through life making the least amount of "waves," leading calm, contented, and composed lives which will have the least impact on others. Yet, not everyone is the same, with the same modest needs. Constant vigilance of the seen and unseen is the price of sharing the world with other intelligent life forms. Most of them are content and similarly inclined, though a few are insidious, ready to infect, divert, or deflect benefits toward their own selfish ends.

Universe

Relying on their own observations, most natives viewed the world (earth) as a flat disk, highlighted by mountains and rivers, with at least one level above it as the sky and another below it as the underworld. In overall shape, this world is a ball, with the earth disk in the middle, an air-filled sky dome above, and a water-filled bowl below. A central tree (sometimes, a pole or pillar) joins together these three domains, along with other mediators such as fire, water, and caves to allow passage between the layers. Certain beings, such as birds and snakes, also have the inherent ability to travel across these divisions.[5]

For the whole of North America, shared among high families interlinked across regions, the universal metaphor is the cross inside a circle ⊕. This unifying tysic is also suggested by the geography around the major confluences of the Ohio and Missouri Rivers entering the Mississippi near modern St. Louis. As if in confirmation of this belief, the huge Mississippian ceremonial center, now called Cahokia, thrived there. It is marked by Monk's Mound, the largest human-made earth platform north of Mexico. Surrounding it are sacred spaces and scattered settlements once presided over by high chiefs and priests, who were involved in a vast complex of trade and ritual relations. In addition to such built sacred centers, the Americas were also marked by numerous, widely-scattered holy sites indicated by landmarks, shrines, rock art, or portable bundles.

5. As Peter Roe, a South American archaeologist, has shown, this world layer cake inside a ball pierced by the world tree was also the cosmic model for lowland Amazonian South America and elsewhere. Indeed, the very title of his book The Cosmic Zygote (fertilized egg with female and male components), further indicates the great importance of gender (engendered life) in South America and elsewhere.

Kinship

Among all human societies, distinguishing social units depended on the size and density of the population. They were conditioned by the local economy, technology, and available foods. Larger kinship networks engulfing families (married pairs and their children, only distinct as an abstracted analytical unit) included three well-known types –

unilateral* (or lineal), bilateral*, and ambilateral*.

Unilateral (one sided) kinship occurs in more complicated and populous societies. It is traced only through the father, only through the mother, or through each parent for different purposes. In these cases, family households were submerged within lineages {* = across generations linkages either through fathers and sons or through mothers and daughters within larger institutions}. But patrilineages and matrilineages were not mirror images of each other because men always held public leadership in both communities. In other words, while men were both leaders and kinsmen because of who their fathers were in a patrilineage, for a matrilineage-based community, kinship depended on mothers but leadership passed from brothers to nephews {MB > ZS}. Their common link was a woman who was sister to the office holder and mother to the inheritor, as described for the Iroquois and Hopi since the 1600s.

Lineages are, in turn, components of larger groupings such as clans, phratries*, and, sometimes, moieties*. While lineages rarely have a name apart from the oldest living grandparent, all of these larger clanship units are formally named. Whether a patriclan or a matriclan, both real and metaphorical kinship was traced among all clan members, so they can never marry.[6] For example, when a member of the Turtle clan travels, he or she will receive a warm welcome and open hospitality in any Turtle clan household, even of another tribe. The virtues of this mystical bond of clanship, therefore, are readily apparent. This wide network of kin, mutual caring, and supportive protection are automatically assumed among clanspeople. If a member is hurt, injured, or killed, men of the same clan as the victim are obligated to take revenge or otherwise seek justice.

Clans, in turn, join into phratries, often on the basis of some logical linkage that also forbids intermarriage among such close kin. Thus, clans called Crane, Frog, Sand, and Willow belong to a Water phratry. Among Hopi, phratries protect clan-owned rituals from extinction. The last official of a dying clan will teach its rite to a man in another clan within that same phratry so it can then inherit the necessary fetish and take over hosting that rite. Since the wellbeing of the whole world relied on such rituals, they should never cease, even if their original human sponsors faded away.

Moieties, whether composed of phratries or only of basic households, divide a community into two halves. They bisect the universe into sky or earth, land or water, right or left, man or woman, night or day, and any other likely opposition. Along the southern United States, moieties called Red or White, symbolic of War or Peace, were characteristic of the sophisticated farmers known as the Mississippians. These were the ancestors of tribes who later entered European history as Creeks, Cherokees, Choctaws, and so forth. Along the upper Mississippi and Missouri River, various Siouian peoples have Earth or Sky moieties, each composed of a number of clans aligned into Land, Water, and Air phratries. Among the Pueblos of the Southwest, Summer or Winter, also known as Squash or Turquoise, are characteristic halves (see below).

Bilateral (both sides) systems include about three remembered generations. They focus around a set of individuals forming a kindred*, a unit also known as an "extended family" in modern American society. Members of a kindred are traced through both mother and father as far as acceptable memory allows. During a lifetime, each member is the center of a personal kindred* of all known relatives. A prestige kindred* involves all those who trace kinship to someone famous, wealthy, or honored. Among tribes, therefore, such kindreds are huge. In practice, however, kindreds function in terms of significant living individuals who guide and direct the membership. Most commonly, a <u>nodal</u> kindred* forms around the node of a married couple. After their deaths, it regroups around a cluster of their children – siblings (brothers and sisters) with their wives and children. A typical example is the *tiyospaye* of the Lakota, larger than a married couple for mutual protection but smaller than a tribe to be more easily fed. In cases where an office or object (fetish) is inherited, serial successors form the descent line of a <u>stem</u> kindred*, as with the transmission of certain sacred bundles among towns of the Skidi Pawnee confederacy.

Ambilateral (chosen sides) descent can be traced through both parents. The resulting discrete units are called <u>septs</u>, though actual residence determines which of the possible septs someone belongs to at that moment. Where special rules, such as primogeniture, apply, high ranks trace membership in a <u>ramage</u>, composed only of privileged linkages. Typically this is first born son to first born son, who in turn marry only first born daughters. The ramages is important in the proper inheritance of high or chiefly rank, as among Wakashans of central British Columbia.

6. In some cases, since clansmembers can never marry, boys and girls not closely related but of the same clan teach each other about sex without long-term obligations nor any possibility of acceptable children.

Arrow Releases

Bows and arrows are part of the " Indian image" favored by Hollywood films and other media. Yet, here as elsewhere, the actual details are complex and fascinating. Native Americans, in all things, want to be precise, as reflected by village, district, river drainage, and tribal customs. A particularly apt example was the manner in which men released their arrows. This simple and vital task involved many cultural differences that serve to distinguish neighboring communities from each other. The four basic variables were the hand, the bowstring, the arrow, and the bow. Their various combinations formed five named types.[7]

"Primary" used the thumb and bent index finger to pull on the arrow, as in the Northeast, Southwest, and California. It was used among Penobscot, Mikmaq, Navaho, Maidu, and Luiseño; along with parts of Africa.

"Secondary" used the same grip to pull on both the string and the arrow, as in the Great Lakes and Southwest among the Seneca, Ottawa, and Zuni.

"Tertiary" plucked the string between the thumb and extended index finger, particularly on the upper Mississippi River among Siouians, along with Menomini, Blackfeet, and sections of Africa and Southeast Asia.

"Mediterranean" was thumbless, pulling the string between the index and middle fingers, as in Southern Europe and among the Eskimo and Seri. Luiseño learned this technique at their Spanish missions.

"Mongolian" involved a leather or iron ring around the thumb to pull the string and was used by specialized archers in Siberia, China, and Turkey. For the Californian Yahi, it was used by Ishi, the last Yahi (Yana) whose final haven was the museum at the University of California in Berkeley.

Bows could be held vertical (straight up) along a standing body, as among the Welsh, or horizontal (crosswise). Along coastal flyways of Brazil, huge bows had to be drawn with the legs to shoot down migrating waterfowl. The archer lay on their backs to shoot upwards.

Across North America, the patterning of these releasing distributions was Tertiary in the center, Secondary around that, Primary around the outer edges, and Mediterranean in the North.

All other basic techniques – such as fire making, house building, pottery styles, and clothing – also required precise techniques both to accomplish the task and to indicate various social identities. These ranged from that of the village to that of the tribe and beyond to the wider culture area.

7. Alfred Kroeber, Arrow Release Distributions 1927.

Languages

Intended to be the most precise of all expressions, languages and rituals expressed an aesthetic of perfection that is especially expected among those high born. Words and phrases were chosen with the utmost care, to convey exact shades of nuance and meaning. The grammars of most native languages required the speaker to specify automatically whether or not any information was the result of direct experience or vicarious hearsay. Long continuous residence in a community is assumed in these languages. News was conveyed by the frequent use of complex pronouns that require strict attention to contexts. Some pronoun referents were marked with verbal tags, such as the Algonkian obviative which specified the "other guy" {= B} in a sentence like "I gave him^a to him$_b$."

For a speaker of the English language, the diversity and complexity of Native American speech comes as a surprise. Befitting from long residence in Americas, many varied tongues evolved here. There never was "The Indien Language." Rather, in North America alone, over half a dozen major language stocks included hundreds of mutually unintelligible languages.

Distinctive and intriguing features of these languages will be contrasted from the perspective of English grammar. Other forms would perplex speakers of other languages. While no detail is absolutely unique to Native American languages, some do have a very limited world distribution.

By comparison with English, Native American sound systems (phonetic inventories) include few vowels but many consonants.[8] These are often "harsh sounding" when produced at the back of the mouth and in the throat. In particular, these include glottalized consonants made by closing off the windpipe. The Pacific Northwest has one of the most complex consonant systems in the world, often stringing several consonants together without any intervening vowels. In some sound systems, the length of time that vowels are drawn out or tones fluctuatied serves to change the meaning of that word. Keresan even has sounds and whole syllables that are whispered, suggesting they are slowly passing out of usage.

Those trained in Amerindian linguistics learn to be sensitive to these and other possibilities, using written characters (letters) derived from the International Phonetic Alphabet (IPA) by Franz Boas (1916), Edward Sapir, and others to transcribe them.

Native speakers who learn several languages modify the sound systems of each to conform to a generalized pattern. Thus, as in the past when leaders spoke many languages, grammars have continued to be modified through the historic period as natives have also learned to speak English. In even more distorting fashion, American speakers have filtered many native place names through the English sound system. Many have lost all but vestiges of their original pronunciations.

Native languages are grammatically complex because, where English would use different words or sentences to convey different shades of meaning, these languages add on a sound cluster or particle (known as a lexical) to express nuance. This segment either might sound unlike any other full words that mean the same thing, or be formed by a standardized contraction of the whole word.

Other grammatical features unfamiliar to English speakers include inflecting (if the language has verbs) for aspect rather than for tense. Aspect expresses types of actions – inceptive (starting), instantaneous, durative, continuative, cessative (ending), and so forth. Verbs can also express different modes (modalities) – indicative, imperative, negative, and so forth.

In all native languages, verbs distinguish between transitive and intransitive forms, although not all of them take accusative objects. Languages such as Tsimshian are ergative, and "work" (from Greek ergasia) differently because what look like intransitive subjects and transitive objects are treated as the same.

In some languages, speakers automatically or inherently, without conscious deliberation, add lexical affixes that specify (like English prepositions) exact locations (beside, near, far, on the water, in the house, upward through the air, etc.), position (left, right, front, back, above, below, etc.), and shape (below).

For example, Navaho[9] has over a dozen inherent shape classifiers whose overall form is here indicated by interconnecting tilde ~, with examples included inside parentheses ( ). These are round~compact (bottle, bow, bread, candy), animal~animate (adenoids, baby, insects, corpse), long~slender~rigid (basket, cornear, dipper, gun), separate objects (dollars, sand, melons, wagons), surface (blanket, buckskin), contained substances (salt, sugar, drink), packed~consolidated material (entrails, mucus), fabric like (paper, bag, sack), parallel objects (bridge, thigh bone), bulky objects (sled, gown), bunched together objects (firewood), granular masses (ashes, bugs, peanuts, puppies, sand, songs), fluffy~vaporous~uncompact substances (cloud, wool, hay), long-flexible objects (belt, cable, death, feather, lightning), amorphous~mushy substances (mucus, mush, wornout hat), and so forth. Navahos delight in word games in which a bizarre shape class is applied. In a famous joke, a hunchback referred to himself as "round~compact" instead of "human."

Instrumentals indicate if something is done by hand, by foot, by mouth, by canoe, with a certain tool, etc. Other affixes might specify whether someone/thing was directly or vicariously experienced, was directly visible or not, and has ever been living or not.

Some languages have different counting or number systems for enumerating manner – such as boxes, canoes, balls, people, animals, or tools – and concepts, such as offices and duties. As the great traders of the Pacific Northwest, Tsimshian used seven different ways of counting. These were either all-purpose, humans, long objects, canoes, humans aboard canoes, volume unit measures (cups), linear unit measures (spans), or animals, including flat objects like hides.

Some languages do not have the English form of plurality. Rather they recognize the singular, dual (pairs, as pants), distributive ("each their own"), and collective ("all their"). A frequent feature is two forms of the first person plural pronoun – the 'exclusive we' (first and third pronouns, s~he and I, but not you) and the 'inclusive we' (all pronouns, s~he, you, and also I).

Another widespread grammatical process is reduplication. This is patterned repetition of certain sounds or words. English uses reduplication in so-called 'baby talk' as an affectionate diminutive in forms such as John-John and lovey-dovey. Many native languages use it to enrich their grammars. In Lushootseed (Puget Salish), different reduplications express different meanings. An example is the word for "American," which is derived from the word "Boston" as filtered through the Chinook trade pidgin. Variants include Boston = pastad; Americans all over = paspastad, American (pejorative) = papastad, American child or Caucasian friend = papstad, and American children = papapstad.

Socio-linguistics studies the social contexts of languages, particularly what are called registers. These range from personal to informal to poetic and eloquent. Usages also include argots and pidgins. An argot* (also called a social dialect) is a speech difference recognized within a community, usually associated with particular roles or careers. Examples might be the distinction of the speech of men from women, old from young, sacred from mundane purposes, and carpenter from fisher.

A pidgin (sometimes popularly called a jargon) is a trading vocabulary and minimal grammar used by people of various linguistic and cultural backgrounds. Pidgins must have occurred prehistorically, but the ones we know best have blossomed and proliferated, if not originated, during the era of the fur trade and European goods. The best known spoken pidgins were each associated with a major river that served as a trade route. These are the Delawarean (below), Mobilian of the lower Mississippi, and Chinookan of the Columbia River.

Delawarean pidgin was spoken along the Delaware River, blending Delaware and Dutch with some Swedish and English. Among its words borrowed into English are wigwam from /wikwam/ 'house,' corn pone from /ahpon/ 'bread', and moccasin from /maksin/ 'shoe'.

Mobilian pidgin was spoken from the mouth of the Mississippi River throughout the Southeast. Like Creole Cajun cooking, it blended Choctaw, French, and other languages, including some from Africa. Folktales with Uncle Remus and Brair Rabbit use Southeastern, African, and European motifs that filtered through Mobilian.

Chinookan pidgin was spoken along the Columbia River and throughout the Plateau and Pacific Northwest, blending Chinookan, Nootkan, French, and English, along with some Spanish and Russian. It probably began on Vancouver Island among prehistoric Nootkan (Nuchahnuth) traders dealing in dentalia tusk shells, but the developing European fur trade along the Columbia River enriched it with simplified Chinookan and European terms.

In addition to these spoken pidgins, the Plains sign language of gestures was ancient enough to have northern and southern dialects.[10]

More than half of the 2000 Native American languages estimated to have been spoken at contact have disappeared. This does not always mean their speakers died off. Some communities have merely shifted to English or to another native language. These shifts in language preference reflect indigenous processes, reported from all over the world.

Western Subarctic and Plateau peoples who lived along rivers emptying into the Pacific have long been shifting to coastal languages and customs. These became successively adopted upstream, village by village, until, to use an English suffix, they "-ized". For example, aboriginal Athapaskan Subarctic communities became "Tlingitized" and "Tsimshianized" over the past century or so.

Our understanding of the underlying semantics of these languages remains inadequate. Especially helpful in this undertaking is a small group of linguistically trained PhDs who are providing remarkable insights into their own grammars as Navaho, Nootkan, and Tohono O'otam Papago native speakers.

8. Consonants are sounds made by the blockage of the air stream by the glottis, tongue, nose, or lips; while vowels are open and only shape the air flow over the tongue or through the nose and lips.

9. Gladys Reichard, <u>Navaho Grammar</u> 1951: 339-351.

10. Brenda Farrell, <u>Do You See What I Mean</u> 1995.

Understanding is growing about the profundity of semantic dimensions for some languages and stocks. For the Salishan family, a pervasive grammatical distinction indicates whether or not the speaker is in control or careful of a situation. Puget Salish lexicals which express care~control (<u>-t</u>) or the lack of it (-<u>duʔ</u>) provide one example. Compare /<u>ukʷalt</u>/ = someone poured it, with /<u>ukʷalduʔ</u>/ = someone spilled it.

Athapaskan and Algonkian grammars include an "animacy hierarchy" based on the degree of mental discipline and willfulness of beings. According to this scale, humans are more deliberate in their actions than horses and, to an even greater degree, than bugs. Significantly, while all share minds, some beings have more mindfulness than others. This does not mean that those with more can or should dominate those with less. For example, animacy makes it impossible to say "The horse kicked the man." Instead, it has to be said as "The man allowed the horse to kick him" because he was not paying attention.

For Algic (Algonkian) languages, grammars inherently distinguish two qualities, named animate or inanimate. But this is not a clear-cut living/non-living distinction. Charles Hockett[11] pointed out that in a Cree story, the word for the skull of a witch, which chased and spoke to children, had an animate ending. He argued that the key feature of the animate was therefore the ability to communicate. But other data do not support his argument. In Ojibwa, 'airplane' is animate, as is 'knee' in Delaware, but both do not usually "speak" – even though knees do "creak" in "old-age" English. Building on the work of Mary Black and others, Miller[12] proposed that the key feature of the Algonquian animate is the ability to move, the property of self-propulsion, self-motivation, self-willfulness.

Recently, scholarly attention has turned to ways in which English is spoken by native peoples, leading to the study of so-called Red or Indien English. Of interest, these versions of English include grammatical features of the original native language spoken by that community. Politeness, constructions of indirection (obliqueness), and expressions emphasizing process enable these speakers to modify English to make it appropriate for existing native contexts. Native languages are supposed to caress, while English as spoken by most Americans is said to poke and prod. It is too direct and lacks subtlety.

In general, native languages are much more concerned with verbs than with nouns – with process rather than product. Indeed, they often rely on "pronoun arguments," assuming that a listener is fully aware of what, who, where, when, how something happened in these intimate communities. In this regard, native pronoun systems are highly complex, incorporating some very specific forms that allow for "switch referencing" so that a hearer will always know which of the several males called "he" is the current topic.

11. Charles Hockett, What Algonquian is Really Like 1966: 62, note 10.

12. Jay Miller, Delaware Alternative Classifications 1975: 442.

Culture

Throughout the Americas, people conformed to the land, not inately, but by compromise and negotiation as among all other life forms. Communities are led, if only for the moment, by those who control specialized knowledge needed just then (sigers). Access to immortals and holy homes provide *puwha*, which, in turn, provide the right to knowledge, by inheritance or instruction. A long, healthy, successful life depends on the control of such knowledge – about geology, history, customs, pedigrees, and, especially, rituals since these embodied all other aspects.

The best informed were those who well understood that *puwha* exists in a web like pattern across the landscape and universe. Within this overall form, each cell includes a <u>matrix</u>, a triple series of nested relationships, such that the exclusive fit within the inclusive and both then into the inclosive. Each might also be called, respectively, marked, unmarked, or mediating. Members of all these categories were engendered as manly or womanly. Most often the manly is the inclusive and womanly the exclusive, though these could be and are reversed in exceptional cases.

Flowing from the tysic, as both source and summary of the web, were sensory, institutional, and cosmic expressions, often engendered respectively as right/left, man/woman, and winter/summer. Enclosive mediators included the heart, hearth, and sun at equinox. While this *puwha* web was shared among the native elite, each culture was distinguished by a particular <u>echo</u>, the apical matrix that pervaded that entire lifeway to provide meaning and order by recognizing overall attributes such as Right / Left, Man / Woman, Animal / Plant, Day / Night, Winter / Summer, Sky / Earth, or some other universal mirrored images.

The Pipe

Among the most potent examples of a matrix series are carved tobacco pipes revered throughout the Americas. Particularly elaborated ones occurred along the Mississippi drainage, made from famous pipestone still mined by natives in Minnesota.

Each pipe has 3 parts. These can only be joined together at the time and place of smoking, often during a ritual. The rounded bowl is womanly and exclusive, the drilled and decorated wooden stem (calumet) is male and inclusive, and the tobacco, providing the divine offering, is mindfully enclosive with fire. Assembled, each pipe was a universe composed of stone, wood, feathers, plants, animals, people, spirits, and complex beauty.

Each material is personified and engendered. Sacred pipe bowls are often made of dark red soapstone from the Pipestone Quarry in southwest Minnesota. In one version, this deposit is the body and blood of a monster transformed to good purpose. Today, saved as a national monument, Santee Dakota retain the right to excavate with hand tools and carve it for sale, much as their ancestors did for the prehistoric trade.

The stem, a straight wooden shaft skillfully pierced through to make a breathing tube or windpipe,[13] was decorated with all aspects of nature. It often had a prepared hide sheath adorned with colored porcupine quills, stone beads, copper pendants, and long feathers, particularly from eagle wings and tails. Paired stems, manly and womanly, known as calumets (Norman French for wand) were the key emblems of the intertribal adoption rite known variously as Hako for Pawnee and Hunka for Lakota.

Tobacco was often believed to be a thoughtful gift from a Creator to sustain or regain his, her, one's goodwill. The first appearance of the plant was associated with men, either from semen among Yuchi or as a replacement for a lost son. It becomes a universal offering as fragrant smoke through the medium of fire, the enclosive mediator most linked with illuminating inner thought, household hearths, and the sun.

A functioning pipe represented sexual intercourse (engendering), so the pieces had to be stored apart in the same bundle. When smoked together, the pipe combined the three culture components represented by a personal smoker (sensory), a ring of people passing it around (institutional), and the potent forces (cosmic), including the Creator – all of these invoked to enjoy this aromatic offering and spread goodwill.

Among many tribes, pipes were central to personal, town, and national bundles. Someone known as a pipe keeper was both holy and a member of the elite by birth, giving, or fame. Despite massive deaths and dislocations, such pipes survived to bless future generations. As solid objects, these artifacts helped natives to remember their past and enforce their identity.

The Americas are vital for the understanding of all humanity because this very flow and flux of *puwha* was given full expression throughout many varied cultures. It was expressed in ideas and in artifacts. Most places in the rest of the world, except Australia, were long subjugated under the rule of one state, one church, and one language. These oppressive institutions, except for Inkas and Aztecs, only came to all of the Americas half a millennium ago. Their imposition included schools and writing. Native scribes used this ability to record final glimpses of awesome native variety, as well as provide glimmerings of creative if painful solutions to on-going survival.

Therefore, avoiding romanticism or other impressionistic biases, Native North America speaks to the human condition of living with the land and each other, in terms of both the virtues of sharing and the dangers of selfish greed and hostility toward enemy outsiders.

13. For natives, proper modesty ignores phallic aspects except in private men's ceremonies.

IIa. *CULTURE AREAS*
Tribal Examples
TENDERS

Across North America, cultural patterns blossomed over time and space. Native peoples – interacting as enemies, kin, friends, and neighbors - cooperated, visited, intermarried, traded, prayed, or fought to create distinctive cultures. The largest units became <u>culture areas</u> {* = regions characterized by predominant foods, housing, kinship, and, most especially, rituals serving both to define and reinforce communal identity}. A <u>province*</u> is a distinctive subgrouping within a culture area, each named for a direction, though the middle one of three or more is designated the "<u>mid</u>" province for clarity.

Language Stocks

Classifying Native American languages into smaller, closer <u>families</u> and into large, remote <u>stocks</u> relies on the comparison of standardized word lists. Matching by means of such "lexical inspection" compares the sounds, words, and meanings. Most groupings have withstood tests of time and shifting intellectual fashions. They have become generally accepted on the basis of a consensus reached among scholars known as linguists.

A language <u>family</u> is constructed of obvious links showing internal similarities. For example, relationships among English, Spanish, and German is reflected in similar words – mother, madre, mutter – with regular correspondences of th = d = t. Similarly, Siouian speakers of the Seven Fires, east to west, call themselves Dakota, Nakota, or Lakota (d = n = l).

A language <u>stock</u> has ancient ties diffused through branching or "daughter" languages. Especially skilled linguists have been able to show abstract, high level, sophisticated relations between remote languages. They can reconstruct a word (as it probably was heard in an ancestral or proto-language) by a combination of lexical inspection and grammatical deduction. To do so, however, requires great insight and deep familiarity with the languages under study.[14]

After a century of coordinated research, linguists have been able to arrange the many languages of North America into over twenty major units. These are equivalent to Indo-European or Chinese in terms of the varieties of speech they encompass. Some covered huge areas, others were regional, and a few, known as <u>isolates</u>,* were spoken in only one locale and can not be readily traceable to any other language.

General texts frequently list these stocks by name only, with no attempt to describe each of them. Linguists working within a stock have a 'general sense' of what features characterize that grouping as distinct from other stocks. These traits are highly technical and likely to confuse a general reader. Still, they bear repeating, with the help offered by the front Glossary.

Edward Sapir,[15] who was unusually qualified by his genius and many fieldwork experiences, attempted classic portraits of various stocks, although scholars continue to debate, deny, or modify it. Indeed, Morris Swadesh, Mary Haas, and Carl Voegelin later made significant strides in clarifying several lacunae. Swadesh made the most ambitious reinterpretation and re-classification. He tried to expand the value of lexical comparisons by devising a formula, using basic 100 or 200 word lists (vocabularies), to suggest the length of time these daughter languages have been separated. The method, called lexicostatistics (or glottochronology), has since been discredited because there are no regularities for all language drift and fissioning.

Many of the names for these language stocks were introduced in 1800s during attempts at classifications by Albert Gallatin, Albert Samuel Gatschet, John Wesley Powell, and other scholars working for the US government or in Europe, using the names of representative tribes. Among these are Siouian (Sioux), Eskaleut (Eskimo + Aleut), Algic (Algonquian, Algonkian, Atlantic + Pacific), etc. Others are named for a word or words shared by all of its members: Na-Dene and Hokan mean 'human,' while Penutian combines shared words for 'two' and 'five.' Sapir suggested that Algic, Salishan, and Wakashan be lumped together in a stock called Mosan for a shared word meaning 'four,' but it has not withstood scrutiny. He also lumped together as Macro-Siouian both the Siouian and Hokan stocks, which others keep separate.

Eskaleut (Eskimo-Aleut) = inflective, with suffixes and greatly elaborated transitive / intransitive verbs, especially for mode* and person.

Algic (Macro-Algonkian) = inflective, with suffixes, some prefixes, reduplicating (repeating) stems, weakly developed noun cases, animate / inanimate nouns, obviative, and transitive / intransitive verbs. The suggested Proto-Algonkian homeland was on Georgian Bay off Lake Huron in Ontario, as evidenced by reconstructed terms for localized species of trees, plants, animals, and fish widely shared among modern daughter languages.[16]

Na-Dene = monosyllabic lexicals in a fixed order of post-positions (at the back), after abstract stems which seem to be essentially nominal rather than verbal. Verbs are active / passive, emphasizing voice and aspect over tense. Many Na-Dene languages have developed tone as a feature of their sound systems. Though the Athapaskan homeland was probably in east central Alaska, this family is remarkable for its far spaced outliers. These members have adopted cultural patterns from neighbors while retaining their own languages. Examples include the Navaho, Apache, Hupa, Plains (Kiowa) Apache ~ Kiłdeen, Nicola, and Swaal ~ Kwaliokwa ~ Klatskanai.

Macro-Siouian = prefixes, active / static verbs, freely compounding stems, and nouns incorporated into the verbs. It includes both Iroquoian and Siouian.

Hokan = pluralizes most nouns by multiplying with verb suffixes, prefixes for instrumental verbs and most pronouns, and has three vowels, with both long and short versions.[17]

Uto-Aztec-Tanoan = suffixes, compounds, reduplication, noun incorporation, and distinct subjects / objects, nouns / verbs. The proposed Uto-Aztecan homeland was in the Upper Gila River or northern Sierra region of the Southwest, based on shared names for local species.[18]

Penutian = resembles the grammar of the Indo-European stock with suffixes having concrete (physically specific) referents, many internal stem changes, and true noun cases. It is the most dubious of Sapir's stocks, aside from the accepted Californian Penutian Kernel. Some extend it to include Mayan, Tsimshianic, and Oregon languages.

Major revisions have regrouped Siouian, Iroquoian, and Caddoan into a Macro-Siouian stock. Similarly, Algonkian, Ritwan, Muskogean, and Gulf stocks can be included in an Algic mega-stock, making it more and more likely that all the inhabitants east of the Rocky Mountains may be traceable back to the same proto-stock, in contrast to the baffling diversity in the rugged terrain west of the Rockies.

The goals and techniques of linguistic prehistory have been discussed with care and insight by Edward Sapir,[19] Mary Haas,[20] and in several summary assessments.[21] The lifework of Haas deserves special mention because she was largely responsible for clarifying the broad framework for several East stocks, especially Algic and its Gulf component of the Southeast.

While linguists and archaeologists have rarely worked together to trace the prehistory of these Amero-linguistic stocks, some regional match ups have emerged. Shared farming rituals across the East, such as the Green Corn Busk, left similar archaeological patterns among diverse languages and cultures, such as Iroquoian, Algic, and Gulf. Mississippians, leaving truncated mounds along their namesake drainages, belonged to diverse stocks such as Caddoan along lower tributaries, Muskogean and Tunican in the south, and Siouian upriver on the Missouri. A Culture and a language were not always paired together. Regional patterns blended many local ones.

In terms of lifeways, regardless of languages, the oldest American occupation involved tenders who "worked with" their own landscapes. They did this first as big game hunters (Paleo-Indiens), then as harvesters of natural crops of plants, fish, and game. Ironically, the most recent natives of the Americas, the Eskimos, live its oldest economy, the hunting of large animals of the sea and land. Tillers who farmed ("worked over") the land developed later. They domesticated the sunflower and other foods, then, over thousands of years, adopted the trinity of squash, beans, and corn from Mexico.

14. Comparison of California Ritwan relations to Algic by Ives Goddard (1975) is a fine example of some of the scholarly complexities involved.
15. Edward Sapir, "Central and North American Languages", Encyclopedia Britannica 5: 138-141 1929.
16. Frank Siebert, "The Original Home of the Proto-Algonquian Languages" 1967.
17. Margaret Langdon, Comparative Hokan-Coahuiltecan Studies: A Survey and Appraisal 1974.
18. Kimball Romney, "The Genetic Model and The Uto-Aztecan Time Perspective" 1957.
19. Edward Sapir, Time Perspective in Aboriginal American Culture: A Study in Method 1916.
20. Mary Haas, The Prehistory of Languages 1969.
21. Thomas Sebeok, Native Languages of the Americas 1976.

Ethnology

Beginning with the hunting and harvesting pattern of the Paleo-migrants from Asia, a variety of adaptations by Native Americans evolved into continental Culture Areas.

For Tenders, these culture areas, from north to south, are the Arctic, Subarctic, Northwest Coast, California, Plateau, and Basin, though these last two are often combined as Intermontane.

Tenders lived off the landscape by hunting, harvesting, and fishing, using skills learned over thousands of generations to cope with the fluctuating bounty of nature. Not all foods were available every year, nor in the same amounts.

The Plains, last haven of the big game Paleo-Indien land hunting tradition, relied on enormous herds of bison, and later added farming along sheltered river valleys.

Ancestral Plains peoples, such as the Caddoans at the core, shifted with the seasons each year from hunting to farming. After Spanish reintroduced the horse into the Americas, tribes spread across the Great Plains. Many gave up farming in favor of full scale bison hunting.

For Tillers, much of the Southwest, Great Lakes, and East relied on farming, influenced by the northern frontiers of Mexican empires and their religious sects. The Valley of Mexico, with its huge population, used rituals and trade as outreaches to attract trade goods and foodstuffs.

Our knowledge of Native American ethnography {* = the descriptions of cultural forms} and ethnology {* = the comparative study of cultural forms} has been best clarified by close collaborations between academic and native intellectuals. Early Americanists often captured insider (member, emic*) perspectives. These were later overwhelmed, though, by museum and academic demands for current fads, theoretical impact, or stark scientific (global, etic*) concerns.

In the rush to save "vanishing" lifeways, scholars were sometimes oppressive, demanding information that natives were unwilling or unable to provide. With the realization of the enormity of the death and destruction (caused by introduced germs even before face-to-face meetings or battles, some academics became skeptical of all ethnohistoric data. In a few spectacular instances, however, close working relationships were forged between a scholar and a native. These often including a bond of adoption or fictive kinship. Important partnerships □ Franz Boas and George Hunt, Alice Fletcher and Francis La Flesche □ provided Native American data that remains vital to our research.

From an etic view, the human adaptation to the Americas involved the interaction of people and habitats. Scholars have again and again been impressed by the congruence between culture areas and natural environments. Overstating this match, however, early Americanists erred by insisting on environmental determinism, best (or worst) represented by George Louis Leclerc, Comte de Buffon (1707-1788), and much criticized by Thomas Jefferson (1743-1826).

Franz Boas and his followers began the shift to a more ecological view. They recognized the possibilities and constraints of any environment to influence (but not determine!) social patterns. Otis Tufton Mason, Clark Wissler, Harold Driver, Alfred Kroeber, and many recent scholars have mapped the similarities between society, ecozone, biome, and culture area. Discussion of the natural areas has been influenced by the work of Victor Shelford[22] on the dynamics of ecosystems and biomes and, as such, is preferable to the older species lists that imply fixed, static biotic provinces.

An ecosystem represents an interacting habitat and community, particularly its nitrogen, oxygen, and carbon cycles. A habitat is a land area with its characteristic climate and mineral constituents. A community is a dynamic interdependence of plants and animals generally viewed as the flow of energy through a food chain of plants, herbivores, and carnivores.

Other facets of an ecosystem are the life spans of community members, the succeeding series (called a sere*) of developmental stages leading to a mature and stable (climax*) ecosystem, and various sensitive intervals needing correct amounts of solar radiation, temperature, and moisture.

Only the prominent members of the community in each culture area will be listed in order to give a sense of its most distinctive, widespread, and culturally significant species. These resources provided the basis for the earlier "food areas" of Otis Tufton

Mason and the classic synthesis by Alfred Kroeber.[23]

Allowing for special area features, each culture area will be discussed in terms of its distinctive *biome*; staple *food* of diet and economy; *labor* by sex and season; basic *bonds* (bondings) of residence and cooperation mobilized by leadership, rank, and descent; *cosmology* with regard to mythic characters and area-wide rituals, and, finally, brief mention of conditions there *today*. Specifics of such culturally sensitive institutions as life cycle (with its crisis or life leap rites) and seasonal rituals will be considered within the context of a representative tribe.[24]

American mythologies were characterized by at least two types of charters. These are founding sagas (or epics) of first creation, or of last reform(ation). In the first, from either a void or primal waters, a universe becomes articulated and populated. In the second, within such a existing universe, reforms establish subsequent alterations until it resembles the modern one.

Before European contact, Native North America had a dense population of several million humans. By 1500 AD, these people, especially on the East coast, had been decimated by epidemics from Europe well in advance of direct face-to-face contacts. Earlier population estimates by Mooney[25] and Kroeber[26] were marred by ignorance of this wholesale devastation. Their approximation of a million people north of Mexico is thus far too low. Estimates for the entire New World hemisphere range from 5 to 100 million, depending on different research strategies.[27]

Upper estimates (by Sherburne Cook, Henry Dobyns), use a general formula based on a standard population ratio of about 25:1 for the hemisphere, which is applied to the nadir (lowest) population estimate for an area. In other words, twenty five people once lived for each individual who survived to be counted. Such high populations, lacking any devastating diseases, could have been supported by available open lands and expanding technologies. Critics favoring a lower population, however, argue that Native American technology was never sufficiently complex to support that many people. Both strategies, however, are in general agreement that populations were most dense on the western side of North and South America and that historic depopulations were the result of despair, slaughter, famine, dislocation, and, most especially, introduced disease epidemics.[28]

In addition to these biological factors, historical ones of church and state have biased Americanist data and interpretations. After the Natives had been set adrift from their aboriginal moorings, missionaries could successfully offer them another rudder in Christianity. Many denominations vied for converts. The least exploitative Indian agents were frequently missionaries, especially Quakers who were also, by and large, more tolerant of traditional beliefs and practices. Most missionaries bettered their own position by relentlessly eroding or suppressing native rituals and religion, or by opposing native prophets preaching replacement beliefs more appropriate to native beliefs.

During the Ulysses S Grant Administration, a program of assigning various reservations to different Christian, especially Protestant denominations, was tried briefly. It is the clearest example of church and state collusion, despite the Constitution insisting they be kept separate. The safeguards of civil and personal liberty cherished by other Americans were rarely allowed among the original ones.

Today, each reservation and region shows the imprint of these competing churches. For example, Catholics, the oldest missionaries, assigned Jesuits to the Northeast, Plateau, California, and Northern Mexico; Benedictines to the Western Great Lakes; Franciscans to the Southwest; and Oblates to the central Pacific Northwest.

Among Protestants, Moravians were in the Northeast and Alaska, Anglicans (Episcopalians) in Anglo-Canada, Baptists in the Southeast, Methodists in the Southeast and Pacific Northwest, and Presbyterians in the Southwest, Plateau, Great Lakes, and Alaska. All of the churches were in the Plains.

A few denominations were more tolerant and accommodating than others. Each generally followed the attitudes of the European nation from which its missionaries came. Catholics allowed a continuation of ritual, song, and dance traditions, while Protestants tended to suppress them in favor of hymns or hymn translations into the native languages. At present, many tribes suffer from opposing Christian / Traditionalist factions, often called Progressive / Conservative. Native communities have always had a broad and diverse approach to outside forces. These factions provide wide options for the whole group. But so-called "pagans" suffer the hardest time of all, because they are out of step with consumerism and media hype.

Today shamans explain that their guardian spirit powers ultimately derive from God, who gave these powers to their spiritual partners to be used for the special benefit of native people. In keeping with this ancient appreciation of all sources of *puwha* beyond the individual, most natives are extremely tolerant of other faiths – believing "The more religions, the better for you." Most natives see little difficulty in being devout Christians, especially on Sunday, as well as sincere healers or medicine bundle custodians, with an ecumenical tolerance more like Asians than Europeans, whose self-righteous bigots have long denied any such calm acceptance in favor of persecutions.

With regard to federal and state governments, as noted, current legal relationships between natives and other Americans is a legacy from the British. It survived, until recently, most strongly in Canada, where status as an Indian or a Native (First Nation) was legally determined by patrilineal descent. If your father is a "legal" Indian, so too are you. Should a native woman marry a Euro-Canadian, she thereby lost her status as a Native and any children become "Non-Status Indians." This is particularly difficult for the matrilineal Iroquois of Ontario and the Haida, Tsimshian, and others along the Pacific Northwest. Someone may be culturally a Native through his or her mother, but legally non-Native through the father. Several traditional leaders have solved the problem by adopting their 'sister's son' and heir as a son according to Canadian law. All of this changed, however, in 1986 when law C-130 was passed to allow each band to establish its own criteria for membership.

Canadian reserves and American reservations developed as a result of the British legal penchant for making treaties. The distinction between Treaty and Non-Treaty Natives remains an important one in Indien law. Thus the history of each tribe and culture area involves various treaties coaxed, negotiated, forced, imposed, and signed over the past few centuries. For the US, these are legally chronicled by Charles Kappler and Felix Cohen.[29]

After the American Revolution, relations with natives were conducted through the War Department.[30] The fledgling USA signed its first treaty, with Delaware chiefs, in 1778. Important early legislation affecting natives included the Commerce Clause in the Constitution. It reserves for the federal government the right to regulate trade with native tribes. From far away DC, US policy decisions, by intent or accident, erode tribal autonomy.

A Bureau of Indian Affairs (BIA) was organized within the War Department in 1824. It was given specific duties by the Indian Trade and Intercourse Act of 1834, and then was transferred into the Department of the Interior in 1849. The legal status of natives has been variously interpreted as that of treaty-making autonomous tribes, of wardship, of domestic dependent nations, of voters via the Indian Citizenship Act of 1924, and of present litigants with sovereignty seeking to recover more of their former autonomy. Long the dominant view, wardship was based on an inappropriate analogy by Chief Justice John Marshall in 1832 that the US was to tribes as a guardian to his ward.

Native relations with their homelands have been damaged or severed by many bad decisions. These include the plethora of treaties, the wholesale removal of Southeastern tribes to Indian Territory (now Oklahoma) in the 1830's, the ignominious Dawes General Allotment Act of 1887, the conscious-salving Indian Claims Commission of 1946, and the reactionary House Concurrent Resolution (HRC) 108 and Public Law 280 for Termination.

Each act reeked havoc. The Dawes Act reserved a quarter section (160 acres) per native adult, releasing the non-allotted "surplus" for immigrant homesteading. The 1946 Claims allowed Indian tribes to sue the government seeking "just compensation" for stolen or vastly undervalued land. HRC 108 was used to "terminate" (read: "abandon") from federal responsibility the Menominee of Wisconsin (since re-instated 1972), Klamath of Oregon, some Northern Ute of Colorado, some Paiute of Utah, Alabama-Coushatta of Texas, and others.

One bright spot in native-state relations came during the New Deal of Franklin D. Roosevelt. The 1934 Indian Reorganization Act (IRA) recognized tribal rights to political autonomy for purposes of determining their own form of government, justice, inheritance, membership, taxes, land use, and internal affairs. The 1934 Johnson-O'Malley Act (JO'M) is intended to improve native educational, medical, agricultural, and social welfare services through contractual arrangements made with the states.

Despite heartless (money driven) shifts in native-state relations, bureaucracy has been remarkably consistent. Common experiences within the (mis)administration of reservations can be seen from the very beginnings of the Brotherton Reservation for remnant Delawares in New Jersey (1758-1802).[31]

In the face of these harmful native-state struggles, a greater cohesion arose among native peoples. Usually called Pan-Indianism, it emerged from an increasing recognition of their shared tribal plight while confronting state-protected settlers. It was reinforced by passive resistance, honed in federal boarding schools, directed against alien ideas and institutions in order to perpetuate their own.

Communities like those at Hopi in northern Arizona have fought bitterly to protect their ancient way of life. After they came up from the Underworld, according to ancient belief, they accepted the great hardships offered by Masauwu, lord of Life and Death, who said "I am living in poverty, but in peace. If you wish to share such a life, you may."

22. Victor Shelford, The Ecology of North America 1963.
23. Alfred Kroeber, Cultural and Natural Areas of Native North America 1939.
24. [* General features of costume, housing, and technology will be left to the pictures that accompany the chapters on each Culture Area. A fuller view of these can be found in Driver 1962 and Whiteford 1970.]
25. James Mooney, The Aboriginal Population of America North of Mexico 1928.
26. Alfred Kroeber, Cultural and Natural Areas of Native North America 1939.

27. T Dale Stewart, <u>The People of America</u> 1973: 35.

28. Some academics have tried to use body size to figure out various migrations into the New World. However, Stewart (1973: 49) has noted that the body size distribution of American pumas parallels the body size of humans throughout the hemisphere. Rather than support migrations, these physical variations support Bergmann's Rule, which holds environment so influences stature that the tallest populations are in temperate regions and the shortest ones in the tropics. Thus, body size correlates with body energy, supplied by diet and, most particularly, its vitamins. Natural foods in the tropics are low in vitamins (rainfall leaches many soil nutrients), yield less energy, and generally dampen activity and growth.

29. Felix Cohen, <u>Handbook of Federal Indian Law</u> 1942, revised 1982 +.

30. Frances Svensson, <u>The Ethnics in American Politics</u>: American Indians 1973.

31. Edward Larrabee, Recurrent Themes and Sequences in North American Indian-European Contacts 1976.

ARCTIC Peoples

Eskaleut (Paleosiberian Stock)
    Aleutic ~ Unangan
      Eastern (Unalaskan)
      Western (Atkan-Attuan)
    Eskimo
     Alaskan
           Yup'ik
            Kogmiut
            Magemiut < marsh
            Kayaligamiut
            Nunivagmiut < Nunavik
            Kuskokwagmiut
            Togagamiut < Togiak River
            Nushagamiut
            Aglumiut < Aglur 'ridgepole' Yukon Delta
            Kaniagmiut
            Chugachigmiut
           Iñupiak
     Canadian (Inuit)
           Kinugmiut
           Malemiut - Kotzebue Sound
           Nunatagmiut - Noatak R
           Noatagmiut - Upper Noatak R
           Kopagmiut
           Point Barrow
           MacKenzie > Siglit
           Copper > Kidnelik
           Caribou
           Netsilikmiut < seal
           Aivilirmiut - Repulse Bay Igulik
           Baffin Land < Nunatsiaqmiut 'beautiful land'
           Kigiktagmiut - islands
           Ittibimiut < other side - East Hudson's Bay
           Tahag Tarramiut < shady
           Suqinirmiut < sunny, south
           Greenlandic
    Polar (Thule)
    West Greenlanders
    East Greenlanders (Ammassalik)

< = name derivations

1. The Arctic Culture Area

Ecosystem

Tundra is the predominant landform. It is covered with ice fields all winter long. Strong winds and severe cold kept this land spare and stark. Ground vegetation, like sedge grass, marsh, and arctic heath, was low, meager, and inedible. Meat was the staple and hunting was the way of life. While nine months of the arctic year consists of cold, white winters, there are some long but muddy summer days. Animals include muskox, Barren Ground caribou, arctic fox, polar bear, and arctic wolf, along with smaller hare, hoary marmots (whistlers), and lemmings. Birds include ptarmigan, snowy owl, plover, and seagull. Coastal rivers offer fish, and oceans provide seals, whales, walrus, and sealions.

These northernmost coasts are occupied by the Eskaleut (Eskimo-Aleut) language stock, spoken from Siberia to Greenland. In the Americas, its major subdivisions are Unangan (Aleuts) along the island chain pointing west; Yup'ik in western Alaska; Iñupiat in northern Alaska; and Inuit.

The natives of this region are best known as Eskimos, though that term has become politicized. Some say it comes from an Algic term for "raw meat eaters", but it probably comes from one meaning "snowshoe wearers" that was introduced into Europe through contact with Basque cod fishers. Throughout Canada, Inuit is the preferred term, but it does not sit well with coastal Alaskans, the largest and densest population of this culture area, who are Yup'iks. Inuit is spoken across Canada and eastern speakers became a Territory known as Nunavut ("our land") on 1 April 1999. These frozen lands discouraged outsiders, though Eskimos battled neighboring Athapaskans or Algonkians.

The arctic has eastern (Greenland), central (Canadian), and western (Alaskan-Aleut) provinces. It is is unique in the world as one of the very few areas where a distinctive physical type, speech, culture, and habitat coincide. Eskimos of the Arctic share distinctive looks, language, lifeways, and locale, before outside contacts and pressures intensified.

Foods

Inuit, most of the Canadian Eskimo, were one of the few human populations to subsist only on meat. It particularly came from seals, along with caribou or salmon. A very strong taboo always separated foods of land and sea. They could not be cooked in the same pot, or misfortune would result.

Labor

The Inuit economy was strictly by age and gender.[32] During the warmer months, Inuit lived in skin tents. During the winter, each province had its own preferred abode. These were a house with sod covered timber frames in the west, igloos (coiled ice block houses) mid, and stone houses in Greenland. Sometimes, a bigger house was built as a men's club for resting, meetings, and rituals. In Alaska, villages had a massive men's lodge, called by a blanket term of <u>kashim</u>. Usually, a married couple and their children, together with stray relatives, occupied a house. An effective hunter or shaman might have more than one wife, who lived together. Aleuts occupied loaf-shaped communal houses (known as barabara generally, ulax in some dialects), partially underground and sod covered like nearby hills.

Every house had a men's and a women's domain. Usually, the hard floor, used as a work surface, and the cold outer storage compartment was used by men. The soft, fur-covered, sleeping platform where the family sat during the day and slept at night was the responsibility of women. The wife was closely identified with the soapstone lamp that brought light, heat, and comfort to the home. It used oil rendered from animals killed by her husband. Respect for the environment, particularly land and sea, was reinforced, as noted, by severe taboos against mixing caribou and salmon flesh in the same pot, for women, or hunting them with the same weapon, for men.

Genders had separate but equal duties. Only married couples survived because a man and woman had to work together to live well. Men hunted, while women processed and cooked the meat that fed her family. Men darted around in sleek, pointed, closed kayaks and women in broad open _umiaks_, moving families, household gear, and cargo.

During seasons of plenty, families might gather together to form "bands" with sigers {* = sig leaders}, but they lasted only a few days until provisions ran low. While respected at all times, sigers came to the fore only long enough to coordinate a particular task, such as net fishing or caribou hunting, and then rejoined the crowd. Larger groupings were known by a geographical or place name and the ending "-miut" ("people of"). Large and complex towns were occupied by Yup'ik near river mouths in southwestern Alaska.

The Arctic sea changed from being open and windy in summer or frozen over in winter, when seals were harpooned at their breathing holes. Hunters waited long hours on the ice to see a puff of air against a downy feather that meant a seal was exhaling below. In a flash, a toggle harpoon was embedded with a jerk of the line. Jerking on the cord rotated this point at a right angle (90 degrees), so it was lengthwise across the hole and embedded in the flesh to secure the seal. After a tug of war, it was hauled out safely. Another dangerous encounter came to a happy end. When seals never came or hunters missed, the specter of famine loomed. Chilling accounts tell how only a few people in a camp survived until spring by a combination of selfishness, sorcery, murder, cannibalism, or being able to digest almost anything.

During spring and summer, animals and birds were hunted from kayak, dog sled, or foot. Fish were taken by hook, leister {* = 3 pronged fish spear}, and trap. Seal, walrus, and whale were harpooned from boats.

In northwest Alaska, umiaks under the command of each _umialik_ ("boat owner") went in flotillas to hunt baleen whales. The wife of the whaler had to stay still on her bed to encourage their prey to be immobile. Once the mammal was harpooned, floats and drags attached to the line provided enough drag and resistance to exhaust the whale. Then hunter(s) could dispatch it, tie shut its mouth, and haul it home.

Inuit and Unangan hunters learned the seasonal and behavioral movements of all these animals intimately well. They made their task easier by driving prey near camp or into shallow bays, shore areas, or other places where they would be exposed. Children were often given young animals as pets to learn species behavior at firsthand.

An especially welcomed food, after a long winter, were fresh eggs taken from the spring nests of waterfowl, such as seagulls. Bands went inland during the summer and fall to intercept enormous caribou herds moving north to drop their young amongst plentiful tundra grasses and moss. Drives were helped by evenly-spaced rock cairns (_inukshuk_). Set in standing rows, each one piled up to human size, they forced caribou down avenues in view of concealed hunters.

Inuit are especially noted for their pragmatism, practicality, and technical ingenuity. They were famous for devising gadgets like the toggle-headed harpoon, ivory wound screw plug, and soapstone lamp. Living in a harsh and unpredictable world of stark, fatal realities, they used ice, snow, skin, bone, stone, antler, and sparse wood in creative ways. Some remarkably gifted individuals invented simple devices that benefited their communities enormously. Such tool-based ingenuity, along with appropriate survival skills, widely appeals to Americans because they are fond of the many gadgets found at Home Depot and other warehouse appliance stores. This kind of living with the land has recently been called TEK {* = techno-environmental knowledge}.

Basic Bonds

Inuit social structure was densest and most complicated at the western extreme in coastal Alaska than in the other provinces. The basic unit was the nuclear family of husband, wife, children, sometimes joined by grandparents, young spouses, and other stray kin. Where and when prey was larger (whales) or more abundant (herds), families camped together and formed a band. These flexible social relations involved a bilateral descent system, often with a patri-emphasis. This is the so-called "Eskimo" system of cousin terminology (which is also shared by modern Euro-Americans), distinguishing siblings from cousins.

With low population numbers, community sentiments were expressed through a series of formal partnerships, involving brief exchanges of wives, good-natured insults, trade goods, names, or specific cuts of meat. People conformed to public expectations because of strong but subtle pressures that were reenforced by ridicule, critical songs, gossip, and snide remarks. If behavior did not improve, slugging contests were held, ultimately leading to ostracism from the community. This was tantamount to death. The worst antisocial behavior resulted in sanctioned murder by close kin. A brother often took care of removing an offending sibling.

Except for awesome shamans, most Inuit recognized only sigers. These men were judged and respected on the basis of their continued economic successes at organizing productive hunts, advising wisely on animal behavior and seasonal movements, and overseeing the equitable distribution of meat by their wives. As long as they remained agile and cogent, older men participated in a community council with considerable public influence. Women coordinated their own activities under the guidance of older women of leading families. The demands of the food quest, however, were such that the very old and very young were the first victims during famine.

The hallmark of a male leader was not only his successes in the economic sphere. It also included his ability to attract and support several wives and to produce numerous, healthy children, especially sons. In this regard, the belief in the greater mastery of the environment given to shamans by their spirit partners meant that they had an advantage in coercing women into marriage. In some camps, a successful hunter reinforced his position of leadership by forming a bond with a shaman. Together, they made an unbeatable combination when bolstered by the usual types of social control.

Ranks

While all Eskimos had shamans and sigers, Alaskans and Aleuts also recognized hereditary ranks of leaders and slaves (war captives). In some areas, particular families were noted for consistently producing worthwhile leaders in the local elite. While most shamans were men, some women also undertook the profession by undergoing the same type of apprenticeship. They learned to acquire and control spirits, to cure diseases, to relieve community hardships, and to rely on feats of ventriloquism and sleight of hand to make people feel better. Women, by and large, kept close to the home and family, traveling mostly to feed and help leadership, authority and prestige.

Shamans had special relationships with *puwha* to cure an illness of a person and any social ills of the community. Certain families produced effective shamans for generation after generation. In the most dramatic of all cures, a shaman mystically journeyed to the ocean bottom to comb tangles out of the hair of Sedna, the fingerless woman in charge of all the animals.[33] Taboo violations, abuse of animals, and ill will among humans caused these snarls. The shaman undertook to soothe Sedna so she would again send animals to hunters. He could only apply the comb to Sedna's hair, however, after someone had confessed to the breaches that caused these problems, such as combining land and sea foods together. This personal confession began absolution for the entire community.

With all of these assertive abilities, moreover, people suspected that a shaman was not adverse to using their powers selfishly. This sinister aspect produced considerable anxiety and fear among their co-residents, all wary and watchful of shamans.

Cosmology: *Myth, Ritual*

For western Inuit, the world was created when Raven "fished up" earth from the sea bottom. Though highly entertaining, Inuit mythology abounds in hostile and dangerous spirits, animals, monsters, and people. Some myths presage present conditions, such as one about women who ate their own babies and became seagulls, a tabooed food. Most mammal food was controlled by Sedna.

The most widespread Inuit ritual came at midwinter when large numbers of people gathered to feast on stored and froze foods, play games, learn from stories, and enjoy competitive games, shamanic performances, and sexual license. Alaskan Yup'ik had a number of elaborate rites centered in the community house and involving masked performances to propitiate animal spirits, honor the dead, and feast kin. During all rites, 4 was the pattern number for men and 5 that for women.

Today

After the Industrial Age arrived, traditional subsistence activities used guns and snow mobiles or lapsed because government subsidies (transfer payments) now provide food, though not the best. The fur trade brought Inuit into the world's money economy, and fur continues to be a source of cash in the north, although this market remains depressed. Instead, Inuit soapstone sculpture now provides steady revenue. Almost all Canadian Inuit and Alaskan Eskimos produce carvings, prints, or art designs for native-run cooperatives selling to the world art market. Politically active, the Inuit Tapirisat (sig) pursues native land and legal claims.

Christianity has engulfed traditional beliefs, but not eradicated them. European nations have imposed police, courts, and written laws. Danish influence and commercial fishing impacted Greenland peoples. Russian and American policies still impose on native Alaskans. Russian rogues brought violence and diseases that severely depopulated the Aleutians. Surviving Unangan men were indentured into the Russian sea otter trade. A few Aleut hunters were even taken to islands off the California coast and "rented" to US hunters during the Russian colony at Fort Ross.

Since 1867, Americans have tried to introduce English among Aleutians, though they were already literate in Russian and their own Unangan cyrillic alphabet. But English-

Only was the bias. In 1971, to gain legal access to Alaskan oil, the Alaska Native Claims Settlement act (ANCSA, amended 1987) assured 40,000,000 acres of land and $962,500,000 to about 200 village and 12 regional corporations. These include seven of the Inuit, three of Athapaskan, one Aleut, and one Tlingit-Haida. Another corporation for natives living outside Alaska was set up in Seattle, Washington, the historic gateway to this panhandle.

32. Nelson Graburn and Stephen Strong, <u>Circumpolar Peoples</u> 1973: 137ff.
33. She has many names, but Sedna serves as a cover term. During famine, her father threw her overboard, then cut off each finger as she tried to hold on. From each joint or digit came one species of animals (land game from one hand, sea from the other) to feed people and save humanity. Sinking to the sea bottom, every breach of a taboo or abuse of animals tangles her hair, until, in anger and frustration, she withholds game from hunters. Eventually, after confession by someone in the community, the shaman, in trance, went to her, combs out her hair, and pleads until she agrees to forgive the offenders and release game animals.

TRIBAL EXAMPLES

Netsilik Inuit of Eastern Canada

Life is difficult and demanding among these five bands of Central Inuit. They are collectively known as Netsilikmiut, meaning "Where there are seal" + people (-miut). Their society is based on bilateral kinship, cooperation by gender and seniority, and formalized partnerships. While bilaterality could be extended to define a large personal kindred, the effective kin group was a nodal kindred. Each is composed of an elderly couple with married children, their spouses, and their children.

While each couple and their children travel together as a unit, their grandparents or oldest elder supervise all closely related families. Significantly, this overall leader is called inhumataq ("the one who thinks"), with his thoughts closely bound up with proper puwha sanctions. Sometimes a shaman, advantaged by his own puwha, led a kindred.

Often, the node was a hunting team of a father and his sons. It then continued as brothers after his death. Variations included a nepotic relation between uncle and nephews, or an affinal one between father-in-law and sons-in-law, leading to a eventually node of brothers-in-law. In all cases, the situation is defined in terms of men because they are hunters, providers of food in an environment where game is abundant and vegetation is scarce. Important meats were seal and caribou. The only edible greens were sorrel and the contents of caribou stomachs.

Women have the vital duties of butchering, preparing, and cooking meat or fish, always in separate containers. Similarly, men butchered caribou, but women cut up seals. Often, the wife of the node leader coordinated the work by all women of that kindred.

Netsilik gender roles were distinct, separate, and complementary. Men had priority as hunters, supplying meat, fish, and grease. Men produced artifacts and utensils from snow, ice, bone, wood, stone, and, more recently, iron. The Polar Inuit of Greenland, though, long had access to iron from crashed meteors, before these were taken to a museum in New York City. Women worked with skin and hide. More broadly, men were associated with the Outside world through hunting, and using hard, pointed, thrusting implements (harpoon, kayak) made of bone, ivory, and wood. Women had bonds with the

Inside world of the camp and house (dish lamp), working with soft, pliable, comfortable materials.

Once finished, each tool belonged to its user. Thus, women became the owners of essential furnishings, made by men, like the oil lamp, ulu {* = semilunar knife}, sewing needles, wooden meat trays, muskox horn spoons, and soapstone pots. Men owned their clothing made by women.

During seasonal transhumance {* = seasonal treks to familiar camp sites}, Netsilik moved to river banks during spring and fall to take salmon trout from weirs {* = fence traps}. Summer was spent inland hunting caribou. For winter, people moved to large seal-hunting camps on the coast. A good Netsilik hunter killed 30 seal per winter, considerably below the average of 200 expected by a North Greenland Inuit.

Genders worked apart. Men ate separately from the women and children, presumably to safeguard their hunting luck. Everyone at a hearth shared the identical fare. For example, the same piece of meat was passed around so everyone could bite off what they wanted. Families {* = commensal kindreds} were defined, hence, by the sharing of home, hearth, and food.

Gender domains were linked through marriages of five types. These were (1) a betrothal between parents to marry their gestating (in womb) or infant children, (2) parents marrying off their adolescent offspring, (3) a hunter arranging his own marriage, (4) taking a wife away from her husband, and (5) murdering a husband to marry his widow.

The preferred arrangement involved the marriage of cousins. Netsilik assumed that relatives were more trustworthy than distant kin or total strangers. In addition, cousin marriage encouraged affines {* = inlaws} to become even more familiar and cooperative. Further, a bride stayed near her own family. In other marriages, a wife removed from her close kin often felt very lonely, with disruptive consequences for all the families involved.

Accidents, starvation, and suicide from dark despair took their toll. In 1923, the Netsilik population was 259. It was reduced both by the starvation of 25 people during a two year period, and by an attempted suicide each year during the previous fifty, with 35 of these being fatal.

Population was also limited by the practice of female infanticide, assuring that more males survived. According to census figures, eighteen couples, responsible for 96 total births, killed 38 female infants.[34] Netsilik justify this by saying that girls do not hunt and when they finally are old enough to help, they marry and move away. Killing a girl allowed a woman to try again for a son.

Such killings, however, depended on local conditions, allowing rescue by someone's intervention. For example, a girl could be saved by giving her a name, thereby providing her with full human status and goodwill from ancestors. Also, she might be adopted and raised by another family, or she could be betrothed to a future husband and saved by such a family alliance.

As cruel as these practices may seem, they were effective (if pragmatic) solutions toward the survival of the larger group in a severe environment. Within the group itself, social flexibility allowed quick response to changing conditions.

Social solidarity was encouraged by various partnerships. Sometimes, these overcame emotions and ambivalences. Partners agreed to apportion fourteen cuts of seal meat among specific families, share identical names, accentuate shyness between two men, or engage in wrestling, ribald joking, antiphonal singing, and wife exchange.

Partnerships esteemed sharing food and comradeship, while also highlighting sources of potential or actual friction to be dealt with.

Sometimes, general ambivalence erupted into hostility or conflict. It might be caused by ill-timed mockery, jealousy expressed through verbal insult or sorcery, anger at another's laziness, minor misunderstandings due to inappropriate jokes, disputed access to women, or just bad moods.

To deal with such points of conflict, Netsilik applied a scale of strategies, ranging from generalized gossip to a formalized confrontation in a ritual fist fight or drum (song) duel. If all were tried and failed, the culprit was judged by community consensus to be incorrigible. A senior close kinsman, usually an elder brother, was then asked to execute him. Since his murder involved only close kindred members, a blood feud was prevented.

One of the most impressive things about Netsilik society is its breadth of tolerance and understanding. Their harsh environment and pragmatic outlook creates a society with great vitality. This is expressed through the concept of _sila_, meaning both "thought" and "outside" because "Thought, to the Eskimo, isn't a product of mind, but the forces outside of men."[35] The Outside remains in check only as long as Inuit apply their own thoughts to it, maintaining a complex dialectic of Mind as both inner thought and outer reality. Neither of which can survive without the other.

34. See Asen Balikci, The Netsilik Eskimo 1970: 148.
35. Edmund Carpenter, Eskimo Realities 1973: 44ff.

Yup'ik of Southwestern Alaska

As with the self-names of other peoples, Yup'ik derives from yuk "person" and -pik "real, genuine" in their Eskaleut language. By far the largest, densest population of Eskimos, they view themselves as part of a web of relations which includes all "persons," both humans and animals, who have ever lived in their region. The souls of all these persons are immortal, provided their remains were treated with reverence after death. This allows for the rebirth of that soul within another body. Throughout this endless cycling, the same soul and name remain together.

Yup'ik culture is based on the respectful maintenance of boundaries and of passages between human, animal, and spirit worlds. It is unlike Euro-American notions that rely on the diversity of individuals united only through self-interest and a concern with essences and core substances. Yup'ik believe in a primordial, undifferentiated universe whose shifting and permeable boundaries depend especially on human action. They keep everything in place, both in public and private, so as to circumscribe and usefully direct any flow of activity. Such human attention to rules, especially about sharing food and other gifts, involve active participation both to create differences and to maintain connections.[36]

Of foremost importance was "awareness" (_ella_), whose ubiquity included that of the universe itself (_ella yua_) and of each and every component (see below). Today, as in the past, Yup'ik out on the tundra "feed the land" by burying food and offerings to show their regard for this greater mindfulness. Everything had to be done with slow, careful deliberation to avoid offense. Berries were picked with individual regard, and a good person always turned driftwood to relieve its tedium and discomfort from lying in one position. This universal watchfulness was decorated on many artifacts as the circled dot motif ☉, sometimes with five rings indicating these levels above the earth.[37]

Each dot was, of course, a _tysic_ {* = nexus of time, space, and affect centering}.

In Yup'ik, such simultaneous fusion of time and space occurs in words such as _ciuliaq_ = ancestor, leader. It is derived from _ciu-_ meaning "the forepart of a body, front area, or time before"; in contrast to _kingu-_ meaning "rear end, back area, or time after".[38]

They were missionized by Russian Orthodoxy in the 1830s, Moravians since 1885, Catholics after 1888, and devastated by epidemics of smallpox (1838) then influenza (1890, 1900, 1918). Yup'ik are now shareholders in their own regional Calista Corporation (meaning "worker," from _cali-_ work) for the Yukon-Kuskokwim Delta. Their cosmology remains vitally integral to their lives as hunters and earth stewards.

The Moravian mission was particularly ironic because of the role of Rev. John Kilbuck, a Delaware Indian descended from famous men like Chief Netawatawas and his son Captain Killbuck, who were active in Ohio during the Revolution. John was raised and ordained by Moravians to appreciate another, more individualized, sense of community. Yet both Yup'ik and Moravians believe that waste is a result of being morally lax, not just of mindless carelessness.

Creatively, Yup'ik became Christians by restating European notions of responsibility and accountability in terms of their fundamental belief in awareness, and of salvation in terms of rebirth, not as separate individuals but within a community of believers. Only the doctrine of original sin had to be wedged into their prior beliefs.[39]

Yup'ik elders have been willing to discuss these tenets because they regard "their words as the conduit for immortal facts about the way the world is", firmly believing "people must not be stingy with their knowledge. They must give away [share] what they know or it will rot their minds."[40]

Two epics reflect Yup'ik views of their universe. The first is about a boy who lived with Seal immortals and came back to teach people how to show respect and regard for these prey. Boys who wanted to become successful hunters were told to keep busy, often shoveling snow away from doorways and entrances, keeping water buckets full, and acting with reserve and decency.

A good hunter focused on making a passage, a clear way, between himself and the animals he hunted. He was constantly thinking about and working hard to attract their attention. By clearing snow away from openings, these animals got a clear view of his face and agreed to benefit him by offering their own flesh. After proper treatment of their outer remains, the spirits of these animals were reborn again. Indeed, for Yup'ik, existence was an endless cycle of birth and rebirth, with the same "persons" (both human and nonhuman) interacting over eons.

The second tale was about the girl who returned from the dead to teach people how to feed and clothe their deceased kin by giving gifts to living namesakes and burning offerings in a fire.

Until 1900, Yup'ik men and woman lived separately, the men in a lodge (_qasgiq_) and the families in a sod covered house (_enet_). The men's lodge was "sweat house, hotel, workshop, medicine lodge, and dance hall."[41] Sea mammals in turn lived in their own underwater lodges with a skylight to watch human actions. These favored proper behavior, right thought, and good deeds by those who were decently restrained and circumspect.

Women and children provided food, clothes, and support. The family or woman's house was variously associated with womb, moon, and holy homes of _tuunraat_ {* = spirit bosses (keepers) of animals}. The purplish spot at the base of a newborn's spine was a mark left by the old woman who was believed to push each baby out of a womb. In general, the lodge represented spiritual reproduction, and the sod house the sexual reproduction of the community.

Everything in these worlds had a _yua_ {* = an in-dwelling human-like, fully-aware being}. Those of sea animals, at death, contracted into the air bladder to await rebirth. Each human had many components, such as breath, mind, vitality, shade, and name, inherited within its own immortal cycle of rebirths. These names were not gender-specific so rebirths as often as not changed sex.

Awareness allowed animals to know the thoughts and intentions of hunters and others. Humans trained throughout life to increase awareness, building upon experiences, stories, instructions, taboos, and religious insights to improve their own minds. Children, in particular, had to be taught to use all their senses to synthesize information during each and every day. Upon awaking, they were sent outside to get a sense of any effects of wind, weather, and wayfarers on the day.

The aim of childhood was ellange-, to obtain awareness as a lasting memory of experiences. After they were five years old, boys moved into the men's lodge, where women brought food every day. When a girl waited for the empty bowl, she too was instructed in moral behavior toward the universe. At her first menstruation, these lessons intensified until she "stood up", reborn as a woman.

Marriage negotiations were not concerned with beauty, wealth, or mere status, but whether the potential partner handled food in a careful, honest, and respectful manner. The groom's family made new clothes for the bride, especially a parka decorated with designs from his mother or grandmother. The foremost rule of any marriage was not to "injure each other's mind."[42] Hardships were shared. A husband restricted his activities every time his wife was in menstrual or postpartum seclusion.

At the beginning, the primordial world was thin when all beings, from humans and animals to extraordinary creatures, interacted more easily. Now it is hardening and thickening. Humans have a greater moral duty to act responsibly to prevent illness because a body reacted physically "to the way a person chose to live life."[43] If standard treatments failed, a patient received a new name to start over.

These extraordinary persons, going back to ancient times when the earth was very thin, include nine beings with more human forms, and eight or more with partial human characteristics.[44]

Those more humanoid are often shape-shifting fantasticals. Their names and attributes follow.

(1) _ircenrrat_ look like humans most of the time, though sometimes only a yard tall, or take outer forms that are half human/half animal, or fully those of wolves, foxes, or whales (orca, balukha). Living in hilly places and gathering into lodges, when humans might overhear their songs, they provide warning of death and disasters, while capture of their artifacts brings good luck;

(2) _egacuayiit_ are tiny people who mimic, echo, and mock humans in humorous ways, and take fish from traps to carry off inside their enormous sleeves;

(3) _cingssik_, derived from "point, tip," are tiny with pointed heads covered by conical hats, sometimes using a thimble for a hat and a shiny needle for a cane to visit human lodges when everyone was away;

(4) _tenguirayulit_ are very fast, move through the air, and like to take out livers from humans they adopt;

(5) _amikuk_ are huge, yet able to travel through everything, whether land or water, though

only in straight lines. For variety, they sometimes take human form pulling a sled as a
(6) *qamulek*;

(7) *qununiq* live out on the ice as a man-like seal wearing five rain parkas, mittens, and boots;

(8) *agiirrnguat* appear from a long distance, attracted by someone waiting too anxiously;

(9) *tengmiarpiit* are giant bird-like people nesting at low hills and volcanic domes, protecting friendly humans, but destroying others.

The other semi-humanoid creatures follow.

(10) *itqiirpak*, a huge hand in the ocean with a mouth in its palm and on each finger to devourer any child who makes too much noise;

(11) *meriiq* (from meq 'water') sucks blood from a big toe if a family carelessly lacks water in the home;

(12) *muruayuli* sinks into the ground while walking;

(13) *arularaq* (from *arula* 'be in motion, move back and forth') has three toes per foot and six toes (not fingers) per hand;

(14) *quugaapiit* live underground, swimming through solid land, where their buried bones suggest a connection with prehistoric mastodons;

(15) *amllit* are abrasive, living in shallow, milky-colored lakes, where, only by stepping over them, never going around, can a human prevent a quick death;

(16) *ingluilnguq* (from half of a pair) are one side of a normal person with only one eye, ear, arm, leg;

(17) *miluquyuli* are teenager size, fond of maliciously throwing heavy rocks at humans;

(18) *ulurrugnaq* is a sea monster that eats whales.

Movements between domains and dimensions, both extraordinary and ordinary, were carefully monitored. Passages were blocked by thoughtlessness. This included clumsy handling of a knife, sleeping late, eating and drinking carelessly, bumbling through a door, being noisy, or wasting personal talents. A proper person was ever concerned to restrict his or her breath, sight, thought, speech, and body movement. He or she carefully wears a belt and hood to bind their actions, deter unclean influences, and hold in their life force.[45] Weapons, tools, and containers were carefully made and decorated both to please that artifact itself and to attract game animals to such a pretty lure.

Before the annual seal hunt, men prepared beautiful gear, while women made them new, handsome clothing. Hunters prepared by fumigating their bodies and tools (sitting mat, pack basket, food supplies, and kayak) so as to smell like the land, which was attractive to seals. During a hunt, the hunter's wife had to remain motionless like the land. This encouraged seals to be listless. If she ate, slept, or groomed, her husband lost his concentration. Their spousal cooperation resulted in formal "ownership" of a slain seal by the husband while it was outside the house, then by the wife once it was inside.

At death, the constituents of a human body separated into mind, breath, feeling, life, warmth, shade, and name soul. The corpse was washed, bound in five places, and taken to a grave. Five stops were made along the way if a woman, four if a man. Similarly, the family remained quiet five days for a woman, four for a man. A surviving spouse was considered "sealed" (confined) for a year to safeguard his or her survival. Over time, a spirit could reincarnate five times within the endless flow of rebirths.

Five major rituals of the traditional Yup'ik celebrated such renewals. Bladder Festival returned to the sea all the air sacks of animals slain by hunters during the previous year so they would be reborn. For five days, men evoked their spirit helpers in song and dance. Each year, with greater elaboration every ten years, a Feast for the Dead invited these shades into the _qasgiq_ to receive fresh water, clothing, and sustenance. The Kelek masked dance invited animal spirits into the lodge to be entertained by men and women reversing normal roles and cross-dressing. At the center of most masks was a tiny humanoid identified as the "thinking part" of that being. A Messenger Feast hosted a visit from another village. The Asking Festival honored cross-sex cousins within one community.

Most significant in all these relationships was the quality of one's mind, as revealed through the senses to enhance "awareness." Appeals to these senses opened passages between worlds as aptly illustrated by two examples. Human "ghosts" craved fresh water, provided by the living during rituals, because their own was too salty from all the tears shed by their kin. At death, mourners wailed loudly to make sure the spirit was awake for its journey to the beyond. Similarly, a seal had to be harpooned while it was awake so its spirit would retract into its air bladder. To kill a sleeping or inattentive seal was to murder it forever.[46]

Immediately after a seal was killed, it was anointed with fresh water in its mouth and on four flippers. Similar regard was shown to land animals, except the five-point anointing used seal oil, because these spirits yearned for the sea. Their separate habitats and desires decreed a firm boundary that kept land and sea foods apart at every meal. In Yup'ik the word for fish also meant food, so many restrictions applied to their handling and preparation, according to whether they were taken by trap or by net.

In everything, Yup'ik observed their duty to carefully perform "acts of differentiation – cutting, binding, covering, circling – to create the possibility of future relation."[47] When approaching boundaries between worlds, Yup'ik prevented any crossover by covering their bodies with gut parkas; by painting themselves with soot, clay, and urine; or by placing grass mats or skins between themselves and the thin earth lest they slip through.[48]

Always, Yup'ik probity showed their active awareness of human duty toward this moral universe, connectinf as community members (not as isolated or alienated individuals) willing to fulfill obligations to other persons by supplying what these lacked, such as fresh water to seals, light and heat to belukha whales, and dry land to fish.[49]

Emphatically, to Yup'iks, "people were social beings first and individuals only if they forgot themselves, in which case their downfall was assured."[50]

36. Ann Fienup-Riordan, Boundaries and Passages ~ Rule and Ritual in Yup'ik Eskimo Oral Tradition 1994: 46, 48.
37. Ann Fienup-Riordan, Boundaries and Passages 1994: 59; 1990, 55.
38. Ann Fienup-Riordan, Eskimo Essays 1990: 202, 212.
39. Ann Fienup-Riordan, The Real People and the Children of Thunder 1991: 367.
40. Ann Fienup-Riordan, Boundaries and Passages 1994: xii, xvii.
41. Ann Fienup-Riordan, The Real People and the Children of Thunder 1991: 53.
42. Ann Fienup-Riordan, Boundaries and Passages 1994: 175.
43. Ann Fienup-Riordan, Boundaries and Passages 1994: 189.
44. Ann Fienup-Riordan, Boundaries and Passages 1994: 62-87.
45. Such restraint was like the moral force of Victorian women wearing a corset, whose stays, not incidentally, were often made from whale bone.

42

46. Ann Fienup-Riordan, <u>Boundaries and Passages</u> 1991: 113.
47. Ann Fienup-Riordan, <u>Boundaries and Passages</u> 1994: 355.
48. Ann Fienup-Riordan, <u>Boundaries and Passages</u> 1994: 360.
49. Ann Fienup-Riordan, <u>Eskimo Essays</u> 1990: 186.
50. Ann Fienup-Riordan, <u>Eskimo Essays</u> 1990: 76.

Inuit Explorers: Hannah and Joe

From ancient times, Eskimos relied on each other's skills for all to survive in the most threatening situation. With the arrival of Europeans, however, these expectations were sorely tested. Eskimos continued to sustain others, even though most strangers were unable or unwilling to reciprocate. Indeed, this unsung dedication by native guides is particularly well illustrated by the ordeals of an Inuit couple from Cumberland Sound of Baffinland. Both were from leading families, and so learned to fulfill their moral and ethical duties. Always hospitable and dedicated, <u>Tukkolerktuk</u>, the wife, was born in 1839 and became known as Hannah to her English and American companions. Her husband <u>Ipilkvik</u> was also known as Joe.[51]

Because they were well connected and friendly, the couple was taken to England in 1858. There, they lived as local celebrities, learning English and wearing European clothing. Once duly married in a church, they dined with Queen Victoria. After almost two years, they went back home. Hannah taught other Inuit women how to knit.

In 1860, Charles Francis Hall, an American explorer directed by a "vision" to learn the fate of the Franklin Expedition (1845-48), came to the region. He became friends with the couple, who taught him to speak Inuit. Together, they visited local landmarks. Joe's grandmother, *Okioksilk*, told Hall about a colony of foreigners that led him to the remains of Martin Frobisher's landing of 300 years before.

In 1862, Hall took the couple and their son to New York, where the infant died. While trying to observe all of the restraints that followed the death of a child – such as avoiding fresh food, not sewing clothes, and not making weapons for a full year – the couple helped Hall raise funds for another expedition to find Franklin evidence.

After two years, homesick, they headed home, but the whaling ship left them off at the wrong place. For nine months, the team survived by living with other Inuit groups, but this was not easy. They were saved from hostile threats by Hannah, before she had another baby that died, and protected from marauding European whalers by Joe. Eventually they did get back home.

In 1868, they sailed again with Hall, who returned a hero. The couple settled in Groton, Connecticut, so their adopted daughter could attend school. In 1871, they tried for the North Pole in the ship <u>Polaris</u>, but, overwrought by an unruly international crew, Hall died. Their vessel became ice-bound, but all survived on meat killed by Joe and Hans Hendrick, a West Greenlander with a wife and four children on board.

After drifting loose, <u>Polaris</u> struck an iceberg. After the captain sent the surly crew of nineteen onto the ice flow, the empty ship floated away. Again, Joe and Hans kept everyone alive by building igloos, making oil lamps of cans, and hunting. Hannah had another child who died. After floating for six months over 2,000 miles, they were rescued by a passing ship. Joe was never thanked nor paid.

The couple returned to Groton, where Hannah died in 1876, a year after their adopted daughter. Joe returned to Baffinland, guiding several later explorers. In all, their training and skills benefited many Arctic explorers, despite horrendous personal hardship.

51. Keith Crowe, <u>A History of the Original People of Northern Canada</u> 1991: 131-135.

Kridlak

Long after the eastward spread of Thule practices, Scandinavians and other Europeans moved west, seeking to trade for furs and hunt for whales. In their wake, however, they left an unforeseen devastation. It was caused by germs spread among native people without any immunity, creating a slaughter worse than the bloodiest battle. Whole communities were wiped out. Though spared, survivors were culturally crippled and suffering.

The resulting desolation made the efforts of missionaries easier. Natives openly questioned the validity of their ancient beliefs in the aftermath of such tragic devastation. Also, practical Inuit readily accepted European healthcare and medicine. These were obviously effective, at least for germ-caused diseases.

In rare instances, however, help came not from outsiders but from fellow Inuit, motivated by both curiosity and concern. The most famous example of such relief was the heroic adventure of Kridlak (Qitlarssuaq), a famous shaman from northern Baffin Island.[52]

During the 1830s whalers told him about other Inuit (Polar Eskimos) isolated in northwestern Greenland. Fascinated, he went into trance and consulted with spirits, who convinced him to find these needy strangers. Kridlak told others about his mission and several families, about 40 people, joined his quest.

Leaving from Bylot Island, they traveled all winter over sea ice. In the spring, they settled and hunted bears. By the second winter, as they decamped, conflicts arose. Old Okik's family became homesick and decided to kill Kridlak so that everyone would turn back. When the shaman and his brother were ice fishing alone, Okik's family attacked, but was driven off. Thwarted, half the people returned to Bylot Island.

Kridlak and the others went on for six years until they came to Smith Sound, where they could see Greenland across thirty miles of frozen water. Moving carefully, they crossed and met two sleds of Greenlanders, who were startled to meet other people like themselves. After a moment of tension, both groups stuck their weapons into the snow and embraced. After several centuries apart, survivors from great distances met together.

Fifty years before, epidemics killed off adult Greenlanders who knew how to make and use snowhouses, kayaks, bows, and fish spears. Kridlak's people retaught these skills and intermarried with Greenlanders to renew the kind of transgenerational community needed for viable survival.

As Kridlak aged, he became homesick and, about 1870, received a vision to return to Bylot Island. Surviving followers, though no longer young and hardy, also agreed to return home. After Kridlak himself died the first winter, they lacked determination, wandering aimlessly and suffering many hardships. As starvation loomed, survivors resorted to cannibalism. Finally, after five years, they turned back to Greenland to stay.

Today, thanks to Kridlak, Inuit on both sides of Smith Sound, whether Danish Greenlanders or Canadian Inuits, recognize a common kinship. It was confirmed by visits westward in 1966 and eastward in 1970. Most recently, Inuit have gone by snowmobile or plane rather than by dogsled. In 1978, however, to commemorate the original trek, five Inuit in three dogsleds from Igloolik traveled 1,800 miles retracing the heroic trek of Kridlak and his kin.

44

52. Keith Crowe, <u>A History of the Original People of Northern Canada</u> 1991: 135-137, 235.

2. Subarctic Culture Area

Ecosystem & Provinces

Woodland forests called <u>taiga</u> grow across this huge area, mostly evergreens such as pine, spruce, hemlock, and fir. Typical species are wolf, lynx, wolverine, bear, and caribou, along with the snowshoe rabbit, marten, and great horned owl. Open areas were marshy meadows called *muskeg* (from a Cree word). Along broad streams, moose thrive on willow, tamarack, birch, alder, and poplar. In high alpine meadows, the pika (related to rabbits) sets out grass and twigs to sun-dry and then store for feeding on over the winter.

Culturally the area can be divided into western (Na-Dene Athapaskan) and eastern (Algonkian) provinces, each their likely homelands. Proto-Athapaskans were probably matrilineal, polygamous, subsistence fishers, who married bilateral cross-cousins, or by sororate and levirate; although some groups shifted to bilaterality quite early.[53] Among Athapaskan-speaking tribes, widely scattered in the Subarctic and Southwest, continuing matrilineal preferences and vague matriclans support this argument about their ancient traditions.

Na-Dene speakers represent the last great movement of native peoples from Asia into the America heartland about five thousand years ago. During the 1200s (probably motivated by a volcanic eruption), some Athapaskans followed the Rocky Mountain corridor into the Southwest to later become Navaho and Apaches. Others settled along the California-Oregon border or linked up with Kiowa on the Plains.

While these Athapaskans retain their own languages, in each case they adopted characteristics of neighboring cultures. Thus, Navaho assumed many features from Pueblos – such as certain clans, sand paintings and weaving – but modified them in distinctive ways once they became sheep pastoralists. The Apaches continued with a mixed economy.

Foods

Staples for the Athapaskans were salmon in the Pacific drainage and caribou in the Arctic drainage. For the Algonkians, prime foods were deer and moose, along with wild rice near the Great Lakes.[54]

Labor

Men engaged in hunting, trapping, fishing, and tool making. Women prepared and stored game and fish, kept house, and carried heavy burdens when traveling. Unencumbered, men could defend the group or take any game that were sighted along the route. Only men drove dog teams. The bulk of hunting was done during the fall, but small-scale winter hunting was made possible by snowshoes. Female subsistence contributions were largest during the summer and fall.

Before European contact, each member of a dog team was attached to the sled by its own cord so that the team "fanned-out" in front. After contact, the tandem hitch was used and each dog "followed the leader". With the fanning out, each dog worked separately, but, much more European, in tandem, according to the Alaskan joke, unless you are the lead dog, the view is always the same.

Tribes such as the Ingalik adopted from nearby Yup'ik the men's house (<u>kashim</u>).

It served as the nexus of the community for council deliberations, sweat baths, cures, feasts, funerals, and elaborate masked rituals. Survival demanded much adaptability and flexibility, as it did among other food tenders.

SUBARCTIC Peoples

Athapaskan Family
  Arctic Drainage
        Bear Lake
        DunneZa (Beaver)
        Chipewayan
        Dogrib
        Hare
        Sarsi
        Slavey Dene Thah
        Yellowknife

  Yukon-Kuskokwim Drainage
        Ingalik
        Koyukon
        Tanana

Cook Inlet
        Tanaina

  Cordilleran
        Babine
        Upper Koyukon
        Gwichin
        Mountain
        Han
        Upper Tanana
        Tutchone
        Tagish[1]
        Kaska
        Tahltan[1]
        Tsetsaut[2]
        Sekani
        Carrier Dakelh
        Chilcotin Tsilhqot'in

Algic Stock
  Maritime
        Wabanaki
        Mikmaq
        Maliseet
        Passamaquoddy
      Abenaki
        Penobscot
        Pennacook
        Wawenock
        Kennebec
        Saco
        Androscoggin
      Algonquian
      Innu (Montagnais)
        Naskapi
      Cree

[1] Tlingitized
[2] Tsimshianized

Basic Bonds, Ranks

Because disease and dislocation devastate small dispersed populations, Subarctic social structure has varied in size. A so-called "atomistic view" emphasized individual autonomy during the fur trade. Later, typologies of band sizes were correlated with seasonal abundance of food resources to feed larger aggregates of survivors.

The basic unit was, most commonly, a **nodal kindred*** sharing kinship and residence with sigs.* The sigers* were known for their consistent hunting success, good character, even-handed generosity, and powerful immortal partners.

Married couples were essential to every community, bridging distinct men's and women's roles. Fishing provided an opportunity for men and women to work together. Otherwise the genders worked apart. Families generally lived together under the influence of an older parent or sibling of the kindred. Leadership depended on the job at hand. The pool of respected elders able to serve as sigers focused on hunting skills, sensible decisions, and spirit allies. Individuals communicated with their immortals via dreams, thereby providing help, heed, or warnings about upcoming events. Always, elders led by example, never by command.

Only shamans had constant authority in these communities. He or she healed the sick, prayed for successful hunts, and directed puberty ceremonies for girls on the verge of womanhood. Their ability, success, and moral intent were evaluated by the number of healthy and productive members in their own families. Any shaman who could keep his or her own family healthy and well supplied clearly had strong *puwha*.

When trading posts of the fur trade were set up in the north, camps and settlements merged into larger groupings called regional bands, each based in the same river drainage, and tribes. These groupings encouraged new types of leaders, who were supported from this outside trading. People along the same drainage often cooperated so that some could hunt for food while others trapped furs. It was difficult to do both and survive. Animals with the best meat to eat never had the best fur to trade.

Tribal organizations were not typical for Athapaskans. Distinguishing tribal names – like Beaver, Carrier, Slavey – were given by Euro-Amero-Canadians because all referred to themselves by variations of "Din-ney," as in the name of the Na-Dene stock. (Naa is Tlingit for 'person.')

Many Athapaskans were characterized by three vaguely defined matriclans and by physically strong and aggressive war leaders. While Athapaskans tended toward the matrilineal, the Algic tribes tended toward the patrilineal. Given the necessary and endemic flexibility of the Subarctic, these social structures might better be described as bilateral with a patri- or a matri-emphasis.

Similarly, social ranks correlated with the effective use of *puwha* and astute knowledge about the behavior of animals, people, and the environment. Generosity incumbent on leaders fostered loyalty and internal cohesion, but a leader could not ask or order anyone to do anything. He could only suggest by example and provide limiting conditions and alternatives. This encouraged people to make a decision that was also mutually beneficial for the community.

Puwha was a prerogative of men, who competed for and with it. Based on study[55] of the Dunne-Za (Beaver) of northeastern British Columbia, the key feature of Athapaskan political process was the "medicine fight" (described below), also common throughout Native America in many variants. Men strove to control each other. Women basked in the reflected supernatural glow of their fathers, brothers, and husbands. Aspects of men's roles were therefore finely specified, but those of women were more general and indirect for both Athapaskan and Algic cultures. Women's *puwha* revolved around giving birth and supporting life.

Cosmology: Myth, Ritual
Subarctic charters include variations on the Earth Diver motif in which an animal

fished or brought up earth from the sea bottom to create the world. More elaborate reform epics feature a transformer, who is generally Raven-like for Athapaskans and Rabbit-like among Algic speakers. Among their most important adventures was the theft of fire for human use. Dunne-Za (Beaver) cosmology was due to the efforts of Muskrat, who dove for earth, and Swan, who set cultural rules.

Throughout the Subarctic, animal species were frequently said to be under the control of a giant immortal leader, sometimes called the "boss." Athapaskans feared Nakhani, a bogey man of the bush, and *Wechuge* (Algic *Windigo*), cannibal giants with ice hearts who transformed humans to be like them. Such an anti-social criminal had to be killed and cremated so as to melt its heart to prevent any chance of reviving.

Shamans had the ability to cure, to lead rituals, to lure game to hunters, to predict the weather, and to foretell the future. These abilities were elaborated in the Great Lakes as the Ojibwa Shaking Tent and Midewiwin enactment (see).

The distinctive Athapaskan public ceremony (except for those of the MacKenzie drainage) is a Give Away. It has aspects of the potlatch,* ostensibly to elevate the status and prestige of the host by confirming his generosity and legitimating his claims to leadership.

As always, these family privileges were sanctioned by an immortal. According to the Tagish of the Yukon, the famous Klondike Gold Rush of 1898 was started by an Indien's encounter with Wealth Woman, who was adorned in marten skins, dentalia (tusk shells), and copper. Traditionally, her long fingernails were also copper, but since the Rush, they have been described as made of gold.

Today

Many traditional economic patterns have been altered because less hunting and fishing is being done in lieu of transfer (welfare) subsidies from the Canadian government. Most Subarctic peoples are now Christian, often Catholic. Guardian spirits continue to appear as angels and the Christian virtue of charity through generosity is strongly upheld. Such change, borrowing, and adaptation is ancient.

Western Athapaskans have long been adopting Pacific Northwest Coast culture styles. Tahltan adopted cremation, moieties, and crests from Tlingits. At least some of the Gitksan villages of the inland Skeena River had earlier been Athapaskan speakers before becoming Tsimshianized. Tsetsaut remnants joined the Nishka Tsimshian as captives, then rose by ability and dedication.

In the eastern Subarctic, Penobscot with other nearby Abenaki tribes and Miqmaq with other Wabanaki formed historic confederacies later influenced by Iroquois, specifically Mohawks.[56] But growing political cohesion was no match for Canadian authority. The James Bay Dam Project by Quebec Hydro, flooded much of this prime hunting territory in the 1970s.

53. Isadore Dyen and David Aberle, Lexical Reconstruction: The Case of the Proto-Athapaskan Kinship System 1974: 428, on the basis of linguistic reconstruction and ecological inferences.
54. James Vanstone, Athapaskan Adaptations, Hunters and Fishermen of the Subarctic Forests 1974.
55. Robin Ridington, "The Medicine Fight: An Instrument of Political Process Among

the Beaver Indians" 1968.

56. Frank Speck, The Eastern Algonkian Wabanaki Confederacy, 1915b.

TRIBAL EXAMPLES

Abenaki of the Maritime Northeast

Among these Algonkians of the far Northeast, often known as Abenaki (or Dawnlanders), their rivers, lands, and families were bound together by a special relationship with an ancestral patron animal spirit. It was created at a moment of transformation when the earth's waters were released.[57] The Abenaki (including Pennacook, Saco, Androscoggin, Kennebec, Wawenock, Penobscot) were organized on the basis of who did and did not share this bond of spirits, animals, humans, and lands.

In their charter epic, Giant Frog swallowed all the waters, causing a drought. Everyone began to die of thirst. People moaned they were as dry as a particular animal – a turtle, beaver, wolf, trout, haddock, etc. Gluskap, their culture hero, killed the Frog, then toppled a birch tree onto to its body to force out the water. Running down this trunk and branches, the flood formed river systems with a lake in place of the leaf at the end of each twig. As water reached ancestors, some of them plunged in to drink, immediately changing into the animal whose thirst they claimed. Others remained human but took their named animal as the sign or badge (totem) of their ancestral lands. These included camps and hunting territory along a particular stretch of waterway.

Penobscot call this section, *nziibum* "my river," while Timagami Ojibwa call it *ndakiim*, "my land." Its boundaries were marked by emblems of the family animal itself, a patron totem called by Penobscot either *baohiigan*, "empowerer" or *ntuutem*, "my parent-in-law, alien partner". Highest in rank were Bear and Squirrel, who provided band leaders for all land totems. Frog and Sturgeon provided water totem band leaders.

This formal relationship was based variously on descent, marriage, or adoption. Inland from the coast, Penobscot patrons (with some of their equivalent English family names in parentheses) were Lobster (Mitchell), Crab (Susup), Sculpin, Eel (Neptune), Bear (Mitchell 2), Toad, Insect, Fisher, Whale (Stanislaus), Beaver, Sturgeon (Sockalexis), Wolf (Polis, Susup), Frog, Squirrel (Attean), Raccoon, Wolverine (Lewis), Mermaid, Otter (Saul, Nicola), Lynx (Fransway), Rabbit (Newell), Yellow Perch (Penewit), and Raven.

Families were expected to inherit some physical attributes from their animal. For example, among Penobscots, "The members of the Whale family (Stanislaus) are pointed out as large, portly, and dark persons, those of the Rabbit family (Newell) as small, timid, and weak, those of the Bear family (Mitchell 2) as orderly and dignified, and so on."[58]

Among the Wabanaki (Canadian Maritime Algic confederates), tribes themselves had game animal emblems depicted as being out in front of two humans in a canoe. The Passamaquoddy pair held paddles and followed a pollock fish, Maliseet held poles behind a muskrat, Miqmaq on either side of a peaked middle gunwale held paddles behind a deer, and Penobscot held a pole and a paddle behind an otter. Settlements and regions among the Miqmaq also had animal logos (see East).

57. Frank Speck, The Family Hunting Band as the Basis of Algonkian Social Organization 1915a; The Eastern Algonkian Wabanaki Confederacy 1915b; Game Totems Among the Northeastern Algonkians 1917a; 2. Malecite Version of the Water-Famine and Human Transformation Myth, Malecite Tales 1917b; "Abenaki" Clans -- Never 1935.
58. Frank Speck, "Abenaki" Clans -- Never 1935: 530.

DunneZa *(Beaver) of Canada*

Initially, the DunneZa world consisted only of a cross inside a hoop floating on the primal waters. Muskrat, as Earth Diver, went for a speck of earth from the bottom of the sea. This mote was placed at the center of the cross, where it expanded into the present earth. The DunneZa are at its center along the Peace (formerly Beaver) River.

Earth's population flourished. Years later, a boy was vilified by his step-mother, causing his father to abandon him on an island. There he encountered a Swan immortal who advised him to use the *puwha* of the Sun to dry and store the meat of migratory birds he was able to kill. In this manner, the boy (himself renamed Swan) thrived until able to avenge himself on his parents.

Thereafter, he went through the world changing monstrous animals who had been eating humans. He placed them under hills or in valley bottoms to be available as immortal partners for future generations of humans, notably the DunneZa. While he was contending with prototypical animals, he changed his name to Saya (meaning Sun), to remind everyone that the sun in the sky is the key to proper orientation, so necessary for a successful life.

The functional hub of the world for any DunneZa was and is the camp. Each camp, regardless of its duration, represented a tysic*. It had to have a stand of pristine bush directly to the east so that visionaries have an unobstructed and untainted route toward the sunrise. Any partnership began when an immortal met a human to give a song and specify the contents of a mystic bundle. Once assembled, such a bundle hung suspended above the eastern or head end of the sleeping area. The owner must sleep with head to the east, under the bundle, so as to receive full benefits of the Sun at sunrise.

Every partnership also involved a specific set of restrictions or taboos that had to be most strictly observed. Generally, these were intended to keep the immortal and the human distinct so as not to intensify *puwha* into a destructive force. Thus, those with Spider *puwha* could not listen to the music of string instruments because these were too much like webbing. If such taboos were breached, even inadvertently, and balance could not be restored, then the human transformed into a <u>wechuge</u>, a monster ogre cannibal from the myth age. He or she had to be killed and entirely burned up, hopefully before eating others.

These and other teachings remind the DunneZa that a good life requires moderation and proper orientation, especially to significant trails. As important religious personages, Sun and Moon are recognized as trail blazers (not as stationary objects), moving along fixed routes attuned with *puwha*. People live best by recognizing these trails and seeking out important intersections.

The means for such identifications is via dreaming. This is a potent force in the cosmos attributed to the Sun – who represents the primordial cross and hoop because it is round, moves east and west each day, shifts from a low in the north at winter to a high in the south at summer, and thereby subsumes all important trails and tracks of *puwha*.

A good hunter must first dream of the intersection of his own trail with that of a game animal in order to be able to kill it. He can only do this by maintaining a proper orientation to the trail of the Sun, which provides an overview of all routes. Remaining attuned to the Sun, therefore, brings health, life, and a supply of meat.

While both Sun and Moon are called by the same word (sa), these planets are distinguishable as day sun and night sun. Further, in contrast to the Sun, immortal Moon has negative associations linked with ghosts and death, moving along its trail with a retrograde (backwards) motion. While the Sun's trail leads into the future, Moon's leads into the past, like a shadow.

All visionary partners learn to follow the trail of the Sun properly. Only the most remarkable ones, known as dreamers (prophets, Swans), learn the trail of the Moon to achieve total orientation and mobility. They are identified with the Swan because its immortal form has the ability to travel beyond the sky dome and yet return to earth intact in the same body.

Humans attune themselves to trails through song. *Puwha* given to a visionary by an immortal is literally called "one's song" in this Athapaskan language. Accompanying drumbeats represent the sound of footfalls along the way; changes in the melodic line are turns and twists. Via dreams and song come knowledge of proper trail orientation, rhythms, intersections, and the patterning of the universe.

By orienting themselves in the larger world, DunneZa trace bonds of kinship with each other, either through consubstantiality (shared substance) or affinity (marriage). Their society is built upon this duality to form **personal kindreds** (both bilateral and egocentric, in lieu of corporate descent groups), everyone tracing his or her own web of relatives on both sides to allow for maximum social flexibility.

In their kinship ideology, those people related to you through same-sex relatives are regarded as consubstantials – consanguineals {* = shared "blood" in American ideology}, while those related through cross-sex relatives were actual or potential affines. Generally, consubstantials comprised mother and her sisters, father and his brothers, then either sisters and daughters for a woman or brothers and sons for a man. Affinals, therefore, were mother's brothers, father's sisters, and the children of sisters or brothers, depending on one's own gender.[59] Among DunneZa, men had priority and *puwha*, but women had their own awesome *puwha* to give life.

Medicine Fight

Local politics are expressed in terms of the medicine fight. This is a contest between the *puwha* of contending visionaries. Success or failure is judged according to relative strengths or lack of vigilance. Pragmatically, it serves to justify uncertainties in an environment where even a good hunter kills only once in four outings.

Such a successful hunter shared his kill with everyone else in the camp, providing a religious basis for accrediting him with authority. In return, others gave their goodwill and support. This thriving partnership with an immortal provided his own family with protection, security, and healthy progeny.

A good hunter became a provider for the whole camp. Others, by accepting his meat, became his dependents. His authority continued as long as the camp was well fed and his children hearty. When he grew too old to hunt, he could maintain prestige by remaining healthy and active, showing that his *puwha* was still strong. Yet such prestige and respect could be tinged by suspicion since an elder could insure a long life for himself and dear relatives by siphoning off the lives of others.

Instead of the interplay of luck, fate, and ability most Euro-Canadians would expect, hunting was an expression of tension among degrees of *puwha*s. A hunter who returned with meat affirmed that his *puwha* was stronger than those who came back empty-handed. Every kill displayed control. Every miss was both a personal failure and a religious setback. Vicissitudes of game and habitat kept everything in flux. There were no consistent winners or losers. The main source of stability was those elders with on-going authority by virtue of their continued fitness and cogent advice. Repeated success by a younger hunter resulted from proper dreams in which his personal trail intersected that of a game animal.

A medicine fight developed when an unsuccessful hunter dreamed of combat between his own animal immortal and another one allied with a more successful hunter, who usually belonged to a different, hostile kindred. Based on this experience, a dreamer made a veiled pubic accusation to alert community sentiment as to their particular circumstances, personalities, political contexts, and general economic conditions.

The accused could respond in two ways. Any misfortune had either of two theories of causation. One was the aggressive use of *puwha* by another. The other was the breach of taboo by oneself. Thus, the camp watched closely to judge by consensus who was triumphant or at fault. Either his accuser brought the trouble upon himself and his kin by taboo violations, or he himself fought his accuser to the death. Thereafter, the contenders concentrated on dreaming a pitched battle between their animal-guised guardian spirits: one's Bear battles the other's Wolverine to the death.

At the time of the accusation, the fortunes of the accused were almost always superior to those of the accuser. If such success continued, the accused won more admiration. If his success vanished and the accuser provided game, such "coming from behind" earned the accuser even greater esteem by effectively mobilizing stronger *puwha* through dreaming. By logic, four outcomes were possible. Neither hunter was lucky (O); both hunters made a kill, negating each other (–); the accused had success (+); or the accuser increased his luck (++) and political base by making good on his accusation.

In all, the medicine fight was a practical justification for the unpredictability of success. Its cultural ramifications guaranteed that a successful hunter will share his dividends with others and that the whole community will have a religious basis for maintaining authority during flux and stress.

While hunters held these contests in the abstract, others with *puwha*, particularly shamans, would sometimes physically act out the fight to fuse together body, mind, and immortal into an effective force for victory.

Ultimately, all of these manifestations of *puwha* were attributed to willful control (as "freedom from risk"), the most scarce and valued resource known to the DunneZa. It was displayed by routine success, the most tangible and useful expression of a strong and binding link of a human to an immortal of the epic age.

59. Warren Shapiro, The Ethnography of Two-Section Systems 1970.

3. The Pacific Northwest Coast Culture Area

Ecosystem

Rain-drenched coastal mountains, thick with evergreen forests, were drained by many waterways. This coastal forest was characterized by a biome of hemlock, wapiti {* = American elk}, deer, northern redwood, Sitka spruce, and, most especially, red cedar. It provided logs for posts and steam-molded canoes, as well as straight grained planks for house sides, bentwood boxes, and essential tools.

PACIFIC NORTHWEST Peoples

Na-Dene Stock	Penutian Stock	Chimakuan Family
Eyak	Chinookan	Chimakum[1]
Tlingit	Wishram-Wasco	Quileute
towns[2]	Chinook	
Yakutat	Klatsop	
Chilcat	Kathlamet	Wakashan Family
Hoona	Clackamas	Nootkan
Auk	Oregon Penutian	Makah
Taku	Takelma	Nitinat
Killisnoo	Kalapuyan	Nuuchahnuth[3]
Sitka	Yamhill	Kwakiutlan
Kake	Tualatin	Northern
Stikine	Santiam	Heiltsuk[4]
Klawak	Yonkalla	XaiXais
Tantskwan	Coosan	Owikeno
Sanyakwan	Miluk	Haisla[5]
Athabaskan	Hanis	Southern
Kwaliokwa	Yakonan	Kwakwaka'wakw
Tlatskanie	Yaquina	
Umpqua	Alsea	Salishan Family
Chetco	Siuslaw	Nuxalk[6]
Tututni		Central
Tolowa	Tsimshian (?)	Comox
Hupa	Coast-Southern (Sküüks)	Pentlatch[1]
	Niska-Gitksan (Gitxsan)	Sechelt
Haida(?)		Squamish
Kaigani		Halkomelem
Masset		Cowichan
Skidegate		Musqueam
Kunghit		Chilliwack
		Straits
		Lummi
[1] extinct		Songish (Lkungen)
[2] tribal town (kʷaan) dialects		Sooke
[3] aka Nootka, AtHˤ		Klallam
[4] aka Bella Bella		Nooksak
[5] aka Kitimat		Lushootseed (Puget)
[6] aka Bella Coola		Twana

Tsamosan
Quinault
Chehalis
Cowlitz
Tillamook

Of note, these planks and basketry materials are~were taken, after giving thanks, from a living cedar tree that was not killed by this stripping process and continued to grow around such scars. Travel was mostly by water because dense undergrowth of thickets, berries, and brambles obstructed land routes, except along river banks.

Its three provinces traced kinship in different ways, northern = matrilineal, mid = ambilateral, and southern = patrilineal. Northern Pacific includes Na-Dene, Tsimshian, Wakashan, and Salishan languages. The last two are limited to this area. Na-Dene includes Athapaskan, a far-flung stock across western Canada and Alaska, as well as outposts to the south. The Salishan family extends from the Pacific to western Montana.

Food

Men and women processed five species of salmon during huge runs (some now near extinction) during the spring, summer, and fall. Other staples were candlefish* (olachen, hooligans) in the north and acorns in the south. Haida and Makah relied more heavily on halibut. Though fluctuating from year to year, food generally grew in abundance and variety, harvested with elaborate skills and technology, such as a herring rake {* = a long pole embedded with wooden spikes, later nails} used like a paddle to impale these small fish and drop them into a canoe. These lush but locally variable resources were evened-out by elaborate social organizations and complex international ~ intertribal relations. For example, all salmon seem to fluctuate in terms of a peak of abundance every seven years, with species peaks.

Labor

Throughout the Northwest, men were concerned with animals and live fish. Women devoted their efforts to plant foods, from fresh seaweeds and greens of spring to berries and nuts of autumn, and to fresh catch. Seasonal mobility took people out of winter towns of cedar plank houses, devoted to feasting and rituals. In the spring, they broke up into small camp sigs* devoted to specific economic (food getting) activities. In some cases, families took along plank siding from their winter house to make into lean-to shelters.

Each sig had a series of summer camps, each conveniently located near their resources for fishing, berrying, hunting, and foraging. In the north, these camp sites were owned by a corporate household. The shift in fall between family camps and communal villages was buffered by festive games, sports, and contests held before they reoccupied their winter home.

Basic Bonds

Pacific Northwestern societies involved graded social ranks and/or classes. While some scholars have argued for rank but not class, others insist on class alone.[60] Most communities, however, recognized three classes of elite, commoners, and slaves. Only the elite had graded ranks, consisting of an upper ten percent of the community in possession of hereditary name-titles and "owned" resource plots. In particular, they knew the appropriate rituals and formulae (dicta) to assure success.

In all provinces, the noble elite class was by far the largest. Overall, these societies suggest the shape of an upside down pear-shape, which has been proposed for the Salishans. It nicely captures the essential organization of Pacific Northwestern societies. The wide top was elite title-holders, the bulbous body was lesser nobles and "good" commoners, and the smaller neck was slaves, who made up another ten percent of the population.[61]

Both freeborn social classes cooperated because they were members of a corporate descent unit. Membership allowed the holding of the ancestral name-titles; displaying of hereditary Crests as designs, songs, and dances; and use rights (called legal usufruct) to resource areas.

The fundamental unit was the household, a "house" (in the same sense as the House of David or the House of Windsor) and dwelling place shared by these three classes. At the rear of the house, beside its secluded storeroom of sacred treasures (masks, costumes, and carvings), lived the nobles who "owned" that house. The eldest man was the leader of the household, but his wife (mid) or sister (in the north) provided other linkages among the members.

Along the sides lived families of commoners, who attached themselves to the house as kin or laborers. Families kept their own fires along the sides. In the middle, however, was a large public hearth used to cook meals for the noble owners or for guests attending a celebration. Beside the front door slept slaves, taken in war or the children of such captives, whose lives belonged to their owner, along with all of their efforts.

Houses owned stories (epics, sacred histories) naming the past people, places, and resources used and thus claimed by ancestors. Some of these house histories can be related to regional patterns known to be in existence for over two thousand years. These involved fishing, berrying, seaweeding, and hunting sites claimed by a specific house. Most stories in the Northwest, therefore, are owned and copyrighted by households. Only a few are phrased in such general terms that they were widely known and used to teach a moral.

Winter towns included a row of big plank houses facing the beach. Each home was inhabited by several related families. In the north, kinship was traced through women of various clans. In the mid zone, it was traced through both parents. In the south, the father's side was emphasized.

Tlingit, Haida, and Tsimshian confederacies were matrilocal, avunculocal for elite heirs, and divided into matriclans and moieties. Tlingit moieties were Raven and Eagle-Wolf, those of the Haida were Raven and Eagle, and the Tsimshian had semi-moieties variously called Raven-Eagle-Frog and Orca-Wolf-Fireweed.

In the mid province, Wakashans and Salishans were ambilateral. An individual chose to activate his or her membership in several possible bilateral descent groups (kindreds). Coast Salish relied on differential emphasis given to four sources of prestige. These were guardian spirit quests, magical words or spells (dicta), the ancestors themselves, and wealth property such as blankets woven of mountain goat or dog wool.[62]

On the present southern Oregon-northern California border, people were patrilineal and patrilocal with noted exceptions. A wealthy family might arrange a less prestigious "half-marriage" for their daughter. It was so-called because the husband came to reside matrilocally with the bride's kin.

Such arrangements indicate the extent to which wealth items (treasures) pervaded these southern (Klamath River) societies. A man could do, say, and commit anything he dared, provided that he had the necessary treasure to reimburse those whom he hurt or offended. Women received status from the treasures shared by their kinsmen. Treasure items were similar to those of the northern Californian province. These were dentalia (tusk shells), beads made from mollusks, red-headed woodpecker scalps, obsidian (volcanic glass) blades, rare albino animal pelts, and ritual regalia. In these societies, every person had a monetary worth equal to the treasured bridewealth (from the husband's family in contrast to her dowry) exchanged for their mother during her marriage negotiations.

Crests, Ranks

Throughout this area, each household corporation held a number of crests (inherited art forms). These included myths, names, designs, songs, dances, carvings, masks, costumes, and the sites of houses, graves, and camps near resources such as berries, beaches, seaweed, shellfish, fish, and game. Every one of these crests was validated by accounts from the myth age recited at public feasts.

As noted, members of the elite were leaders, along with their close kin, who inherited a limited number of name-titles mentioned in such epics. Name-titles were ranked and the holder of the apical (top) name was manager (or steward) for the corporation. The word for these name-titles often translates as "real-names". Among Tsimshians, their holders are called "real people."

Crest inheritance varied by province, but such corporations were always localized in households. A large and successful one would include several households that were ranked among themselves. The rank of a household correlated with the rank of its crests. Succession to a "real name" position of leadership needed the approval of a council of corporation and community elders. On rare occasions it was possible to elevate a name-title to a higher status by continuous lavish giving by a successive series of its holders.

Wakashans gave preference to inheritance by the first-born male, forming "ramages" composed of a senior line, eldest sons of eldest sons. Kwakwaka'wakw (Kwakiutl) and Tsimshian allowed a few eligible women to inherit names and positions.

Tlingit crests were kept behind a wooden partition (screen) at the rear of the house. In large Tlingit corporations, the household of the manager contained the highest ranking crests, and lesser houses had minor ones. But crests could be borrowed for use by any member, depending on the magnitude of the event planned by a host and household.

The holder of the most prestigious name-title in a community was its chief. Northern tribes recognized moiety chiefs, Salish tended to follow strong, wealthy, and renowned personalities as sigers, and southern tribes valued the owners of treasured heirlooms. Segmentary (branching) lineages were most formalized in the north. In all areas, members of the elite or aristocracy displayed high rank, intermarried, and traced their genealogies as carefully as do European royal houses.

The leaders attracted followers who were commoners holding so-called "kid's ~ made-up names." Leaders were idealized as stable, responsible, and entrenched. Commoners were unreliable and fickle, formerly moving from one household to another wherever they thought they could receive a better living by working for that leader. Commoners could rise above their station, especially as shamans able to amass personal wealth. Others could become famous warriors, carvers, or craftworkers.

At the nadir (lowest) were slaves, war captives and their descendants gained by capture or trade. Slaves were invariably commoners. Elite captives were ransomed by their kin or quickly married by their elite captors to avoid any moral taint.

Leaders could be wealthy and generous because they had several wives, in addition to slaves. Their labor force produced food and luxury goods necessary to maintain a successful community of contented people.

More tightly than other culture areas, knowledge was personally or corporately owned in this region. Most important information could only be "whispered to close kin." Several corporations may appear to have the same epic, but seemingly minor details or variations (featuring a clam, sea urchin, or crab, for example) were sufficient in the native view to make them different properties, if not completely different myths.

A northern leader would immortalize the deeds of his predecessors or himself by selecting a number of crest designs from those of his elite ancestors. He then instructed a "hired" carver to place them on a sculpted pole (which Henry Schoolcraft first called a "totem pole"). This column served as a portal into a house, a supporting pillar for the remains of a deceased relative, or a memorial on the beach.

In contrast to this northern "formline" style, mid province art decorated smaller objects and was more concerned with representing personal guardians, while southern art included shaman's paraphernalia and tiny effigies.

Cosmology: *Myth, Ritual*

Northwestern reform charters are well represented by the epic series in the northern province. These describe how Raven, a humanoid trickster + transformer, stole fire, set the tides, scattered foods, and otherwise altered the world toward its present form.

Mid tribes had distinctive transformers and tricksters (variously called Raven, Bluejay, Xhaals, Changer, or Coyote), who prepared the world before it "capsized" and humans appeared. A few creational charters were recorded as fragments from the southern province, but transformers called Bluejay, Ice, and Coyote were more vital for remaking the world.

After Raven came a host of changers, shapers, transformers, or finishers. Broad contrasts of this protean world became the backdrop for details and particulars added by these reformers. While Raven usually worked alone, transformers came in teams, although only the most prominent member was named.

Most such reformers came from elsewhere. Some simply appeared on earth. Others descended from the sky, or were born as the offspring of marriages between animals and humans. Transformer cycles ranged from the Straits of Georgia to the Oregon coast, featuring Mink toward the north and Bluejay toward the south. Both are renown for their amorous adventures and improprieties.

Reformers created much of the contemporary landscape, set the ancestry of names and privileges, invented useful tools, and gave animals their present forms and attributes. For example, when transformers met people sharpening weapons to attack them, they used the very same weapons to change these people into animals. Thus, a spear became the tail of mink or otter, while a knife or paddle transformed beaver.

Eventually, changers went away. Other replacement teams no longer arrived. According to the Quinault and Quileute, they turned into rocks near the mouth of the Columbia River after they finished. They had created various tribes from wolves or dogs, made mouths with the slash of a knife, and reversed certain people to the upright who used to walk on their hands and carry things with their feet.

Among tales that thrive to this day along the North Pacific are fearful accounts that deal with the dangers of the sea and of the impenetrable forest bramble. Monsters still live in these remote places, ranging from Land Otter People (Kushdaka) of the north to Wild Men (Sasquatch) of the south. For the Tlingit, Haida, and Tsimshian, Land Otter Men still transform those who drowned into Otters, who are still identifiable by their human fingernails. Land Otters can mimic the appearance of someone, often a sweetheart, that a human alone in the woods is thinking about or longing for. They can be led into danger because they should instead be concentrating on their quarry. A hunter should be single-minded, like anyone else engaged in an activity.

The Kwakwaka'wakw recognized a Wild Man (Bukwus), who captured people by offering them food when stranded on a beach or near freezing. He arrived standing in the bow of a canoe, along with Land Otter paddlers who look like the victim's relatives, minks who acted as paddles, and a skate who was the canoe itself.[63] The Fraser River Salish have a similar being called Sasquatch, who stole women and food.

The source of humans was often left unspecified. Tlingit were said to come from a place called Tlin. Most Tsimshian once lived at Prairie Town on the upper Skeena (below). Kwakwaka'wakw lived at Crooked Beach. Nuxalk founders of an "ancestral family" descended from the sky house wearing their crests as outer garments to alight on certain local mountain peaks and walk down into the human world. Greater cultural concern was given not to these generic charters but to the ponderously detailed tales about how particular crests were acquired by specific ancestors.

With potlatches, the other major areal rite is the Winter Dance. It is held to display crests in the north and guardian spirit powers in the south. Puget Sound Lushootseed's especially dramatic cure was a simulated canoe journey by four to eight shamans to the Afterworld in the West, a fire arrow fight with the ghosts to recover a stolen soul, and, after their eastward return, restoring it into the patient.[64]

During recent centuries, a series of secret guilds (cults) was diffusing north and south along the coast from the Heiltsuk (Bella Bella) and Nishga Tsimshian as royal privileges. Examples from the southern limits appear among the Quileute isolate.

Today, copper, dentalia (tusk) shells, and abalone retain their great value along the entire coast. Among northern tribes, spirits still able to confer treasures included a giant Beaver with copper eyes, claws, ears, and teeth, or Wealth Woman now adorned with gold.

Today

Northwestern natives remain primarily fisherfolk even now. They devote the summer months to economic activities and the fall to native festivals with canoe races and salmon bakes. These communities, both in the past and present, still achieve full expression during the winter months. In the past, winters were spent in crowded villages where the ranks, classes, and potlatches held full force. Now there are no winter villages, except in the north. People nonetheless gather together in updated plank houses for feasts, potlatches, namings, spirit dances, and *puwha* displays.

Through the early 1900s, potlatching of the traditional, non-rivalry style continued surreptitiously, often as Christmas parties, despite American and Canadian bans. Since 1951, potlatching has enjoyed a public revival especially among Tlingit, Gitksan, Kwakwaka'wakw, and Canadian Salish.

Most Pacific Northwestern peoples are now Christians. They are primarily

Russian Orthodox in coastal Alaska; Catholic, Anglican, and United Church of Canada in British Columbia; and Catholic, Protestant, Mormon, and Pentecostal in the United States. Any eroticism of Raven is now largely muted or denied. Traditional stories of a flood or other events congruent with the Bible have grown in popularity.[65]

Among the Nooksack and other Salishans, the very first objects on the earth were "power boards" which (who) occur in five varieties of Man and Woman pairs, as do most plants, animals, and magical spells.

In a few cases, spiritual belief syncretized aboriginal and Christian beliefs. The Indian Shaker Church was founded near Olympia, Washington in 1882 by John and Mary Slocum. Like the Midewiwin of the Ojibwa, it represents a democratization and socialization of an ancient individualistic shamanic belief. John Slocum returned from the dead with the message that the Christian God existed for natives as well as others. Later Mary Slocum received "the shake" as a gift. This unique feature of church membership enables healers to tremble with their hands and bodies. Church teachings blend native curing and *puwha* beliefs with candles, crosses, altars, school bells, and prohibitions against smoking, drinking, adultery, and unkindness. Generally during cures and services, women play a more limited role, but, as indicated by Mary Slocum herself, women have vital and strong roles in this faith.

60. See Tom McFeat, <u>Indians of the Northwest Coast</u> 1966.
61. According to Wayne Suttles, <u>Coast Salish Essays</u> 1987: 12.
62. According to Wayne Suttles, "The 'Coast Salish' of the Georgia □ Puget Basin □ Another Look" 1977.
63. Franz Boas, Kwakiutl Mythology 1935: 146.
64. Jay Miller, <u>Shamanic Odyssey</u> 1988, <u>Lushootseed Culture and the Shamanic Odyssey</u> 1999.
65. Christian suppression of older beliefs has altered the texture of native communities. For example, when James Deans (1891, 284) visited the Haida village of Skedans in 1872, he saw a totem pole topped by a carving of a phallic shaman, representing the *puwha* of *Skaga Modeve*. (*Skaga* means *puwha*, orca, and doctor) When he next returned in 1889, this effigy was "respectable" so he made inquiries until someone told him that the missionary said it was bad, "So a number of us loaded our guns with bullets and fired until we shot it off."

TRIBAL EXAMPLES

Potlatch

Distinctive to this area was and is the "give away feast" before witnesses called the **potlatch** {* = a formalized redistribution of crests, privileges, people, and resources in the presence of elite witnesses and guests, who were given food and gifts to validate changes in the social fabric of a Pacific Northwestern community}. The name comes from the Chinook Wawa "to give". It balanced out fluctuations in local resources, kept track of the allegiances and movements of commoners, and legitimated the assumption of name-titles. A noble family dramatized their clan crests and treasures (via songs, dances, masks, effigies, and natural rarities). In return for witnessing and accepting the copyrights of these nobles for names and privileges passed on to their children, guests received abundant food and gifts. Later, guests would host their own potlatches and reciprocate their former hosts.

Potlatches were held at critical life junctures (leaps) that varied by nation. Tlingit and Tsimshian held them at the death of a leader, Haida at the house dedication of a mature leader and at his death, Wakashans at the assumption of increasingly more prestigious name-titles, and Nuxalk at life leaps associated with naming, marriage, and death.[66] Among Salishan and southern province tribes, potlatch-like Give Aways ("Invitationals") were held to elevate the status and esteem of families of leaders and shamans during other ritual events.

Unfortunately, outsider officials willfully misunderstood the potlatch. Canada, under pressure from Indian agents, missionaries, and zealous native converts, outlawed both potlatch and spirit dances between 1884-1951. Over time scholars have grappled with interpretations of the potlatch. It has been analyzed as an elaborate game, as a banking system with doubling interest payments, and as a historical and exceptional extravagance fueled by trade goods.

Each of these interpretations provides only a partial answer because so much has happened to native peoples and their traditions. The Northwest Coast was decimated by severe measles, smallpox, malaria, and other epidemics. Among the dead were the proper claimants to the limited number of name-titles. In their absence, lowly commoners took a chance to claim titles that had been previously impossible, amassing property that was used more like bribes than as gifts.

The Hudson's Bay Company was buying furs. Commoner could work hard to gain funds to potlatch and validate a name-title. Some villages and tribes congregated around forts and trading posts where they began unprecedented daily interactions.

In 1834, nine Coast Tsimshian villages setup separate neighborhoods outside Fort Simpson, British Columbia. In the process, village chiefs appointed heirs to manage these neighborhoods. Older leaders remained in their Skeena River villages, becoming tribal chiefs since each directed at least two villages. Rankings among these chiefs became contested. They began to hold special "rivalry potlatches" in order to sort out their relative status. The holder of the name-title of Ligeex emerged from these contests as the Tsimshian chieftain (grand chief), dominating the Skeena River fur trade.

Similar "rivalry" potlatches, noted for the wholesale destruction of goods and valuables to indicate limitless wealth, were hosted to sort out the internal ranks of the Kwakwaka'wakw tribes who settled about Fort Rupert on Vancouver Island. In the face of this challenge, a rival had either to destroy equal or greater wealth or slip further down in the emerging ranking system.

While the medium of exchange had earlier been lush animal pelts, the Hudson's Bay Company two-point blanket became the new currency. Some especially treasured items such as the "copper" became a repository for vast wealth. A copper was a heraldic shield differentially valued in the northern and central provinces. The Tlingit assigned to a copper (which they named "Dene" for its Athabaskan origins from Copper River ore), a reasonably stable value of five or six slaves. The Kwakwaka'wakw increased its value with each transaction so that a copper, each named and considered alive, might be worth tens of thousands of blankets and now have to be kept in a bank vault when not "brought out" at a public event.

Raven

Not surprisingly, Raven is an important figure of legend on both sides of the

Pacific, not just North America but the Siberian coast as well. Raven's wide appeal derives from the complexity of his character, which allowed an audience to ponder possibilities ranging from identity to catharsis. His important characteristics include superhuman abilities, social license, entertaining incongruities, and delightful paradoxes. For example, he convinced Bear that a stone had insulted it, or he was swallowed by a whale and lived inside by stripping off and cooking its meat. He reformed larger distinctions (fire, tides, foods) of the modern world by skill, cunning, and incredible feats of wonder and stupidity.

Humans can identify with his omnipotence and craftiness, while holding up his disgusting lapses to scorn. As a bumbling host, an amorous interloper, or a devious glutton, he provided abundant negative examples. Like Raven, a narrator had complete license to say the unsayable, plot the unthinkable, exalt the lowly, and defame the mighty.

The Raven cycle is remarkably open-ended, as alive today as ever. Louis Shotridge, a Tlingit noble and scholar, remarked that serious transforming episodes should occur in a logical order, while the humorous or trickster incidents could occur anywhere that a narrator felt his audience would appreciate them. Viola Garfield, another important scholar of the region, made the point that Raven's own life cycle established a chronology for this series.

In brief, Raven was born in the sky from an unfaithful wife. He descended to earth as a shining youth, but became humanized both by ritual adoption as well as being tricked by slaves into eating scabs. In effect, this ingestion made him voracious, motivating all of his subsequent adventures. Oblivious to humans, his greed led him to differentiate the world by tricking various owners into releasing the Sun, Moon, and Stars; Fresh Water, Candlefish, Tides, Fair Weather, Fire, Death, Salmon, and Dry Land. He gave many animals their present attributes, painting colors on birds and cutting out the tongue of Cormorant. In still other episodes, Raven was humiliated, teased, and maligned. Always, he sought food. Finally, Raven moved out to sea, invited sea monsters to the first potlatch, feasted and entertained them, and either received their promise not to harm humans further or turned them and, lastly, himself into stone.

66. According to Abraham Rosman and Paula Rubel, Feasting with Mine Enemy 1971.

Tlingit Traders[67]

A vast and ancient trade network linked the Northwest Coast with the interior Athapaskan Subarctic tribes. More exotic items, like copper and special woods, were even traded from Inuit in Siberia and Alaska, who received dentalia shells indirectly from Vancouver Island in exchange. Subject to religious obligations like all other activities, traders had to prepare by fasting, consulting a shaman, and then hosting a feast. Before leaving, he or she applied face paint to appear their most attractive.

Tlingit also traded among themselves. For example, to island peoples, men and women from mainland Tlingit villages traded rabbit or marmot skin blankets, moose hide shirts, skin trousers with feet, dressed hides, cranberries in oil, pressed strawberry cakes, candlefish oil, horn spoons, woven blankets, and spruce root baskets. In return, islanders gave sea otter pelts, dried venison, seal oil, dried fish (halibut, salmon, herring), dried seaweed, clams, mussels, sea urchins, herring spawn, cedar bark, baskets, greenstone, and dense yew wood for bows, boxes, and batons.

Among neighboring tribes, Tlingits would travel 300 miles to the south to acquire large Haida canoes and Tsimshian candlefish oil, carved dishes, painted boxes, and woven fabrics of mountain goat wool and finely shredded cedar bark. Once Europeans occupied the coast, some Tlingits canoed over a thousand miles south to Seattle.

Fueling this entire enterprise was trade with the interior. Certain Tlingit chiefs retained hereditary rights to trade with Athapaskan leaders. These bonds were perpetuated each generation through the marriage of men of particular Tlingit noble houses with Athapaskan women of high degree.

From the interior came moose hides, fine moccasins, birch wood bows wrapped with porcupine gut, dressed caribou hides, leather thongs and sinews, snowshoes, and copper ore; from the coast came cedar baskets, fish oil, shells, and smoked seafoods.

Trade routes went up river valleys (Taku, Stikine, Alsek) and over mountain passes (Chilkat, Chilcoot). Goods were taken in canoes upriver as far as possible, then transferred into male slaves' backpacks. These were made of a large basket with shoulder and forehead straps, holding 100 pounds or more. In large groups, women carried packs weighing 50 to 80 pounds, and dogs had saddle bags holding up to 25 pounds. A wise trader always included a shrewd elderly woman to act as bargainer, calming influence, and arbitor of exchange values.

Every packer had a wooden staff for pushing away summer underbrush or knocking off packed winter ice from snowshoes. During winter, markers were set along the trails. Preferred campsites, with water and firewood nearby, were indicated by an upright flat stone that served as the deflector for a fire. While trudging, travelers snacked on dried salmon, augmented by fresh berries during the summer and fall. The only meal was eaten at the evening camp.

Chilkat Tlingit went into the Yukon River to trade in May, after candlefish but before salmon runs. Only men undertook winter treks on snowshoes that lasted a full month in January and February. When these Tlingit arrived, they bent branches along the trail to indicate the number in the party and their intended direction of movement. Lacking clear signs that people were nearby, they built a smoky fire or ignited a large tree to serve as a beacon.

Athapaskans knew to expect their Tlingit partners at certain seasons and so were ready to trade. First, however, they exchanged gifts and made speeches of welcome. In time, the Tlingit language began to replace the languages of some of the interior towns because it was associated with the prestige of the coast.

Tlingits were, understandably, very possessive of their trade contacts, diligently keeping Athapaskans away from Europeans. For example, when a Tahltan chief wanted to see a European vessel anchored at the mouth of the Stikine River, he had to pay a Wrangell Tlingit household 500 beaver skins to do so and was never let out of their sight.[68]

Tlingit made a huge profit from the interior, particularly during the fur trade era. Everyone there wanted manufactured goods, such as guns, powder, shot, hardtack, flour, rice, beans, pants, shirts, yard goods, blankets, tobacco, molasses, steel traps, knives, hatchets, needles and thread, paint, and jewelry.

But Tlingits did not assume that Europeans were obviously superior. Instead, they regarded all strangers as fair game. Natives quickly learned to use tea to dye red fox skins to look like more valuable pelts. Fierce international competition encouraged such tricks. When the Russians tried to use dentalia as a kind of money, the Spanish and Americans glutted the market by bringing many of these shells up from California.[69]

67. George Thornton Emmons, The Tlingit Indians 1991: 55-57.

Tsimshian of British Columbia

As master traders and trend setters of the north, Tsimshians long lived in their home territories along the Skeena and Nass Rivers. By 10,000 years ago, obsidian {* = volcanic glass, often black} was being traded from Mt. Edziza, north of the Stikine River, throughout northern British Columbia and the Alaska panhandle. About 5,000 years ago established trails, now paved as modern highways, spread trade goods throughout the region. After 3,000 years, this trade included exotic goods suggestive of a ranked society like that of the modern Tsimshian. Wealth differences in grave goods (amber, jet beads, and shells) suggest their ranked use among the living, since these occurred in some graves and not others. Wear on front teeth indicates both men and women wore labrets {* = plugs of stone or inlaid wood buttoned under the lower lip}. In recent centuries, however, only women wore labrets.

Armor and weapons also appear in these graves, showing increasing warfare. Trophy heads and rod armor imply rippling influence from the Old Bering Sea complex on both sides of the Pacific (BC 1000) traced to Shang China (BC 1600).   Over time, Tsimshians, of course, developed their own styles and meanings.

Plank houses and towns increased in size. Woodworking tools became more varied, suggesting the growth of the formline art style for which the Tsimshian are famous. Social ranks were indicated by differences in house size and exotic goods. Just as in historic times, the largest houses were in the middle of the row of dwellings facing the beach. The chief of a town, now as in the distant past, lived in the center of his (or her) people.

Raiding and warfare also increased, as indicated by broken bones and fractures, due to spreading military strategies. These rippled across Asia toward the Eskimo, then Tlingit, who used them on the Tsimshian, who, in turn, used them against Haida Gwai (Queen Charlotte archipelago) to the west and various Wakashan tribes to the south. Taking slaves was a strong motivation for these attacks.

By 2000 years ago, communities along the Skeena settled in. Economic territories were obviously claimed by houses. They used these resources to feed gatherings that fostered a cosmology shared among the regional elites.

Thus, according to Tsimshian belief, the earth was a flat disk supported on a pole resting on the chest of _Am'ala_ ("smokehole"). All future people and animals lived together at Prairie Town (_Temlaxam_) on the upper Skeena River near modern Hazelton. After a flood and other punishments, everyone left Prairie Town to move to separate towns over a huge area.

Animals retained their human forms only within their own holy homes. When a male bear had his fishing line break or a female bear had her tumpline {* = forehead strap} snap, they had been killed by a human hunter. After a few days, however, he or she would return to Bear Town provided that they had been treated with proper respect and ritual by the hunter and his kin.

On the edge of the earth, Pestilence Chief, his daughter, and maimed people lived together in a house. Ocean surrounded the earth, abounding in fish and sea mammals. Orcas were divided into the same four semi-moieties (phratries or clan clusters) as are the Tsimshian themselves. They displayed their crest membership by the shape of their dorsal fins.

Across the ocean were different worlds inhabited by dwarfs, birds, ghosts, and salmon. In the Salmon Country, each species had its own town. The Spring Salmon were furthest away, and the Silver, Steelhead, Humpback, Coho, and Trout successively closer to the ocean and the earth.

Spring Salmon sent scouts up the Skeena River to see if what they called their "salmon" were spawning. When a positive report came back, Springs started out announcing the good news to the other Salmon Towns as they passed by. Silvers, Humpbacks, and Dogs announced that they would follow shortly; Cohos that they would wait until fall. Trout asked to accompany the Springs; and these two together continued on to meet the Steelhead who were already returning down the Skeena. What the Salmon called their salmon, humans saw as cottonwood fluff floating in the river.

Spanning this earth realm was the Sky World. Various immortals, generally called "shining youths," descended to earth during four flashes of lightning and four claps of thunder in order to help or to marry a mortal. One of them, known as Wiigyet ("big man"), became Raven.

In the early 1800s, a major series of changes began as Tsimshians left the sites of their winter villages to move to the trading post at Fort (later Port) Simpson run by the Hudson's Bay Company. Town chiefs appointed heirs to manage either the new neighborhood or the old town. They thus elevated themselves into the role of tribal chiefs. These new ranks had to be confirmed, in the old accepted way, by lavish generosity at public potlatch displays. But these now took on aspects of rivalry and confrontation so as to sort out the graded rankings among tribes and chiefs.

From this melee emerged a Tsimshian high chief named Ligeex, of the Eagle crest. The previous name-title for this tribal chief, Nisbalas, had been shamed when its holder was beheaded by insulted chiefs of the Raven crest. Therefore, a foreign name from the Kitimat, inherited through marriage, was substituted as this new tribal chiefly name. While potlatching the Ligeex name into public acclaim, his Gispaxlo'ots tribe moved to the forefront of the nine Coast Tsimshian tribes, and he assumed a previously unknown position as high chief.

Other changes were introduced in religion. For several years after 1800, a series of prophets called Bini ("mind" in Athapaskan) preached an accommodation of European and traditional beliefs. These attempts did not last long because in 1857, William Duncan, a remarkable Victorian lay missionary, settled among Coast Tsimshians. He learned their language, and created a model cooperative Christian community that still exists. In hindsight, Duncan's success was a benefit of his replacing Ligeex, who did convert, as chieftain of the Tsimshian.

For millennia, therefore, the Tsimshian have displayed an elegance of culture in the midst of changes. The beauty and acclaim of their abilities are apparent to all. What has complicated the analysis of Tsimshian genius, however, has been this facility to adapt to new conditions by modifying old ones in diverse and creative ways.

A Tsimshian Potlatch

Sunlight gleamed on the paddles as the slaves brought the huge canoe into the bay where the potlatch was being held. The Orca chief, Sharp Fin, sat in the middle of the canoe with his wives and children. Noblemen acting as messengers had come to the Orca town a month before to issue a special invitation to this event hosted by the Ravens.

Sharp Fin recalled how a lower ranking Raven chief had stood in the bow of that canoe, wearing a Chilcat robe, shaking his carved raven rattle, and singing a *puwha* song accompanied by hidden whistles. He called out the name of Sharp Fin three times, inviting him (and his people) to the Raven potlatch. The fourth time, the chief himself responded by sending a messenger out in a canoe to invite the visitors into his house. There, he fed them and gave them gifts to take to the impending host, Moon Raven.

Now, as they entered the bay in front of the Raven town, Sharp Fin looked at the row of houses. There, in the middle, was the home of the host, Chief Moon Raven. Painted along the entire front of this house was an enormous Raven with a moon in its bill, his famous heraldic crest.

Sharp Fin ordered his canoe to halt in front of the beach, as was proper etiquette. The chief stood up and held a crystal in his hand, flashing light onto the house front. Suddenly the stillness was broken when the carved raven's beak protruding from the house opened up and a woman stepped out. She was the sister of the Raven chief, and a leader in her own right. She was elaborately clothed in a dress and cloak woven with Raven designs. Over her face was an amazing mask that represented one of the great *puwha*s of her house. It was called Calm Heavens and looked like a human face, with wings painted on the cheeks. Whistles, heard from the woods behind the home, acted as the voices of related spirits.

With graceful movements, Raven's sister came across to the beach, where she flashed a crystal to show that her family was as powerful as that of Sharp Fin. A line of women appeared in front of the house and sang a welcoming song.

Sharp Fin sat and waited. He wondered if men would come to lift out and carry his canoeful of people to the house, as was sometimes done. Instead, the masked woman called to the house and slaves came out carrying furs, which were laid out in a line to make a path to the beaked door.

Ordering his slaves to beach the canoe at one of the runways cleared through the rocky beach, the huge canoe backed into shallow water. Dozens of small canoes were already pulled up onto the beach, along with six large canoes belonging to great chiefs. Landing, his slaves carried Sharp Fin and his senior wife onto the shore.

Other members of the party stepped out and waited to follow behind. While Sharp Fin and his wives led the procession into the house, his slaves began unloading boxes of food and gifts, carrying them to the house where the Orca chief would lodge.

When Sharp Fin got to the door, the beak opened. He stepped inside and paused, waiting for his wives to join him. His eyes took time to adjust to the firelight inside. The speaker for the Raven chief announced the name and tribe of these Orca visitors. Then an usher came to escort Sharp Fin to his seat.

As he walked down the center of the house, he mused on its splendor. Like all Tsimshian houses, the walls were made of finely adzed boards slotted into a framework of squared beams. Four carved posts held up the roof, which had a ridge pole along the peak of the gable. Wooden bunks, over a yard wide, lined the lower walls. Each family had space along these bunks where they slept and kept their provisions stored in wooden boxes. Ordinary people lived along the sides. The chief and his close relatives lived at the far end. Slaves huddled by the door, where they were exposed to cold drafts and vulnerable during enemy raids.

Sharp Fin kept his head up and his eyes ahead. He did not look at the sides filled with those far beneath his exalted rank. Instead, he looked at the carved and painted screen that filled the back of the house. It depicted another scene from the sacred history of the house in which Raven pretended to be a human baby so he could steal the light that became the Sun, Moon, and Stars. A small round opening in this screen led into the cubicle protecting Raven house treasures. Just now it was empty because all of these treasures were out on public display for all the guests to admire. Lined up along the platform before the screen were masks, feast bowls, woven blankets, armor, and helmets.

In front of these, chiefs sat during the potlatch. A space just to the left of Moon Raven was reserved for Sharp Fin. He walked to it and sat down. He saw his wives take seats with their Wolf clanspeople in the rear left corner of the house. The right side was reserved for the Eagle crest since Moon Raven's father was an Eagle, and these people had special obligations to perform for their inlaw.

Sharp Fin was the last important chief to arrive. Now the festivities could begin. One after another, masked figures danced into the house, each an inherited privilege and spiritual claim of the Ravens. Special songs were sung and Wonders amazed the guests.

After a few hours of these displays, Moon Raven called for food. Many bowls and dishes were passed out, each holding fish, berries, meat, or shellfish from a location owned by the house. The Ravens showed everyone that they were wealthy and well supplied. All ate as much as he or she could to honor that house. Ordinary people ate great mouthfuls, Nobles ate with small bites, discrete chewing, and closed lips.

By the time the meal was over, it was late. Visiting families went to their host houses, talking until the wee hours of the morning. Ordinary people camped on the beach, supplied with wood and food by the Ravens.

The next day, late in the morning, a picnic feast was held on the beach. That night, everyone again gathered in the Raven house to hear Moon Raven "one-up" his guests. He was boasting of his ancestors, while subtly belittling everyone else. Important guests like Sharp Fin were singled out to receive huge ladles full of candlefish grease mixed with snow, brought from the mountain tops. Regardless of the consequences, chiefs had to drink all of this oil.

To underscore the implicit hostility of this offering, Raven warriors, with their hair bound up, rushed into the house and made threatening gestures. When no one flinched, the Ravens quickly lightened the tone by scattering eagle down as a sign of peace.

When calm was restored, some gifts were distributed, accompanied by jokes about the shortcomings of the guests. Every item was counted out to songs, all the better to overwhelm the guests with the generosity of the Ravens. Many goods had been kept hidden behind a rear partition, and these were now tossed into the room. Soon the pile was so high that the roof boards had to be moved aside. Truly, the Ravens were great.

Now the moment had come when the Ravens explained the source of this bounty. An Eagle chief, uncle to Moon Raven, spoke for the Ravens as a gesture of respect to his inlaws and to highlight the ultimate modesty of the Ravens.

"Ladies and Gentlemen," he intoned, "Moon Raven has asked me to speak to you about his ancestors and the sacred history of his house. We all know that Raven was a powerful spirit who came from the sky as a shining youth. Here on earth he learned to eat food and became ravenously hungry. He would do anything to get fed and sometimes he did things that have helped us to this very day. He gave us fish and game. He taught us to respect other creatures. He taught us to pray to Heaven Above. But more than these, he brought us out of darkness. He got light for us.

"A great chief called Raven Upriver kept the Sun, Moon, and Stars in a box. Raven wanted them. None of his usual tricks would work. He pondered what to do. He turned himself into a pine needle and had Raven Upriver's daughter drink it. Soon she was pregnant and her household awaited a miraculous birth. Raven did not disappoint them. After he was born as a human child, he was pampered and spoiled by everyone, particularly his grandfather. Raven became fussy and cried a great deal. Nothing would pacify him until the box of daylight was given to him. Then he was content. Eventually, no one thought to protect the box or guard the child.

"At that moment, Raven changed back into his bird body, and flew with the box through the smokehole. People tried to hold him back with their powers, but all they could do was halt Raven long enough for his feathers to be blackened in the smoke. All ravens, thereafter, became black and shiny.

"Raven tried to trade the box for fish and for adulation from people fishing in perpetual twilight, but they wanted nothing to do with his tricky deceit. Instead, he smashed open the box and released the Sun, Moon, and Stars. The world changed forever. Light shone.

"All people admire the work of Raven, but the people of the Raven clan are particularly close to him.

"In this house where you are being cared for, they honor the Moon as a special gift of Raven. This is because, ages ago, a woman of this house was lost in the forest. She was high class and knew how to take care of herself. She prayed constantly and made offerings, although she had almost nothing. Just when she thought she would die, she received a great gift, one that she brought into this house.

"It was late when she came upon a stream in the woods. A full moon reflected in the water, allowing her to see many fish swimming there. These salmon saved her from starving. The next day, she followed the stream to the shore, and discovered where she was. In a short time, she was home. She told the story to her people and they went back to the stream, where they caught many fish. Today, the house of Moon Raven still owns this stream and you have eaten of the salmon that thrive there.

That is some of the sacred history of the house of Moon Raven."

Next, all of the treasures of the house were shown to the people, one at a time, and their individual histories were told. Since the potlatch was being held to confirm the greatness of this Raven house, mourning songs were sung for the old leader who had died the year before. Then the man who had taken his place as the holder of the name of Moon Raven introduced the members of his own family. Any Raven women who were then pregnant were given both a boy or a girl name so the newborn would become known as elite as soon as he or she arrived.

Finally gifts were passed out to the visiting chiefs, who responded with elaborate, clever, and thoughtful speeches of thanks. A last meal was served and then everyone left for home, pleased that the Ravens had been so lavish in their generosity. Sharp Fin hoped to do as well when he hosted his own potlatch the next year.

68. George Emmons, Tahltan, 1911.
69. Kalvero Oberg, The Social Economy of the Tlingit Indians 1973: 105-113; Aurel Krause, The Tlingit Indians 1956: 128-137.

Maquinna and John Jewett

In 1778, while charting around the world, Captain James Cook visited the North Pacific, in part to counter Spanish and Russian claims there. At the Nootkan (now called

Nuu-chah-nulth) town of Yuquot, also known as Friendly Cove, Cook's men exchanged pewter and beads for sea otter pelts. These were highly valued for their luster and feel since they have about 1000 soft hairs per inch, the densest number of any mammal. When these sailors reached China, they were offered huge amounts of money for each pelt. Thus the trade in sea otter skins to Chinese Mandarins was inaugurated. Though the British government tried to suppress knowledge of this valuable trade to exploit it after the American Revolution, a few rogue crewmen published their journals. Soon, ships from France, Portugal, England, Spain, New England, and Russia crowded the coast. The trade made local natives more wealthy, but at the cost of wholesale epidemics, prostitution, famines, and other disruptions of social life. When a Spanish garrison was sent to Yuquot to assert national claims to that coast, the huge native plank houses were demolished and the town forced to rebuild nearby.

By 1800, the sea otter trade was worth millions of dollars. In 1802, two American brothers decided to refit their vessel Boston, and cash in on the trade. At Hull, England, the ship took on the largest amount of goods ever assembled for the trade. Joining the crew was a reasonably well educated young man named John Jewett to act as armorer (or weapons smith).

When they arrived, however, the trade did not go as planned. The captain insulted the local chief, Maquinna. These natives had already suffered many abuses from visiting ships. Villages were depopulated by foreign diseases, four chiefs had been murdered by the Spanish, canoe crews had been shelled by English cannon, and pelts had been stolen out of native homes by sailors.

After the Boston's captain used the wrong tone of voice and belittled Maquinna, vengeance was swift. Offering the use of a salmon stream, Yuquots were able to divide the crew and kill them all except for two. Since he had visited on the ship, Maquinna knew the value of Jewett as a maker of iron weapons and goods. He alone was spared, though wounded, on the promise that he would become the slave of the chief. He did so and earned the goodwill of his capturers because of his good humor and kindness, particularly to children.

By sheer luck, another man, John Thompson, was also spared. At the time of the attack, he was working below mending sails. The next day, when warriors returned to flush him out, Jewett saved the older man, who was almost forty, by pleading with Maquinna that Thompson was his father. Indeed, it was probably his age rather than this made-up kinship that saved him because, by all accounts, Thompson was gruff and feisty. Still, native respect for age, and his abilities as a tailor, kept him alive.

Though the ship burned before everything could be salvaged, much of the loot was used to enhance the social position of Maquinna. He gave lavish potlatches and bestowed many exotic gifts on regional nobility, including the kin of his many wives. Both captive sailors were able to supply themselves with tailored clothes and food stuffs for a considerable time. More importantly, Jewett saved the Captain's writing desk and was able to keep a daily diary. The Book of Common Prayer provided succor.

Finally, after 28 months of captivity, Jewett and Thompson were rescued in 1805. Though a native of Boston, England, Jewett went to the US, married in 1809, settled in Connecticut, and supported his family by peddling the account of his adventures at Yuquot. His diary was published in 1807. While it is very useful as a spare chronology of food-getting activities, unexplained rituals, and the chief's whaling expeditions, it was not exciting reading. Therefore, with the literary help of a local millionaire, his diary was revised and published as a compelling narrative in 1815. He sold it from town to town. In 1817, he even starred in a play, with music, about his adventures. Jewett died in 1821, thirty-seven years old. Maquinna died about 1825, about twice that age. Both have left descendants who carry their names, and those called Maquinna still lead at Yuquot.

Chinook Traders *of the Columbia River*

At the emporium at the Dalles (Long Rapids) along the Columbia River, thousands of people gathered to fish and trade during summer salmon runs. Set at the gateway between the lush coast and the dry interior, this fishery intersected routes along the sea, upriver, and across land in all directions. Small items as exotic as pipestone from Minnesota, turquoise from the Southwest, galena from Montana, and copper from Alaska and the Great Lakes were traded there.

The bulk of the materials were regional, however. From the coast came dried shellfish arranged in standard units by being impaled on two-foot long sticks of salmonberry wood. Upland hunters provided mammal furs and dried meat in tule rush bags of standard size. Dried berries provided a variety of tastes and condiments. From the interior came dried roots like camas and the potato-like wapato. From further east came the skins of elk, deer, and occasional buffalo, along with dried meat. From California and Oregon to the south came slaves raided from small villages.

Local Chinook traders provided dried salmon, pulverized salmon flour, dried sturgeon, dried smelt, dried seal, and canoes, which carried this water borne exchange. Occasional beached whales provided blubber and exceptionally large bones for tools and weapons.

Most valuable of all were tusk-like shells called dentalia (*higua* in Chinook Wawa or jargon) from the West Coast of Vancouver Island. Ordinarily these shellfish lived deep in the ocean. Off this shore, though, they were only a few hundred feet below the surface. Traders had marks tattooed on their arms to measure standard lengths of strung shells. They carefully appraised the quality of each.

So significant were these shells that they had a supernatural aura. According to Chinook, the insides were the food of people so tiny their mouths could only eat dentalia. After sucking out the meat, they gave the outer shell to their tiny slaves, who strung them in standard lengths to be traded by their noble masters to humans.

Practicalities of gathering these shells were much more ingenious, however. Important families of the Nuchahnuth (Nootka), over centuries, had closely guarded the secret location of dentalia beds. Landmarks along the horizon were used to triangulate a canoe so a round brush could be lowered over the side. Many handles were added on, one joined to another, until the tips rested on the bottom. Stone weights with a hole in the middle were fitted over the end of the handle and allowed to sink until they forced the bristles to close up. Then the entire apparatus was laboriously lifted to the surface, as each handle was detached. If the collector were lucky, the brush clutched a few shells.

In this way, dentalia were gathered for trade across all of western North America. The further from the source, the more mysterious was their origin so that they became truly wondrous items.

Even so, their mystery conformed to cultural expectations of a stratified society. The tiny people, like all other communities, were divided into ranks of freeborn and of slaves. Throughout the region, the shape of the head physically distinguished these classes. A freeborn baby was bound in a cradleboard with a sloping plank pressing against the forehead so that the skull would grow into a wide, wedge shape.

The skull of a slave child grew normally. As dentalia were the measure of standard value, slaves were the units of prestige. Every important family had several slaves, as much to indicate their social standing as to perform drudge work. Most slaves were children purchased from their captors, and raised within the household of leading families. They did tedious, sometimes distasteful, work such as getting water, firewood, and clams. If slaves had children, then they too were slaves. Most slaves were commoners taken in raids. Important people, invariably adult women, if captured, showed by their conduct that they would not perform menial tasks. They were more valuable if ransomed by their kin. In some cases, captured noblewomen married into the elite of their captors, forming a diplomatic alliance between their two communities.

Local people might also end up as slaves under unusual circumstances. Inability to pay debts, murder, or other failures to compensate would generally mean that a person had to forfeit his or her freedom, either for a stated period or for a lifetime. Orphans without kin to protect them also became slaves at the insistence of their chief, who used the purchase price for his own needs.

A slave had no standing in the community, nor any distinct identity. Their only designation was that of their tribe, which also served to insult and denigrate all these other people. The life of a slave could be forfeit at any time. Alternatively a master could free a slave or accept a price for his or her freedom. In a few cases, devious owners had male slaves act as henchmen, ambushing, poisoning, or killing rivals in secret.

When European ships arrived on the coast, slaves were sent to taste their strange food and drink their mind-altering alcohol. Since they survived the experience, and some even liked it, their masters knew that these new items were reasonably safe.

Slaves were traded far from home so that escape was virtually impossible. Most were well treated. Those who lived in elite households were well fed, although they ate by themselves because of their tainted status. Slaves who ran away only to be recaptured were punished by having their ears cut off. Even when he or she reached home, however, they still carried the stigma of having been a slave. Unless a form of rehabilitation, like a feast or potlatch with lavish gifts, were held, such a non-person would be shunned.

At the other extreme of these communities were the elite families with molded heads and prideful bearing. Their influence was only limited by their ability. Some governed because they were kind, generous, and skilled arbitrators. Others were feared because they were haughty and suspected of controlling reserves of great *puwha* that could render their enemies maimed or dead. It was such chiefs who had their slaves act as henchmen and poisoners.

An effective chief managed a vast network of kin, trade, and alliance, in a few instances backed by loyal warriors and bodyguards. This "muscle," however, was otherwise out of keeping within the region. Profitable free trade required wide access and unrestricted transport. Injuries or murders were quickly adjudicated by chiefs to dampen hostilities. Deep-seated antagonisms more often led to secret sorcery than to overt attacks.

Leadership passed from father to son, though Chinook kinship was characterized by considerable flexibility. People claimed as many noble ancestors as possible on both sides of the family. Only matters of residence restricted these linkages since members of a household cooperated more fully than did other relatives. People might live in several households during a lifetime, thus cementing ties of kinship through a large network of birth, domestic, and marriage relationships.

Prestige factors influenced succession because an important leader had both slaves and many wives, and their children inherited certain privileges and restraints. A chief added to his influence by having a large family, not all of whom had the same status.

The children of the senior wife had the best chance of assuming leadership roles, unless other factors and abilities intervened. Women from coastal villages outranked those upriver because coastal communities were more cosmopolitan, wealthier, and better connected. Personal ability also played a role. A wise and patient child was often groomed for leadership. An older sibling who was angry, sloppy, or careless was passed over.

Prestige was a key to successful leadership. Thus, the son of a chiefly coastal mother and a father from upriver was more entitled to lead than a man of distinguished but lesser ranked parentage. Some of these women were quite powerful, controlling vast trading privileges.

Chinook leaders coordinated activities, more than directed them. He or she would announce when the villagers would move to resource areas to take seasonal foods. Generally, a man of chiefly family initiated moves to fishing and hunting camps. Elite women led berrying and plant gathering tasks. When a beached whale was found, nothing was done until a chief indicated where the first cut was to be made and what slices would go to which people. While commoners and slaves did the actual work, they could not commence until sanctioned to do so by the chief or his representative. More a manager than a martinet, the chief and his family set the tone for transactions between people, land, and spirits. His ability was judged not so much as due to his pedigree and training, though this was important, but rather to his special relationship with *puwha* via immortal allies over many generations.

4. Plateau Culture Area

Ecosystem, Provinces
Framed by the wide trough between the Cascades and Rocky Mountains, the Plateau, like the Basin, includes sagebrush desert, mountain coniferous forest, and alpine communities. It is populated by whitetail and mule deer, wapiti (American elk), moose, mountain caribou, cougar, coyote, grouse, ptarmigan, spruce, fir, and pine.

Plateau speakers, aside from the Kootenay isolate and Nicola Athapaskans, belonged to two provinces. These were Salishans in the north, and Sahaptians in the south.

Foods
Plateau staples were root crops such as camas and bitterroot gathered from spring camps, and summer salmon taken along the Columbia and Fraser Rivers and their tributaries. The greater reliability of salmon meant that Plateau social organization was more complex and sedentary. Leaders occupied elite positions that were usually hereditary. At the primary Plateau fisheries, major trade centers thrived.

Labor
During the winter, people lived in villages of semisubterranean pithouses and extended mat-covered lodges. The largest homes of leading families hosted councils, deliberations, rituals, Winter dances, and feasts, all involving both men and women. A leader excelled at oratory, generosity, maturity, and exemplary moral behavior. Often, elite families also included shamans, who worked closely with civil leaders to maintain

community wellbeing.

PLATEAU Peoples

Penutian Stock
  Klamath-Modoc
  Cayuse ?
  Molala
  Sahaptian Family
  Nez Perce
  Sahaptin
  NW Yakama-Klickitat-Kittitas
  NE Walla Walla-Wanapum-Palus
  S Umatilla-Tenino

Salishan Family
Interior Salish
  North
    Secwepemc ~ Shuswap
    Nlaka'pamux ~ Thompson
    Stl'atl'imc ~ Lillooet
  South
    Coeur d'Alene
    Flathead(Selish)-Kalispel-Spokan
    Lakes-Colvile-Sanpoil-Nespelem- Okanagan
    Columbia(Sinkiuse)-Wenatchee Entiat-Chelan >
      Methow

Athabaskan Family
  Nicola

Isolate
  Ktunaxa ~ Kootenay (remotely Salish)

- represents linguistic closeness
( ) represents a tribal synonym, alternate name, or quality

In the spring (about March), the village broke up into smaller, mobile groups. The largest one accompanied the chief. Generally only the young and active went to the summer camps. Women gathered prickly pear fruit, and men killed fowl and rabbits. The old and infirm stayed behind in the main (winter) villages.

Each year, the readiness of every harvested resource was signaled by a communal meal. After a First Roots Feast (April), chaste women gathered camas roots from moist ground, dug bitterroot in arid areas, and took them to nearby camps. There, they were peeled, cleaned, and prepared for drying and storage. Men enjoyed leisure until the fish runs (May), beginning with sturgeon and followed by trout and salmon.

After the First Salmon Rite, people moved into summer mat shelters and set up weirs, traps, and scaffolds. At the Dalles and Kettle Falls fisheries along the Columbia River, thousands gathered to process salmon. Fraser River runs included a large one of bright red sockeye.

Chinook at the Dalles (see Northwest) and Colvile at Kettle Falls were important traders linked into extensive networks. The trading center at the Dalles-Celilo Falls area was truly international. It involved Plains bison products, Nootkan dentalia from Vancouver Island, Californian slaves, local fish flour pounded up from dried salmon, and more. Far upriver, the Kettle Falls trading center was secondary but predominantly Salishan.

As salmon passed various fishing sites, people moved upstream to other camps until the runs had peaked for that season. While men did the actual fishing; women laboriously prepared, smoked, dried, and stored all fish. By fall (September), fishing camps were vacated, women dried berries for storage, and small groups moved up into the mountains to hunt. Others went upriver to fall salmon sites to catch and smoke lean fish.

After mid-October, people reoccupied their winter villages, sharing their bounty with any one less fortunate. Women cleaned out their houses, while men made repairs, cutting building timbers for women to pack home.

During quiet winter lulls, men and women engaged in craftwork, gambling, and story telling. At midwinter, visionaries in public and private were revisited by their immortal guardians, who compelled them to sing their *puwha* songs. During the winter religious season, dramatic performances and *puwha* contests engaged shamans. Among Interior Salishans, *puwha* is called <u>shumish</u>.

Despite the Plateau orderly seasonal cycle, their ecology was unpredictable, due to floods, volcanic eruptions, and earthquakes. During periods of famine, sacred deposits of salmon and animal bones were scavenged to make soup. When these were not available, old hides and pelts were boiled to provide a meager broth.

Basic Bonds

Plateau social organization was generally intergraded from informal to more formal organization. It was characterized by sigs, winter settlements, shared drainages, and linguistic diversity. Ideally, each village was completely autonomous, under its own chief and council, but, in practice, smaller villages had to depend on larger ones located downstream.

The two strongest Plateau cultural values were equality and pacifism, but with certain allowances. Everyone was ideally equal, but members of certain leading families were allowed to assert their priority during most events. Nevertheless, distributions of food and gifts seem to have been remarkably equitable among Plateau peoples, especially during famine.

Similarly, while intertribal hostilities were minimal, they did flare up. Plateau tribes remained remarkably pacific, even after some tribes, most notably the Nez Perce and Salishan Columbians, acquired horses and Plains trappings. Intratribal or intracommunity arguments sometimes developed, but the only acceptable recourse for recurring anger or displeasure was to pack up and move somewhere else.

Necessarily, Plateau individuals seem to have been quite mobile, even to the point of joining another tribal settlement. Residence was usually patrilocal and descent was bilateral. Leadership was supposed to be hereditary, but the village council of men and women always carefully considered the abilities and generosity of all candidates before approving an heir.

The most important duties of a chief were to arbitrate disputes and render judgments of mutual benefit to all, even if he had to give away many of his own goods to settle an angry disagreement. If his office became a burden, a chief could abdicate by moving elsewhere. Potential heirs usually served as subchiefs, to gain leadership practice. In historic times, many Plateau tribes had a "lasher," who publicly enforced the judgments of a chief by whipping offenders.

Perhaps based on earlier prototypes, several intertribal confederacies emerged by 1800, relying on newly introduced horses. They drew together large numbers of people so that they could safely hunt bison on the turf of Plains Blackfeet and other enemy tribes.

The Columbia, Entiat, Chelan, and Methow tribes of Interior Salish formed a confederacy under a patriline of Columbia chiefs from Suktalkosum (Split Sun, the father), Patsksteeweeya (eldest son), and Kwiltninok (son) to the famous Chief Moses (1825-1899), youngest son.

A late 1700s Yakama (Yakima) Confederacy of the Kittitas, Yakima, Wanapum,

Klickitat, and Palus Sahaptians was founded by Weowicht, then led by a Palus-Yakama chief called Kamiakin, who attacked settlers in the aftermath of treaties coerced in 1855.

The premier rank of the families of these confederacy chiefs encouraged their children to intermarry. Other historic integrative factors were various waves of "prophet cults" initiated by Sahaptian speakers. Smohalla, a Wanapum who founded Washani, and Jake Hunt, founder of the Seven Drum and Feather, were the best known. Skolakin had a Sanpoil following. These and other sects were Christianized variants which grew out of aboriginal beliefs. Thus, God became the capstone for ancient *puwhas*.

Ranks

Except for a few Plateau tribes who kept war captives as slaves, the only clear ranks were those associated with leadership and shamanism. Everyone was judged on the basis of ability, character, and generosity. Rigorous training during childhood, demonstrated capability, and descent from a recognized leader increased one's prestige. Generally, sigers were distinct from hereditary chiefs. The most visible position was that of the siger of a nodal kindred and camp. His authority was based on seniority, credibility, and moral example, rather than coercive authority. Arrow Lakes and Southern Okanagan accepted women as chiefs. Indeed, the greatest Lakes leader was a woman who served as an advisor to other chiefs. Special status was accorded to the founders of various prophet cults and the leaders of Plateau confederacies.

On the Plateau, as elsewhere, ability was an outward sign that someone had appropriate *puwha*. Leadership was derived from the ability conferred by a spirit partner to control the environment and humans.

Shamans had special status. A Plateau Salmon Priest (Tyee) had both received a Salmon partner and inherited the spells (dicta) that enabled him to coordinate the activities at a salmon trap for the benefit of all. Women stayed away from the trap because fish were known to abhor menstrual blood.

Ordinary shamans were expected to be more selfish and greedy, so they were usually wealthier than other people. While they were paid for individual cures, some also served as public servants safeguarding kin and community. These included the Antelope shaman and Salmon *Tyee* (a term for chief or siger in Chinook jargon).

Transgenders, usually men taking on the female role (but occasionally the reverse) seem to have been barely tolerated. They had no clear function, and so lacked the prestige in regions were they did outstanding work.

Cosmology: Myth, Ritual

During the myth age, ubiquitous and wily Coyote reformed the world. He decreed how humans were to observe many traditions within a new landscape featuring the Columbia River, salmon, self-awareness, and, through his own fault, incest. Aptly for a region with a staple of underground root crops, Coyote's long-suffering wife was Mole. One of the few creation epics was the Sanpoil account of how Sweat Lodge made things ready for humans before Coyote finished details. Other important Plateau mythic figures were Raven, Salmon, Wolves, Mourning Dove, Bullhead as shaman, and other personified animals.

Important Plateau rites were the Winter Dances (involving the performance of guardian spirit songs and shamanic dramatizations in a sequence of villages over a two month period), first food rites, give aways, prophet cults, Blue Jay rite, and a Sun Dance imported from the Plains. Plateau shamans also performed a version (called Blanket Rite) of the "shaking tent," described in the section on the Great Lakes area.

Plateau Salmon priests conducted the First Salmon rite, and coordinated activities at weirs and traps during the annual fish runs. During Winter Dances, Plateau visionaries communally thanked their spirit helpers and renewed the world.

Today

While Plateau people are now located on reservations, traditional values of flexibility, adaptability, and integrity remain strong. More traditional families still travel by car to resource areas. They gather seeds, roots, and berries, and hunt in order to satisfy their desire for native foods, supplementing food bought in supermarkets. Almost everyone is Christian. In some areas, most particularly those missionized by Jesuits, shamans and traditional cults and beliefs flourish within a Christian context.

On the Plateau, guardian *puwhas* are now believed to be a special gift from the Christian God to native people. Several of the prophet cults continue to thrive, most notably the Seven Drums religion among Sahaptians on the Yakama, Warm Springs, and other Columbia River reservations. The Indian Shaker Church, based in Puget Sound, also has churches in the Plateau and northern California.

Some groups have asserted a more traditional orientation under the influence of a famous figure. The Wallowa band of Numipu (Nez Perce) followed Chief Joseph through surrender in 1877 and their devastating ordeals in Florida and Oklahoma before they were returned to the Plateau. They settled on the Colville reservation of Washington State, rather than the Nez Perce reservation of Idaho, where many men had unfair warrants against them. Wanapum have remained culturally conservative through their adherence to the teachings of Smohalla.

Pentecostal and other ecstatic denominations have gained converts through the Plateau. The current, albeit New Age, interest in Native America has encouraged many younger natives to return, to revive, or to invent cultural forms of their ancestors.

TRIBAL EXAMPLES

Sanpoil of the Upper Columbia River

Along the upper Columbia River, Interior Salishan villages, such as those of Sanpoil, were each led by generations of hereditary chiefs. Other members of these elite families provided particularly skilled sigers and individuals "blessed" by an appropriate immortal to sanction an endeavor.

During an individual's quest at remote places in the mountains, spirits appeared in human form to confer *puwha* before changing into their outer species form as they departed. Personal good looks and a strong human body were particularly attractive to spirits, who departed as one became old, weak, or sickly. When a mortal partner died, the spirit became a spirit-ghost in quest of another human, preferably from the same family unless it was lured away by a shaman.

A child received *puwha* at eight to ten years of age. This encounter was forgotten until the partner returned about fifteen to twenty years later and the visionary then took sick, feeling lonely and despondent. A shaman was called to fix that spirit inside the patient, allowing him or her to sing the song signaling their bond. When winter came every year, the patient sang his or her song during special public dances.

Spirit *puwha*s included both animate and inanimate forms, such as driftwood and fish traps. Among the most awesome were Grizzly, Wolf, Badger, Skunk, Flying Squirrel, Pack Rat, Spider, Hawk, and Eagle. The most dangerous *puwha*s, because they sometimes took over a human partner, were Grizzly, Bear, Wolf, Cougar, Badger, Summer Weasel, and Rattlesnake. Rabbit and Magpie were weak *puwha*s, usually, but nothing was ever absolute. *Puwha* could not be prejudged.

The most powerful spirits gave the sanction to cure particular ailments. They enabled shamans to heal persistent and spiritual illnesses. These included wounds from animals, fevers, mental upset, sudden spirit return or loss, and magical poisoning by a jealous woman.

The shaman, either a man or a woman, arrived at the home of the patient and began treatment by first smoking a pipe. Helpers got things ready. One of them brought a basket of water for the shaman to use for washing his or her own hands. Then the basket was emptied and refilled. The shaman sang, accompanied by the audience, while examining the patient. Once a diagnosis was made, the shaman began other songs, sprinkled water, and used brushing hand motions or sucking to extract the disorder. When a spirit or poison was clasped, helpers forced the shaman to the basket and submerged his or her cupped hands to neutralize (drown) the strength of that intrusion. In return for this cure, the shaman received a generous payment that was already agreed upon in advance.

Winter dances were and are the most important religious ceremony. They are held every January and February to express personal bonds with immortals. Families host them in rotation at each of the reservation districts. Modern homes with a large fron room are now used. In the past, a large mat house was cleared, poles hung sideways to hold gifts, and a cut tree with only its top branches, decorated with wrappings and dangles, was set up in the center. Led off by the host, each visionary, in turn, grasped the pole and sang his or her song.

Cooking or eating was forbidden during a Winter Dance. Specially empowered men, called Bluejays and Owls, wearing only breechclouts despite the bitter cold weather,

Tenders Basin

sat in the rafters watching for violations. After serving all winter long, they were ritually captured and restored to normal lives. By early spring, these dances were also devoted to drawing upriver the warm melting winds called "chinooks."

Inside, men sat on the right and women on the left. The host was usually a powerful shaman able to protect everyone. Any less confident display of *puwha* encouraged theft by unscrupulous doctors. A speaker acted for the host and others, announcing intermissions to drink water and smoke. On the last morning, gifts were distributed by the host to other singers, and to the audience, as quantities allowed.

In public, a novice proclaimed renewed ties with his or her partner by dancing. He or she was protected by the sponsoring shaman. He or she was particularly vulnerable because their link was so new. After this initial display, the visionary would briefly describe the circumstance of the vision during a later intermission, or, alternatively, ask for guesses about what his song and gestures evoked.

In addition to this generalized world renewal ceremony, thanksgiving rites were held throughout the summer as various harvests began. Among the most important to be acknowledged was the first salmon to be caught every spring. It was preceded by a number of rituals to thank the many aspects of nature providing stakes, cords, nets, spears, and scaffolds needed to trap these fish.

First, in series, was a ceremony held in the forest to thank trees. These were then cut and laid in a row. When these poles had seasoned, another ritual signified that they were ready to be moved to the river to build the weir*.

While men assembled the trap, women gathered sunflower leaves to put on the roof of a sunshade like a summer mat house without walls. The ground inside and outside this shade was also covered with leaves. When all was ready, women, children, and young men withdrew for 5 days. Men stayed beside the river and wore no clothes in obvious supplication. The Salmon *Tyee* (or priest) spent five nights at the trap praying and singing to consecrate its use.

Every morning, men appointed by the Tyee carried salmon from the trap, placing them on the leaves. These salmon were gutted, with intestines hidden away. During these four days, men, using a special triangular spoon bent from a willow twig, ate only salmon flanks, boiled the first two days, then roasted.

Salmon heads, tails, fins, backbones, and roe were placed upon a woven willow platform to dry until the fifth day. Then they were mixed into a soup with serviceberries, camas, and bitterroot. This was the holiest meal of the rite since it included water and virtually all staple foods. Every man ate as much as possible.

When not fishing or feasting, men gambled, joked, and played. Religious ceremonies, even very sacred ones, were always mixed with joy. After the fifth day, men dressed, women rejoined the camp, and fish processing began. Thereafter, women resumed their usual duties of cooking all meals, caring for families, and processing all fish.

As every other resource became ready for harvesting, a similar ceremony thanked that food as fresh examples were served at a public feast. Then everyone was free to gather as much of that staple as they needed without waste.

With the same intensity as Salishans knew and appreciated their land, they upheld the virtues of gender equality and pacifism. While men and women did mutually supportive tasks, no sanction prevented a man or a woman from taking on a role, skill, or activity of their own choosing. Women were as active in politics as men, but generally they did not take the more public positions in favor of time with their families.

Tenders Basin

Warfare was strongly discouraged, except for some defensive efforts. Leaders preached that retaliation would not bring back the dead nor avenge wrongs. If villagers came to blows, the chief would make them fight on slippery ice, during the winter, or in mud, at other times, so they would look as ridiculous as possible in front of their family and friends.

Nez Perce ~ Nimiipuu

Long resident on the eastern Plateau, the Nimiipuu (in downriver dialect Nuumiipu) lived along the confluences of the Salmon and Clearwater Rivers on the middle course of the Snake River. In 1800, there were 70 villages with between 30-200 members, using 300 named places.[70] Like the Kootenay, the Upper Nez Perce were more Plainsized, and the Lower Niimiipu more like others of the Plateau. Their uplands extended from the Bitterroot Range to the Blue Mountains on the west. They shared Grande Ronde Valley with the Umatilla, and the Moscow (Idaho) camas meadows with the Palus.[71] Their enthusiastic breeding and trading of horses gave them great influence over a vast region.

Local resources included stone for knives, points, scrapers, awls, ground pestles, mortars, and mauls. Elkhorn provided wedges and handles, animal bone was used for flakers, fish spears, gouges, and markers for the disk game; bird bone was cut into beads, and sandhill cranes provided whistles used in battle. Horn was steamed into spoons and cups. Bows were shaped from syringa or yew, and usually had sinew backing. Wood was used for drum frames, shafts, and tally stick calendars. Hemp bast was woven into soft basket pouches and cordage. Cornhusks were woven into bags, later made with yarn. Women wove their own basket hats, made coiled baskets on a willow framework, and sewed cattail mats. Hides were tanned using the animal's own brains, sometimes smoked to become waterproof. Rattles were sewn up pieces of deerskin.

Typical housing included a winter mat long lodge, summer skin tipi, underground menstrual hut, birthing hut, sweatlodge, and a brush arbor when hunting. Unmarried men above the age of 14 slept together in the sudatory, which was 3 feet deep, 12 feet around, and entered by a ramp. Diversions were and are hand game, dice, shinny, and mocking teams facing each other in lines.

Their territory was and is rich in a variety of foods. Important roots are camas, kouse, lomatiums (desert parsleys), bitterroot, and balsamroot. Fish include many species of salmon, trout, eel, lamprey, whitefish, sucker, and sturgeon. Game are elk, deer, moose, mountain sheep, bears, mountain goat, otter, beaver, rabbit, squirrel, badger, and marmot. Birds are many ducks, geese, sage hens, and raptors killed for feathers and body parts used in ceremonies. During bad times, famine foods include pine lichen and inner bark.

Hunting relied on fire surrounds, decoys, and deadfalls. Rattlesnake poison was sometimes applied to arrow tips. Snares were used for small game and birds. Fishing relied on hooks, spears, harpoons, dip nets, spread nets, weirs, traps, and dipping platforms, as well as gaffs in historic times. Each person ate 500 lbs of fish a year.

Winter villages broke up in the early spring after the cache pits were empty to undertake communal game drives in the river valleys, or hunts on snowshoes in the mountains. Once salmon run s began, men caught them and women processed them to smoke and sun-dry. Women then dug roots in the lower elevations. By midsummer, people moved into the cooler uplands and by mid-August dug the higher roots. In the Fall, they pick serviceberries, gooseberries, hawthorn berries, thorn berries, huckleberries, currents, chokecherries, pine nuts, balsam seeds, and black moss. After being prepared, these dried foods were stored in baskets and rawhide envelopes (parfleshes) that were placed in deep winter caches lined with bark and grass.

After 1700, the horse was given pride of place and 1000 people would venture out to hunt bison in Montana. Close allies were Cayuse and Flathead, while enemies were Blackfeet to the east, Bannock to the south. Gear included a low saddle for men, and a high pommel for women to hold suspended cradles. With the horse came other influences from the Plains, including clothing. Men wore a shirt with long fringes, leggings, clout, belts, gloves, gauntlets, moccasins, and a blanket; women wore a wing dress decorated with elk teeth and seashells, basket cap, and knee-high moccasins. Adornment relied on dyes, quills, teeth, and beads. Warriors wore armor made from elkhide to provide a helmet, tunic, and shield.

For travel, people used oval snowshoes or dugouts carved from red fir. The Crow name for the Niimiipu was paddlers, while most others referred to the men's pierced noses or pompadour hairstyle. As horse traders, men covered a large region and, after 1800, Niimiipu became the language of trade and diplomacy.

Winter villages were set along streams and allied with others on that tributary into a band, which sometimes joined with others, such as the composite bands at Kamiah on the upper Clearwater, and at Lapwai, Grande Ronde, and Alpoway on the Snake River. Each village and band had a council made up of senior men who advised the local headman, who was expected to be a moral exemplar, skilled speaker, fair judge, and welfare aide. Crimes included murder, theft, and adultery, with the worst punishments being execution, banishment, or exile.

The band chief took care of defense, ceremonies, and coordinated harvesting of the area. The leader of a composite band was usually the siger of their intertribal bison hunt. Chiefs were drawn from leading families and confirmed by popular election or council decision. They constituted peace / war leaders, and sponsored gifting and feasting to show their generosity. A scalp dance was held after a successful raid or battle, with ears often taken as trophies.

Specialized guilds drew together shamans, craftswomen, and warriors of larger bands who took a pledge of "no retreat", anchoring themselves on the battlefield by planting a special staff. Slaves were war prisoners, such as Itskimzekin, traded from Northern California and mentioned below.

A life cycle varied according to the wealth and prestige of the family. A pregnant woman retired to an underground hut for a few months before and few weeks after the birth, when she was attended by a midwife and female kin. Twins were considered lucky. The baby's cord was attached to its cradleboard. Once the baby teethed, he or she was weaned to soft foods, and taken off the cradleboard when able to walk. Childcare was taken over by the grandparents, who freely joked and shared the same kin terms with the child. The grandfather had primary care for boys, and the grandmother for girls. Older disobedient children were punished by the community whipper, a specially designed old man. Relations with the parents became formal.

Each day, a child wakened in the predawn to bath with uncles or aunts, then listened to stern lectures, undertook training exercises, and followed instructions. A child began to contribute to the home from the age of three, using toy utensils, and made singular contributions after the age of six, when rites were held for the first kill of a boy, or the first berry or root of a girl. As a subteen, the family arranged for a formal private lecture by an honored elder that indicated their prestige. A child was named for an ancestor, with the name changed in recognition of later accomplishments.

About puberty, a boy or girl of good family was sent out to quest for a vision. Meeting a spirit provided access to *puwha*, a song, and a bundle that was and is vital for all success. Those with allied spirits formed guilds, such as the Waptipas whose immortals were elk, deer, wolf, or cougar, conferring the ability to handle live fire and draw game close. Each winter, in a public setting, visionaries gathered together to enter trance and sing for their immortal partner.

Greatest *puwha* belonged to the shaman (*tiweet*), both men and women, who specialized in fishing, hunting, curing, prophecy, weather control, or finding lost goods. Massage, herbs, sweating, and dicta were all used in cures. A sucking shaman could remove a curse lodged inside someone's body. Some used their *puwha* for sorcery, providing a kind of social control.

A girl's puberty was and is celebrated. In the past, she entered a special hut and was urged to keep busy, have good thoughts, and eat from a separate plate at her own fire. She could only come out briefly at night, and had to use a carved scratcher. At the end, she was given gifts and new clothes.

Families arrange a marriage on the basis of their relative prestige. A woman go-between moved into the home of the girl to watch her closely. If she was accepted, then a trial marriage began. If it lasted, it led to two decisive ceremonial exchanges between the inlaws, which continued on throughout marriage. The first featured meat from the groom, and the second served plants from the bride. The groom's kin gave horses, hunting and fishing gear, and buckskin; while the bride's kin gave root bags, baskets, beads, dibbles, and plant foods. Thereafter, the groom respected his inlaws, especially the wife's mother and brothers, but freely joked with her sisters. The bride respected her husband's father and sisters, but joked with her brothers-in-law. This joking eased an eventual sororate or levirate marriage after the death of a spouse.

As death approached, elders tried to settle their own affairs. The town herald announced the death, and female kin wailed. The body was washed, dressed in fine clothes, and the face painted red. It was buried next day in a talus slope or upon a nearby hill, marked by a cedar pole, and, if the person was wealthy, a favorite horse killed. A shaman ritually blocked any return of the ghost. At a following feast, all of the deceased's possessions were given away. His or her mat house was dismantled and moved, or sometimes destroyed. Close kin mourned for a year, wailing and wearing short hair and shabby clothes. Then the surviving mate was given new clothes and a new spouse, if possible, from same family.

Over eons, prophets arose among the Nimiipuu to predict or warn of coming events. They told of new machines, missionaries, and other stresses. In mythology, Coyote was a key figure who also influenced the future. Horses arrived in the Plateau after 1700 and the Niimiipu undertook a successful breeding program. In 1805, when Lewis and Clark appeared, the Nez Perce were 6,000 strong and the largest nation on Plateau. In 1900, they numbered 1800; in 1994, 3000.

They became heavily involved in the fur trade until local beaver were obliterated by 1846. In 1831, inspired by Iroquois traders, a delegation of Nez Perce and Flatheads made it to St Louis to ask for "the great prayer" [Mass] of Catholic priests. Instead, Presbyterians came first and grew to dominance until the Whitman Mission was massacred by the Cayuse in 1847. Rev Henry Spaulding fled the region and did not return until the 1870s to establish a printing press for texts in the native language that were enthusiastically used by lay leaders. In time, Catholic Jesuits converted the last of the traditionalists to found Slickpoo Mission.

Niimiipu leaders forged a nation by 1830, largely during the bison hunts, and missionaries in 1842 encouraged the establishment of a legal code with a head chief and 12 subchiefs, each with five policemen. The US forced a series of treaties in 1855, 1863, and 1868, which shrunk their land base. Negotiators, including future president James Garfield, acted fraudulently, leading to the flight (July to September of 1877) by Young Joseph, leader of the Oregon Wallowa Nez Perce. After a successful retreat, they were halted just south of the Canadian border. Exiled to Oklahoma, where many died of heat and despair, survivors moved to the Colville Reservation in 1885, avoiding the arrest warrants waiting for them in Idaho.

Among the unlikely warriors was a slave named Itskimzekin. To punish him for stealing, his Yakama owners locked him in irons. One bitterly cold night, the metal froze to his body and three badly frostbitten limbs had to be amputated. His remaining left arm and leg stumps resulted in many ironic nicknames. Joining the Niimiipu, he fought on the 1877 retreat by rolling around to take cover while firing a pistol.[72]

The Nez Perce Reservation in Idaho was allotted about 1890 under the terms of the infamous Dawes Act by early anthropologist Alice Fletcher. Herbert Spinden researched there in 1907 for the Harvard Peabody and in 1908 for the American Museum of Natural History. In 1948, a constitution set up the NPTEC, Nez Perce Tribal Executive Committee. Periodically, Wallowas try to resettle in Oregon, returning to their stolen lands.

70 Deward Walker, Nez Perce, Handbook of North American Indians, Plateau, Vol 12, 1998: 420-438.

71 Herbert Joseph Spinden, The Nez Perce Indians, American Anthropological Association - Memoir II (Nov) Part 3 1908: 171-274.

72 Scott M Thompson, I will Tell of My War Story, A Pictorial Account of the Nez Perce War, Seattle: University of Washington Press, in association with The Idaho State Historical Society 2000.

5. Basin Culture Area

Ecosystem

The Great Basin was a cold desert of sagebrush, scadscale, and kangaroo rat, in addition to rice grass, saltbush, pronghorn antelope, great horned owl, mule deer, and many tasty insects.

Throughout the Basin, water was a vital concern. Most rain and rivers drained down into but never left the bottom of valleys, staying in "sinks" to form ponds, lakes, marshes, or salt pans. Great Salt Lake is a prime example. The Basin was filled by Numic speakers, except for Hokan Washo at Lake Tahoe.

Foods

Basin staples were various wild seeds, especially pinyon nuts. Other edibles included rodents, insects, and a few large mammals. Fish known as cui-cui rose from the depths of Pyramid Lake each spring to spawn in the Truckee River. To protect the food supply for humans, no dogs were kept in the central Basin.

GREAT BASIN Peoples

Aztec-Tanoan Stock
  Numic Family
      Western
            Northern Paiute-Bannock
            Mono
      Central
            Western Shoshoni
            Goshiute
            Panamint
            Lehmi-Wind River-Comanche (Plainsized)
      Southern
            Ute
            Kawaiisu-Chemehuevi
            Southern Paiute

Hokan Stock
  Washo

* - represents linguistic closeness, ( ) represents a tribal synonym, alternate name, or modification

Adaptability

Basin communities testify to the human potential to adapt and to survive in the face of difficult environments with stark ecological conditions. While every bit as conceptually complex as all other cultures, these societies provide prime (the original meaning of primitive) examples of human interaction in close cooperation with local ecology. Kindreds scattered or congregated as economic and ritual communities in direct proportion to the available supply of foods.

Married couples sheltered inside brush windbreaks. Men hunted animals and women tended plants. During seed or fish harvests, couples worked together, as also happened during communal net drives for rabbits, antelopes, or birds. Men manufactured tools, built traps, and coordinated their families during an annual cycle of seasonal movements among ripening foods. Harvests allowed people to gather together. The fresh availability of each resource was greeted with a first food feast to confirm their reliance on it. Sigers arose according to situational needs, sanctioned to be successful at some task.

Labor

Except for a few rivers, springs, seeps, and sinks, the only sizeable Basin water sources were Pyramid, Walker, and Honey Lakes where populations were larger and more sedentary in response to available fish and waterfowl. Some central Nevada tribes were also able to sustain larger populations by scattering seeds in damp areas and later harvesting that crop.

Within modern eastern California, the Owens Valley Mono sowed wild seeds in irrigated plots. Like other hunting, gathering, fishing, and protofarming (advanced tending) peoples, Basin inhabitants intimately knew their local plant and animal species.

Southern Paiutes classified plants as "bloomers" and animals as "movers". Interspecies kinship terms used deer as the referent (Ego) for the artiodactyles (hooveds), such that mammals larger than deer were called "elder brothers", while those smaller were "younger brothers."

Throughout the Basin, men hunted game animals for meat and furs, manufactured most utensils, gouged out any irrigation ditches and broadcast seeds, constructed fish traps, and held leadership positions. Women collected seeds, roots, insects, and other ripe foods; made baskets, rabbitskin blankets, huge nets, and other tools particular to their own activities; maintained home and family; nourished their kin, and sometimes made pottery or tended tobacco plants. Both sexes collectively worked to provide firewood and water, harvest pinyon nuts, drive rabbits into a net, entice antelopes into a corral, and ambush mud hens, deer, and mountain sheep. The seasonal round moved among set (transhumant) camps at or near particular resources.

Basic Bonds

Great Basin societies were more "elegant", in the sense of basic and streamlined, when compared to many other areas of Native America. Except for plentiful micro-environments around lakes or enhanced seed crops, the residential unit was a camp occupied by a **nodal kindred** {* = a bilateral kinship grouping composed of parents, siblings, and spouses led by a node (intersecting knot) of parents and children or, after the death of the parents, among siblings}. According to the availability of resources, these camps were larger in winter than during other seasons.

Because of the small size of these kindreds, they were particularly influenced by factors of demography and ecology. Therefore, maximum flexibility provided a survival advantage through various means, particularly marriage choices (polygamy) to assure continuity. Strategies included sister exchange, cross-cousin marriage, sororal polygyny (sister wives), and fraternal polyandry (brother husbands). Bands emerged only among the Ute, Northern Paiute, and Northern Shoshoni in response to the adoption of horses, increased mobility, and Plainsization. This shift introduced tipis, bison hunting, war honors, and the Sun Dance. In more central areas of the Basin, the arrival of a stray horse meant only that natives had a good meal.

Ranks

Basin leadership arose as needed, under the care of sigers. Certain families seem to have had strong ties to immortals "owning" a particular homeland and especially used rare commodities like turquoise. Only shamans were noted for their skill in various endeavors. In the Basin, a specialist shaman lured antelopes into a corral so that hunters could kill them. Such a shaman was given *puwha* to do this by Antelope, though the species is notoriously curious to its own harm.

Cosmology: *Myth, Ritual*

As a marplot, Coyote rearranged the features of the Basin, sometimes aided by Eagle or Hawk. Shamans often received their *puwha* from three special mythic figures called Water Baby, Little Man of the Mountains, and Elk. Goshiute attributed local rock art, both petroglyphs and pictographs, to Little Man and other Short Giants. Much of the Basin flora and fauna were personified in myths, particularly Frog, Cottontail, and some women culture heroes. Any abundance of food was the occasion for a gathering of families to hold a Round dance or a fandango (a term borrowed from recent Basque sheepherders) to give thanks for their bounty. Smaller and more personal were kindred celebrations held at birth, girl's puberty, and death.

In 1870 and 1890, prophets arose in the Basin and Plateau whose doctrines were carried across Native America. The most famous of these was Wovoka (Jack Wilson), from Walker River in Nevada, who preached a return to ancient traditions through the Round Dance. His message spread through the Plains, aided by free railroad passes, and, despite the massacre of Lakota at Wounded Knee in 1890, continues to influence native beliefs in Western America. For an area of great hardship, the Basin has had an inordinate impact on the rest of Native America, much as the Arabian desert has had on the rest of the world.

Today

Small, scattered native populations were settled by federal officials at reservations on or near homelands, and at "colonies" (land parcels) within towns so natives were available to whites for domestic and wage work. Traditional families still travel by van to gather seeds, roots, and berries. Almost everyone is Christian, particularly Mormon (Church of Jesus Christ of Latter Day Saints) like their neighbors, although their dark skins set them apart from "whitesome and delightsome" full membership.

TRIBAL EXAMPLES

Mono Paiute of **Owens Valley** California

While all tribal elites knew of the web of rings and rays reflecting the flow of *puwha* in the world, for Great Basin peoples, *puha* {* = *puwha*} followed the distribution of moisture through this arid landscape. Falling as rain on mountain peaks and lakes, flowing down as streams and rivers, the upward return came from both evaporation and gushing springs. Dwarf spirits called Water Babies lived in these waters, with their homes under hot springs that were said to be heated by their cooking fires. From small camps, Basin people gathered when and where water collected to harvest foods and to celebrate.

The source and summary of this flowing was and is the Creator. It is Sun Father in the northern Basin, and Ocean Old Woman on Charleston Peak near Las Vegas in the south.[73]

Unlike much of the arid Basin, however, Owens valley was a huge oasis sustaining 2000 people. The valley is 80 miles long and, in places, 10 miles wide, drained by the Owens River (once 20 miles long, 50 feet wide, and 15 feet deep) to end in Owens Lake. This "sink" is a dead saline pond whose brine flies and brine shrimps (sold as water/sea monkeys) sustain migrating waterfowl. Such an abundant and reliable source of water, though undrinkable, enabled greater social stability, with cultural elaborations showing fascinating links with the Southwest and eastern California.[74]

Like other Basin peoples (with the sole exception of Washo), Mono, along with Northern Paiute, belongs to the Western section of the Numic branch of Uto-Aztecan. At the southern or lake end of the valley, autonomous villages and hamlets were located near the alluvial fans of creeks. In the northern or river section, villages were more numerous and dispersed, grouped into 5 districts, to take advantage of streams and marshy meadows. In nearby arid valleys, people lived near springs.

Within Owens, traditional foods gathered in summer were seeds of ryegrass, wild rye, needlegrass, blazing star, chia, lovegrass, sunflower, pigweed, and bullrush. In the fall, root crops ranged from wild hyacinth corms to nutgrass and spikerush bulbs.

An aboriginal irrigation system mourished wild plants in the north valley. Using check dams and thin feeder ditches built communally, sustained watering was the job of one man in each district. Once elected, the insignia of this office was a "water staff" (*pabodo*) used as a lever to control water flow. Bishop Creek, the largest tributary, was dammed to flood grassy lowlands. Only women belonging to that district could harvest these foods, though untended areas could be gleaned by anyone.

From the valley, people resorted to the Sierra Nevada mountains for pinyon nuts, the Basin staple, along with acorns, the California staple. Caterpillars of the pandora moth were taken in alternate years on a 20 year cycle. After feeding on the needles of the Jeffrey yellow pine, these insects descend in late June to pupate. Trees were circled with trenches where the caterpillars were trapped, gathered in open-twined baskets, baked in hot ashes, sun-dried, and stored for later consumption and trade.

While Northern Paiute relied on communal drives for waterfowl, Owens Mono took them individually. The only fish available were suckers, minnows, and the Owens pupfish, which was sun-dried for storage. Their lake also teemed with brine shrimp, brine fly, and other tiny animals. Fly pupae were processed and traded as a winter food supplement called *kutsavi*. Deer, mountain sheep, and antelope were hunted, sometimes in drives like those held for rabbits.

Through intermarriage and trade, people from the Bishop area moved across the mountains and became the Monache. They included the Northfork Mono on the upper San Juaquin River, intermediaries between Owens valley and the upland Miwok, Yokuts, and Tubatulabal. A polyglot native population resident in the Sierra Nevadas facilitated these intertribal contacts.

From native California, locals adopted notions about the territorial ownership of resources, like the fishing and collecting rights of San Juaquin triblets. Equally important was the assembly lodge (*muusa*, a Yokuts word), distinctive of California, used by Owens community men for sleeping, meetings, gambling, story telling, and singing. The construction and use of the *muusa* was the responsibility of the tribal or district chief, as in California. While the patrimoieties of California (Miwok land/ water, Yokuts upstream -

Eagle/ downstream - Coyote) had yet to be adopted, nicknames distinguished "Eagles" in the south valley and "Magpies" in the north.

Religious dances and shamanic rites were held within large, roofless, bush enclosures, along with the Cry, an annual mourning ceremony borrowed from lower Colorado River tribes like the Mohave. Indigenous festivities included the Round Dance (fandango), with hired professional singers and skilled dancers.

Unlike the meager brush houses and shades of the rest of the Basin, Owens Valley had seven building types, including the _muusa_. Houses were conical, with or without a ridgepole, covered with mats or thatch. Other shelters were pole lean-tos, ramadas (sunshades), and stout log food caches at winter camps in the mountains.

Technology was spare, including slow matches (punks), fire drills, sinew-backed juniper bows, sagebrush sandals and socks, women's digging sticks (dibbles) of mountain mahogany, and a great variety of baskets. Heavy items like stone metates, mortars, and grinders were left cached at the camp sites where they were ready to be used. The winter garment was a fluffy blanket woven of strips of rabbitskin, typical of the Basin.

A specialty of the Owens Mono was cooking pottery, unique to the Sierra piedmont. It was probably inspired by indirect contacts with the Southwest about 1650. Made by coiling, the pots were sun-dried and lightly fired to absorb a watertight coating made from mallow leaves or acorn mash. The final color ranged from dull red and grey to brown or black, in shapes like those of basketry. Made by only a few women, their wares were traded for food, baskets, and shell money.

Isolated, Owens Valley was not colonized by Americans until the 1860s, when settlers were duly impressed by the existing irrigation networks. Precipitate skirmishes over land and water rights fostered the leadership of Captain George in the south and Joaquin Jim (a Yokuts) in the north. In 1863, 900 Mono prisoners were marched to Fort Tejon (in Grapevine Canyon along Interstate 5), disrupting native life forever. Within three years, however, all prisoners had drifted back into the valley.

The greatest disaster, however, came when the City of Los Angeles Department of Water and Power began buying up water rights throughout the valley after 1905. The first aqueduct was finished in 1913, and, by 1933, the city owned 95% of the farmland and 85% of the towns, strangling their growth. To gain native compliance, local men were hired for manual labor. Land and water contracts arranged by Bureau of Indian Affairs personnel showed neither interest nor competence to protect native foods and ancient territories.

As a result, Owens valley is now as arid as the rest of the Basin. Native people have concentrated at modern towns like Lone Pine, Independence, Big Pine, and, particularly, Bishop. It was long an important aboriginal center and is now the location of an intertribal museum. Mammoth Lakes, a skiing spa, draws many tourists into the region.

73. Jay Miller, Numic Religion: An Overview of Power in the Great Basin of Native North America 1983.
74. Sven Liljeblad and Catherine Fowler, Owens Valley Paiute, Great Basin 1986.

Chemehuevi of the Lower Colorado River

Chemehuevi culture and language was presented, with great skill and insight, by Carobeth Tucker Harrington Laird. She began writing at 75 years of age, based on the knowledge of George Laird, a Cherokee well versed in Chemehuevi traditions. Initially, Carobeth was sent by her then husband, John Peabody Harrington, an obsessive linguist and anthropologist, to collect data on this little known group. By good fortune, Carobeth met George, they married, and their collaboration filled her life until she died, at 87, in 1983.[75]

The Chemehuevis expounded on the all-pervasive role of oral literatures in defining every facet of native society. Through males, Chemehuevis inherited certain songs that provided "ownership" of territory and abilities. The two most important of these were named for Mountain Sheep or for Deer.[76] Those who inherited the Mountain Sheep Song evoked a trail along the west side of the Colorado River in terrain called "my mountain". Those with the Deer Song, went along the east side of the Colorado, following a trail through "my land".

Owners of Deer Song also possessed Salt Song, which was made up of garbled Mohave words. Salt Song was particularly noteworthy because it went directly through Mohave territory, just outside their own traditional lands, but "claimed" it in a mischievous sense of fun. This was intended to suggest that Chemehuevis were true cosmopolitans, playing with foreign words and ranging boldly through enemy territory. The bird-song gaiety of the tune made Salt Song peculiarly appropriate for use at festive occasions.[77]

With equal bravado, this loosely democratic society included a "high chief". His few symbols of office included the right to wear turquoise and eat quail beans (black-eyed peas), together with the sole use of "real song" and "real speech." As owner of "talking song", he was THE exemplar of highest morality throughout the entire community.[78] Presumably, he and his family had special bonds with the land and its immortals.

For most activities, Chemehuevis lived on the landscape as members of a kindred company (*yunakaim*). Each was led by a siger coordinating natural harvests to sustain life that was "repetitious, monotonous, yet always surrounded by mystery and spiced with danger."[79]

Mirror and Pattern is especially good for the linguistic details so often overlooked in the study of oral literatures, particularly speech signatures.[80] Each character used a word, sound, or phrasing distinctively his or her own, just like cartoons where Daffy Duck speaks differently than does Mickey Mouse. Thus, for Chemehuevi, Coyote prefaces his remarks with *haikya*, while Skunk inserts *haikyaikuku'u*, Rattlesnake has hoarse *kwaagwaiwl*, Chipmunk uses *kwivi'i*, and Duck intersperses *kingko'o* into its remarks.

Of special note, Laird sensitively noted all-pervading spiritual aspects of native life, for humans, shamans and others. She clearly indicated that the relationship between mythic and present time went only one way – "The mythic era spills over into the human era, but the reverse is not true," and added the insight that "Mythic persons have breath and minds, but they do not have [or need] souls."[81]

75. After reentering California anthropology, Carobeth described her life with Harrington in Encounter With An Angry God 1975; her confinement in a nursing home in Limbo 1979; and her years with George, who died in 1940, in The Chemehuevis 1976, and

Mirror and Pattern: George Laird's World of Chemehuevi Mythology 1984, based on archival copies of their early work together.

76. Laird, The Chemehuevis 1976: 11, 14.
77. Laird, The Chemehuevis 1976: 16.
78. Laird, The Chemehuevis 1976: 24, 27.
79. Laird, Mirror and Pattern 1984: 123, 259.
80. Laird, Mirror and Pattern 1984: 297-301.
81. Laird, Mirror and Pattern 1984: 17, 18, 133, 268.

6. California Culture Area

Ecosystem, Provinces

California has a summer drought ecosystem. Its arid resistant (sclerophyll) plant community was composed of a dozen oak species, sagebrush, chaparral, and bunch grass. Animals include mule deer, grizzly, chipmunk (ground squirrel), kangaroo rat, pocket gopher, rabbit, wood rat, hawk, quail, and many reptiles. Much of its ecological integrity is long gone, like the bear on the state flag.

Native California intergraded into south, mid, and north provinces. It was the area of greatest social diversity, occupied by tribelets, because its high mountains and deep valleys fostered isolation around the more open Central Valley. After much research, linguists have included many of these languages into either Hokan or Penutian stocks. Tiny scattered settlements termed "rancherias" were the California norm, with kinship highly varied, though it was more patrilineal in the north and matrilineal in the south. Like the Tohono O'otam of the Southwest, these rancherias gave allegiances to larger settlements or focal towns of the tribelet that had a shrine or a large rotunda (community hall, diagnostic of the region) belonging to their leader.

CALIFORNIA Peoples

Hokan Stock
 Palaihnihan
  Achomawi
  Atsugewi
  Shasta
  Karuk
  Chimariko
  Yana-Yahi
  Pomo
  Salinan-Esselin
  Chumash
  Diegeño
  Kamia
  Yumans

Athabaskan Family
 Hupa
 Kato
 Mattole
 Tolowa
 Wailaki
 Sinkyone

Numic Family
 Tubatulabal
 Takic
 Serrano
 Cupan
  Luiseño-Juaneño
  Cahuilla-Cupeño
  Gabrieleño-Fernandeño
 Numic

Algic Stock
 Ritwan Family
  Wiyot
  Yurok

Tenders California

Penutian Stock	Isolate
Californian Kernel	Yukic
Yokut	Yuki-Coast-Huchnom
Miwok	Wappo
Costanoan	
Maidu	
Wintun	

Housing in the north, including separate men's houses, were made of wooden planks, while those in the south were built of bark, branches, earth, and fibers.

The three provinces will be typified in terms of Klamath River tribes for the north, Pomo for mid, and Luiseño for the south. The Yuki isolate are also mid.

Foods

The staple was acorns, using a complex technology to leach out their toxic tannic acid. Interestingly, this tradition was not strictly necessary since the acid was removed by cooking. Considerations of flavor and granular consistency, however, probably accounted for all the effort. Diet was also augmented by locally available plants, insects, and shellfish; by salmon in the north; and by seals on the south coast.

Labor

Californian sexual dichotomy was profound. It was especially so in the north on the Klamath River, where men lived in sweatlodges and women and children lived in domestic houses. Men hunted as women and children gathered. Both cooperated during the fall acorn harvest before the women ground, leached, and stored acorn meal. Women, especially among Pomo, wove exquisitely fine baskets. Men sometimes wove coarse openwork ones. Both types stored food from foraged plants, mammals, shellfish, reptiles, birds, and insects, depending on local preferences.

Leaders held their position through a combination of heredity, generosity, eloquence, and wealth. Leaders were men with great supernatural *puwha* and material wealth, who were usually polygamous. Typically, a strong personality and the possession of these attributes might entitle someone to leadership without additional qualifications. Such a candidate had only to dominate the field and be acceptable to other elite families. A leader's house was the largest in the community, serving as rotunda, church, and community hall for the wider region.

Material wealth was more emphasized in the north, heredity in the center, and generosity in the southern province. Treasures in the north included paired red, black, or colored obsidian blades a yard long; red-headed (piliated) woodpecker scalps; albino or unusual deerskins; shell beads; dentalia; olivella shells; abalone; and baked magnesite cylinders (called "Indian gold").

Throughout California, especially in the north, women were often shamans, conducting important female puberty ceremonies, and representing the female principle as complementary to the male one.

Cosmology: *Myth, Cults*

Public first foods observances, particularly before each acorn harvest, were held throughout the year. Men joined esoteric guilds (cults). These were world renewal + public wealth display in the north, Kuksu for mid, and Chungishnish in the south. Along the Klamath, prehuman immortals prepared the world before some of them sank into the ground at places that became sacred. These were visited during the world renewal ("fixing") held yearly, ending in wealth displays like the White Deerskin Dance or Jump Dance.

Southern Californian charters emphasized creation from a primal void or water. The Cahuilla and other southern tribes believed the universe was created by a collision of two swirling forces within this void – one male and one female. After colliding, a great web (not chain) of being was created, maintained, and differentiated by graded amounts of *puwha* (* = _ayelkwi_ for Luiseño). Males and females possess and bestow different aspects and intensities of this "vitality + knowledge + force + power."

Today

Throughout California, Man was often equated with Sky and Outside, or Woman with Earth and Inside. But these orderly worlds collapsed under the impact of European (starting with Spanish) "contact". Native Californians suffered planned genocide and cultural suppression. Tribes in the southern province were converted to Catholicism and herded to missions (in part to protect the Manilla Galleon (1565-1815) bringing loot back to Spain across the Pacific). There, they were repeatedly devastated by epidemics, Spanish arrogance challenging traditional leaders, and the arrival of new sources of *puwha*. Shaman's children often were among the earliest converts because they hoped to learn how to control this alien *puwha*, manifested in trade goods, only to succumb to unexpected aggravations, stresses, and abuses.

More serious disruption (social and psychological) occurred with the decline of the mission system after 1825 and its secularization in 1834. The disastrous plight of the southern province received national attention in the famous novel Ramona (1884) by Helen Hunt Jackson. This led to various reforms.

Tribes and people in the mid and northern provinces were devastated by the influx of desperate Americans during the Gold Rush of 1848. Demoralized settlers and miners raped, raided, and enslaved natives.

Most mid tribes did not survive these attacks. This fate was personified by the last southern Yana (or Yahi), known only as Ishi, their tribal word for man. He lived out his final days in a San Francisco museum, as living display and handyman.

The northern province tribes were devastated later than mid province peoples. They are currently in the midst of a cultural revival.[82]

82. cf G-O Road, News from Native California.

TRIBAL EXAMPLES

Klamath River

This northern California drainage is a world-famous example, in contrast to the uniformity of the Arctic, of linguistic diversity amidst cultural similarity. It involved neighboring Yurok (whose language belongs to Ritwan within Algic), Karuk (Hokan), and Hupa (Athapaskan). Though each tribe spoke unrelated languages, they nevertheless cooperated fully with the others to celebrate major rituals, and share wealth treasures.

In this province, *puwha* is not so much equated with knowledge and position as it is embodied in material property as "treasures." Unlike Pacific Northwest tribes, northern province tribes constantly accumulated this wealth for display rather than to give away.

People had considerable autonomy, with each individual's fixed worth set by the brideprice given for his or her mother. Every act had a potential value attached to it. Insults, feuds, murders, incest, and spouses all had a negotiated worth. Men had marks tattooed on their inner arms to measure standard units of dentalia and other bead strings. Leaders were wealthy men, serving as bankers, judges, and arbitrators. They expected to receive or give a percentage of the wealth involved in any transaction.

The sexes were extremely segregated. Men shared a communal, semi-subterranean sweatlodge. Women and children lived in houses scattered at the edges of the settlement. A primary theme among the Yurok was a quest for "balance" within person and world. Everything had two sides, often equated with Man and Woman. Paired obsidian blades were considered a mated couple, while the immortal Great Dentalium was considered a man.

Being a "real man" involved long and strenuous training by fasting, praying, esoteric instruction, *puwha* quests, personal control, and overcoming fear. By these criteria, a woman, especially as a shaman, could also become a "real man." In this way, she learned to manage *puwha* and to cure the "pains" believed to cause disease. A pain was a blood-filled, splinter-like being that was responsible both for illness in a patient and for the *puwha* of a shamaness. This balance between men and women, wealth and treasures, and patients and curer expressed the importance of gender.

World renewing wealth displays of the Klamath River tribes required much cooperation. Frequently, the required mate to an obsidian blade was owned by a member of another settlement, tribelet, and language group. Its owner was asked to allow its use in a White Deer Skin Dance or a Jumping Dance. Such requests were rarely, if ever, refused because of mutual self-interest and family honor.

While strong individual autonomy was the rule and wealth compensation standard recourse, cooperation was the understood norm. It enabled the building of a fish weir or a wealth display ceremonial at any of the seven Yurok, four Karuk, and three Hupa sacred town sites. In the absence of a more formalized social organization, these tribes focused on specific locations within their landscape as centers of and for social cohesion, ritual, and *puwha*.

Pomo

Mid Californian societies like the Maidu and Yokut were divided into foothill and valley segments. A much wider spectrum of terrains belonged to the Pomo, who had seven major dialect divisions, about 75 focal towns, and about 500 satellite villages, each shifting between winter concentrations and summer dispersals.

The leader of a focal town was a member of an elite called "great chiefs". He was selected on the basis of proven ability and control of *puwha* by consensus, patrilineal descent or, very rarely, matrilineal claim. Satellite towns had subordinates called "surrounding chiefs," each leading a resident patriline. Main duties of any leader were welcoming visitors, providing hospitality, supervising ritual work done by others, holding ceremonies and moralistic preaching, and judging disputes.

Among Pomo, women held various high statuses. These included titular leadership, shamanship, and, in rare instances, membership in a cult. On the whole, men occupied the graded, specific positions and women filled more general, community ones. Elite families were expected to intermarry and were labeled by special terms, particularly among northern Pomo groupings.[83]

Kuksu (or Big-Head) probably diffused from the Patwin Wintun, and was closely associated with Penutian tribes. Rites were held in a rotunda that featured a foot drum made from an 8 foot long wooden slab placed over a trench. Salinans and northern Yokuts belonged to both Chungishnish and Kuksu.

Kuksu seems to have had two major divisions, with perhaps a series of internal degrees. The first division was a male puberty initiation when immortal embodiments performed at a series of winter dances to strengthen younger boys and renew the world.

Second division initiation involved older, perhaps married, males who voluntarily submitted themselves to rigorous fasting in return for detailed instruction from cult leaders. These esoteric doctrines on cosmic order and meaning were expressed in ever more elaborately detailed tellings of their creation epic. Second degree men (l)earned a very comprehensive cosmology with privileged esoteric knowledge. The Yuki isolate was typical of the mid provence.

83. Alfred Kroeber, Handbook of the Indians of California 1925.

Luiseño

Luiseño were confined at and named for the Catholic mission of San Luis Rey. Devastation took a heavy toll on their lives and culture. They formerly had a complex series of patri-inherited leadership positions, devoted to war or religion, that were intersected by some sort of matri-moieties, distinguished as coast or mountains and perhaps named for Wildcat or Coyote.

The basis for this hierarchy was an esoteric belief in *puwha*. Here it is called ayelkwi, and regarded as omnipresent, imperishable, immutable, and causal. Everything that manifests *ayelkwi* is called a "person" and represented a link in a web of beings. Female *ayelkwi* is generic, general, diffuse, undifferentiated, inclusive. Male *ayelkwi* – as possessed by men officials or initiates – is specific, particular, and exclusive. Both intermeshed as men joined finely graded hierarchies set within more open matri-moieties.[84]

The last immortal involved with the distribution of ayelkwi was Chungishnish (named "*saon*" as a boy, "*tobet*" as initiated shaman, and "*quoar*" as prophet).[85] Kuksu did much the same for mid California. The Chungishnish cult seems to have diffused from the Gabrieleños (at Mission San Gabriel).

84. Raymond White, Luiseño Social Organization 1963; Lowell Bean and Florence Shipek, Luiseño, California 1978.

85. James Moriarty, Chinigchinx: An Indigenous California Indian Religion 1969: 13.

Luiseño lived in fifty separate villages, each with its own hunting, gathering, and fishing places to feed about 200 members. Women gathered plant foods, men hunted and fished, and all helped with the acorn harvest. Ownership of resources was vested in the whole village, a family, or a chief. Communal property included trails, camps, rabbit drive locales, quarries, shrines, and a sacred brush-fenced enclosure (wamkish). In addition, villages owned mountain oak groves providing acorns. Private property consisted of a house, tools, treasures, trade items, eagle nests, songs, and special knowledge. Some households tended gardens of conveniently transplanted wild foods, medicines, and tobacco.

Elaborate rituals within and near the enclosure drew together villages and districts. Sand paintings depicting the universe were used to instruct Chungishnish initiates. These were both boys and girls, who were fortified by drinking a datura (jimsonweed) infusion. Death was also a time of ritual attention, with a dozen rites held within each memorial series.

Membership in the cult involved a series of progressive initiations symbolizing death and rebirth. At six or seven, a boy was encouraged to acquire a guardian by fasting, crawling on his hands and feet, and, at night, drinking mixtures of tobacco, urine, and lime called _pibat_ or of Jimsonweed called _mani_. The cult was sometimes named "toloache", another term for Jimsonweed (Datura). After they revive (and a few never did) from narcosis, initiates were given a series of lectures on cult origins and meanings.

At the next stage, boys walked through a trench containing a string figure representing a corpse in a grave. Next they were made to lie on ant hills, after which any attached ants were whipped from their bodies with stinging nettles. They were given further detailed instruction in myth and cosmology, illustrated by sand paintings, dances, and costuming.

After life-long membership, at a final memorial service, his feather headdress (an insignia of initiation), was buried in the center of a dry sand painting to release his spirit to become a star.

IIb. *CULTURE AREAS*
Tribal Examples
TILLERS

TILLERS (Farmers)

Careful tending of the landscape, over time, evolved into the farming of crops. These plants were both locally derived and, for the trinity of corn, beans, and squash, spread from Mexico with appropriate rituals. Such farming, alongside the tending of natural crops, distinguished the culture areas known as the Southwest, Plains, Great Lakes, and East.

7. Southwest Culture Area

Ecosystem

The Southwest (Oasis) biome had a mixture of woodland, brushland, and hot desert communities. This arid climate, preserving the most fragile of human evidence over centuries, made water a primary concern. People's reverence for water pervaded all worship. Rivers and rain made life possible, though sometimes strained. Antelope, rodents (kangaroo rats), and fish occur in the lower desert, with cactuses, other succulents, and insects. Deer, cougar, and bear live in the mountains.

Over thousands of years, many separate regional traditions thrived, shown in a full range of perishable artifacts made of fiber, skin, and wood. A priest~temple~bundle complex stretched throughout the Southwest and southern California.[86] Every main community had at least one official who lived in a large house used for councils and rituals. He also had custody of a bundle holding various holy objects. Particularly well developed in these regions, this triple complex extends throughout Native America.

In the lower West, it grew out of the more personal association based on a vision that told an individual what to assemble into his or her bundle. These special items betokened a particular spirit partner, an array of objects, and special locale. Among members of leading families, moreover, such bundles were expected to influence the larger good of the community.

Hence, the priestly leader of a district drew upon *puwha* vested in the bundle of sacred items and revered in a central rotunda, serving as the temple. While the relationship between a family, a spirit, and a place was expected throughout the Americas, this more institutionalized complex of a priest(hood), tribal bundle, and temple was characteristic of farming communities with denser populations and more political controls.

Along the Colorado River, the farming and gathering way of life of Quechans (Yumans) benefited from an annual flooding of the banks (like the Nile) that enriched their soil and crops. In the arid south, the O'odam (Pimans) gathered and farmed around an oasis spring or river allowing irrigation. Along the Rio Grande and other rivers, Pueblo peoples lived in elaborate towns under the control of priesthoods. These worked ritually and politically to even out fluctuations in the climate by supervising irrigation networks and work parties. Throughout the Southwest, men were the farmers, probably because irrigation and flood control were labor intensive.

SOUTHWEST Peoples

PUEBLOANS

Aztec-Tanoan Stock
 Tanoan Family
  TEWA
   San Juan
   Santa Clara
   San Ildefonso
   Nambe
   Tesuque
   Pojoaque
  TANO (Southern Tewa)
   Hano (at Hopi)
  TIWA
   Taos
   Picuris
   Sandia
   Isleta
  TOWA
   Jemez
   Pecos(at Jemez)
 Numic Family
  HOPI
   First Mesa
    Walpi
    Sichomovi
    Polacca
    Hano (Tano)
   Second Mesa
    Shimopovi
    Shipaulovi
    Mishongnovi
   Third Mesa
    Old Oraibi
    Kyakkotsmovi (New Oraibi)
    Hotevilla
    Bacavi
    Moenkopi

Penutian Stock (?)
 ZUNI

OTHERS

Hokan Stock
 Yuman Family
  QUECHAN (Yuma)
  COCOPA
  MOHAVE
  MARICOPA
  WALAPAI
  YAVAPAI
  HAVASUPAI

Aztec-Tanoan Stock
 Uto-Aztecan Family
  Piman
   O'OTAM (Pima)
   TOHONO O'OTAM (Papago)

Na-Dene Stock
Athapaskan Family
 NAVAHO
Eastern
Western
 APACHE
  Llanero
  Chiricahua
  Mescalero
  Jicarilla
  Lipan
  Western
   Tonto
   White Mountain
   San Carlos
   Cibicue(Coyoteros)

Isolate
 KERESAN

Eastern	Western
Cochiti	Acoma
Santo Domingo	Laguna
San Felipe	
Santa Ana	
Sia	

Over six hundred years ago, Southern Athapaskan (Dene) ancestors of the Navajo and Apache came to the Southwest from a distant homeland near Great Slave Lake in the western Subarctic. Their livelihood mixed raiding and farming until the 1680 Pueblo Revolt released Spanish livestock. Then Navajos separated from fellow Apacheans to take up sheepherding as pastoralists. At first living in brush houses, Navajo later built octagonal or round houses called "hogans." Those with rounded forms are regarded as "female", those with peaks are "male". Families live in both styles, but each gave certain advantages for nurturing or protecting.

Foods

Maize was and is the staple for farming tribes, sharing the trinity with beans and squash. Wild foods, wood rats, pronghorn antelope, deer, and, sometimes, fish contributed to the diet. As noted, productive farming relied on irrigation, regulated by seasonal rituals led by specialized priesthoods.

Provinces

A rich mosaic of different cultures, the Southwest consists of four provinces. These were the Puebloan, Piman (O'odam), Yuman, and Athapaskan (Dene). The first three farmed, while the last foraged until the Navaho became distinct as sheep herders.

Most Southwestern tribes lived communally. Yuman rich men along the Colorado River built large houses where people wintered. During hot summers, a sunshade (ramada) was all that was needed. Pimans lived in large oval brush houses clustered in villages. The home of the hereditary leader was larger than the others because it provided the "temple" where men gathered each night to smoke and lecture.

Puebloan peoples developed distinctive apartment-style houses, with the stories made of stone and adobe. Families lived in a suite of rooms extending from front to back, often with rooms also on lower and upper stories. Most of the time was spent on the open rooftops.

Kinship was very complex. The clan with the most members in a community usually provided its leader. His home was the "temple" used for village councils, and his family was the custodian of sacred objects associated with local lands and mythic events.

Often, Pueblo clans were traced through the mother and grouped into phratries of related or similar kinds of things. Villages were divided into halves (moieties), and arranged by membership in **kivas** {* = underground churches, often circular, sometimes square, associated with men, particular tasks, or priesthoods}. Sometimes, clan and household membership came through the mother, while religious affiliation came through the father, as among Keresans who are well known for such dual descent.

O'odams and Yumans emphasized the paternal line for households, clans, phratries, and moiety halves. Clans owned particular territories and fields that their members were entitled to use.

Dene Athapaskan migrants kept their Na-Dene languages, but borrowed from local traditions. In Navaho ritual, cosmic harmony and health concerns replaced Puebloan prayers for rain and town solidarity. Unlike Pueblos where men were weavers, Navaho women wove blankets and rugs. Throughout, Navaho culture has proved to be remarkably resilient despite Hispano-Anglo-American pressures. With the adoption of sheep herding in the late 1600s, Navahos diverged from their Apache kin, who continued a mixed economy that included some farming, harvesting of wild crops, and raiding.

Priesthoods had the responsibility to remember and enact aspects of the life of twin heros, sons of the Sun. The community itself performed elaborate masked dances reliving features of their ancient history when these Katsina spirits (who now animate these masks) actually lived among them and personally brought rain. Their full *puwha* was too dangerous and lethal so now Katsina masks are worn. A thousand years ago, the ceremonial center at Chaco Canyon held similar re-creations of the world orchestrated by entrenched priesthoods.

Prehistory

After Paleo-Indian times, the Southwest was occupied by Archaic (Desert or Picosa Complex) foragers. These are subdivided by archaeologists into the Pinto Basin complex of southeastern California and the Cochise complex of southern Arizona. About 7,000 years ago, some of the Pinto Basin people split off and moved east to become the San Jose complex of west central New Mexico. The first two letters of the names for these complexes provided the acronym Pi-co-sa. This era (**) spanned the developments from the Archaic to the Ceramic periods, when farming and pottery making became hallmarks.

During the ceramic era, Pinto Basin residents became the Hakatayan ancestors of the Yuman tribes, Cochise branched to become the Hohokam ancestors of Pimans and Mogollons, and San Jose became the Oshara component of the Anasazi complex ancestral to the Keresan Pueblos.

Mogollons migrated north and adopted Anasazi patterns after AD 1000, establishing the ancestral sites of Tanoan Pueblo towns. This was the domain of Chaco Canyon, a complex of over a dozen massive towns. Casas Grandes later became the center to the south. Then Mesa Verde flourished in Colorado, before its descendants later moved into the Rio Grande. For Pimans, Snaketown was a major hub for centuries.

Labor

In contrast to the East and Plains, men farmed in the Southwest, raising the trinity and cotton. Men wove textiles and worked with stone, bone, and wood to make tools. Women tended kitchen gardens, cared for their households, and made the most colorful pottery north of Mexico.

Fields were irrigated. In the spring, everyone cleaned and repaired the water ditches under the direction of priests. Summer was spent raising farm crops and gathering wild foods, while winter was a relaxing time devoted to crafts, elaborate rituals, trading, and traveling.

Among the Apacheans, men were hunting (and raiding), while women collected wild fruits. Navaho couples also foraged, and some families farmed. The old and young herded flocks of sheep.

Puebloans (Tanoans, Keres, Zuni, Hopi)

All Pueblos (Spanish for "towns") share a farming economy, multi-story apartment houses, theocratic rule by priesthoods, rain-bringing rituals, masked god (Kachina) enactments, and a complex ceremonial system focused on Mother Corn, kivas, public plazas, and shrines oriented upon their landscape. Culturally, each town emphasizes its own difference.

Pueblos, despite their common name, belong to four different language stocks. These are Tanoan, Keresan, Zunian, and, for the Hopi, Numic, the languages spoken in the Great Basin. Tanoan is related to Uto-Aztecan, a vast stock whose speakers stretched from the Valley of Mexico to central Oregon, and included the entire range, from the most basic (Basin Numic) to the most complex (Aztecs), of societies in North America. Eastern Pueblo villages emphasized paternal descent through the father, while western towns were matrilineal. In many cases, clans also provided leaders or members of governing priesthoods. Among all Pueblos, such a theocracy, which safeguarded ritual and esoteric information, encouraged social ranks among men that excluded uninitiated women and children. Men progressed through grades of membership such that leaders of each town were fully "ripe" initiates, while lesser degrees included mature men who were "cooked" or those youngsters who were "raw."

Tanoans *(Tewa, Tano, Tiwa, Towa)*

Each Tewa town has a single large kiva, jointly used by members of the Summer and Winter moieties, which recruit through males, generally fathers. The masked deities of the Tewa are not Kachinas, though they look similar. Summer and Winter pervade all of the Tewa world. According to the matrix, Summer is womanly and generic, while Winter was male and specific. Mediating between these two sides are the Made People, a hierarchy of priesthoods serving the entire town.

Tiwa have a single town kiva and moieties that recruit through either parent, often in alternation. Towa have two kivas, like the Keresans, recruiting paternally, and are governed by priesthoods linked with particular matriclans. The Tano (once Southern Tewa), perhaps from Hopi influence, have two kivas drawing members from each of a pair of matriclan phratries and hosting Kachina performances.

Keres *(Isolate)*

Keresans balance manly kivas, priesthoods, and male bondings beside womanly households, matriclans, and family bonds. Keresan Bear or curing priesthoods influenced many other Pueblos, who adopted their songs or rites in ancient times. *Puwha* for Keresans is called *iyaanyi*.

Zuni *(Isolate)*

Modern Zuni has 6 kivas, one for each direction, recruited through sponsoring "fathers." Matri-households were basic units, with those of elite families maintaining sacred fetishes and town officers. Complex linkages among kivas, clans, priesthoods, and households fused each pueblo into a coherent whole. Since there were 6 separate towns at the time of Spanish arrival, modern Zuni (named Halona 'ant hill at the world middle') seems to represent their amalgamation.

Hopi

Each Hopi community has one town kiva (called <u>Mung</u>), recruiting through a "ceremonial father" who sponsored the initiation of a boy. Matri-households formed into clans, phratries, and kivas. The leading household of a primary clan owns sacred emblems (<u>tiponi</u>) and official positions in the town theocracy.

Pimans
(O'otam, O'Odham - Pima, Tohono O'otam – Papago)

Both Pimans and Yumans are patrilineal, with O'odams patri-moieties called Coyote (also Bear, White Heart, White Ant) or Buzzard (also Cougar, Red Heart, Red Ant).

The Piman world consists of concentric rings divided in half on the basis of gender. The Rain House of the Keeper of the Smoke is at the center {tysic}, houses and women are inside, and fields and men are outside. For an individual, the heart is his or her center, the right hand is called "inside" and the left one "outside."[87]

Pimas became hispanicized due to Spanish pressure on their choice riverine farmlands. Living in desert valleys, Papago were largely ignored by colonists. Within their four dialect regions, each community had a focal town near a rotunda-like Rain House. The family living in it was led by the Keeper of the Smoke, who guarded the plaited basket holding the town's sacred fetishes. Scattered throughout the valley were allied towns and seasonal hamlets, who gather at the Rain House for meetings and ceremonies.

The local elite was~is composed of influential families with proper sanctions from *puwha*. A Piman visionary is called a "meeter," and a Coyote meeter could cure diseases caused by this canine. A man could also acquire *puwha* by killing an eagle or hawk, by reluctantly slaying an enemy, or by gathering salt from the Pacific Ocean. After each deed, a 16-day purification was required before someone emerged as a successful meeter, eagle killer, enemy slayer, or salt pilgrim. A few men led the solitary life of a deer hunter, living in the hills for months and wearing a stuffed deerhead as a disguise to get closer to the prey.

A woman gains respect by well caring for her family and carefully secluding herself during menstruation. After menopause, women could become shamans specializing in the illnesses of women and children.

Shamans were the result of a special creation during the beginnings of the world, and activated their abilities when quartz crystals were believed to grow inside their bodies.

Quechan *(Yumans)*

The Yumans both farmed and foraged the bounty made possible by the periodic flooding of the Colorado River. Every village had both a summer camp and a winter home in one of the massive earth-covered houses. In addition to the farmed trinity, and tobacco, while wild foods included mesquite beans, screw beans, and grass seeds. Fish were taken with arrows, cactus spine hooks, drag nets, dip nets, and traps.

Quechan patriliny was strong. About twenty exogamous {* = marrying out}, totemic patriclans formed about four phratries. A woman bore the name of their father's clan, along with a nickname to distinguish her alone.

Yuman culture relied on "dreams," a belief so pervasive that a fetus began dreaming in the womb. A village leader combined a proper dream with skill and wealth. He was assisted by the Brave Man, acting as younger war leader and directing a staff of runners, noted for their reliability and endurance, to carry plans and messages. Male family heads formed a council to advise these leaders.

Among Yumans, institutional cultural elaborations included militarism (particularly among Mohave), cremation, and homosexuality of both men and women berdaches (called two hearts today).

Athapaskans *(Dine = Navaho, Apache)*

With over 150,000 members, the Navaho are the largest single tribe in the United States.[88]   Families are widely scattered in sheep herding camps and hogan compounds. Matrilines pool their sheep into a common herd that is watched mostly by children.

Matriclans were and are vital social units. Everyone was considered to "belong to" the clan of their mother. But this was not a rigid matrilineality. They were secondarily "born for" their father's clan. Married couples occupied a hogan, which was built near the houses of other close relatives to form a "compound" or an "outfit." These relatives lived, herded, and ate together. When a member was ill and needed treatment at a "sing", kin contributed to the cost of feeding guests and compensating the singer (yataali), who knew the proper chant to restore harmony in the patient and the world. Often close members of the same family took the same medicine when the patient did, showing their mutual interdependence.

Navaho culture was and is pervaded by a symbolic tension between static / dynamic. It is further expressed as exclusive balance, order, control, speech / inclusive beauty, harmony, creativity, and thought. The static was also linked with man, ritual, culmination, and inner form. The active was associated with woman, life, change, and outer form, particularly the culture hero Changing Woman. The inclosive was expressed as Mind acting through wind {* = air in motion}.

Navaho believed that plants, animals, rain, mountains, ceremonies, hogans, directions, and much else had male and female forms, ultimately due to the work of First Man and First Woman. The swirling together of black and white made First Man, as yellow and blue made First Woman. Because they were distinct by gender, they were mutually attracted to each other.

Cosmology: *Myth, Ritual*

Most tribes of the Southwest shared the use of dry sand paintings, large community houses, priests, and mystic bundles associated with clans, sweat lodges, and initiation cults. Many different creations were recognized among Southwestern people. Such charters trace the world from either primal water or a void, with subsequent reforms to prepare it for modern human life.

The O'odam world was first fashioned by Buzzard and Earthmaker. Then Coyote and Elder Brother I'itoy, both helping and hindering, made it ready for humans. After killing many monsters, Elder Brother provided their petrified hearts and limbs to be sacred objects placed inside the village bundle of each Keeper of the Smoke.

The Yuman world was made by two brothers who came from the sea. Their vital rituals concern thirty or so Dream Journeys, recited over several days. Each describes in minute detail the travels of a spirit husband and wife as they visit, name, and arrange huge stretches of homeland.

Puebloans have elaborate epics of how their ancestors emerged from successive lower worlds until they topped out in the present one. Pueblo creators were often women, associated with plants and maize, who made a world that is further prepared for humans by hero twin boys.

Navajo creation included many incidents also in Pueblo and other neighboring literatures. Yet the Navajo telling is bold, innovative, and engaging, emphasizing distinctive features of their own life and culture.

Pueblo rituals include feasting, elaborate Katchina dramas and dances, retreats by the priesthoods, and calendrical ceremonies renewing all or some aspects of the world.

The Piman world was periodically renewed at a _Wiigida_ (Vikita, Prayerstick) ceremony as specially-composed songs greeted ingenious litter~floats of clouds, healthy crops, and mountains carried around the inside of a sacred enclosure to avert flooding.

Yumans cremated their deceased in emulation of the original funeral of their Creator. About 1890, the Quechan adopted a memorial "Cry," rite from Californian Diegeño, featuring the burning of child-size effigies of the dead.

Female puberty observances, widespread in the Americas, were particularly important for Athapaskans. In addition, Navaho celebrated a complex series of "sings" (chants), each directed to a particular malady to restore harmony, health, and well being. By embodying Holy People in sand paintings and songs, the patient and community were restored to balance. Because these paintings trapped _puwha_, they had to be scattered by sundown to return this energy back to the cosmos.

Among Apaches, their major ceremony was held whenever a family invited others to celebrate the coming of age of one or more of their daughters. Navajo also had this ceremony and it too celebrated the efforts of Changing Woman or another female creator to make the world ready for humans. During a girl's puberty ceremony, she was explicitly equated with this all-powerful woman creator.

Today

The Southwest is noted for its obvious cultural conservatism. Native languages are learned from birth, clans determine life choices, and rituals are celebrated throughout each year. Outside pressures were deterred or delayed by the dry climate. Tourists visit but do not stay, leaving money behind. Puebloans remain extremely reluctant to deal with most outsiders. Their priestly hierarchies have kept firm control of each town. The best way to attain personal freedom, for those who want it, is to leave the community and move to a city, the further away the better.

Navahos are responsive to change. To receive leases for oil and minerals on their reservation, a Navajo Nation government was set up in the 1920s. It blended local autonomy with federal oversight. Their huge reservation was divided into a hundred Chapters, each electing local representatives to the tribal council at Window Rock, Arizona.

The tourist industry has done much to encourage the preservation of crafts and skills. Natives do a thriving business in blankets, pottery, silverwork, baskets, and jewelry, providing steady incomes in some very remote locales. Nevertheless, water rights, land claims, contested jurisdictions, and strip mining remain real issues for natives and other Southwest residents.

Spanish suppression and abuses took their toll on the native peoples. Reprisals, murders, and punishment of native priests and the destruction of native sacra are bitterly remembered. The ancient determination of native peoples to survive in the Southwest continues today, partially in reaction to this earlier abuse. Their entrenchment has benefited from slow European settlement, Spanish land grants that guaranteed village sites as an indigenous land base, tight control by the priesthoods, complex social structures, inhospitable environments, and the in-home transmission of Native cultures.

86. Duncan Strong, Aboriginal Society in Southern California, 1972 [1929]: 346), cf An Analysis of Southwestern Society 1927: 1-61; Elsie Clews Parsons, The House-Clan Complex of the Pueblos 1968 [1936].

87. Ruth Underhill, <u>Social Organization of the Papago Indians</u> 1939: 143.
88. Ojibwe are much larger and occupy more territory, but live internationally in both the US and Canada, which is used to count against them. Go figure?

TRIBAL EXAMPLES

Tohono O'odam ("Desert People," Papago) of Arizona

Floating in a dark void, two beings met four times to encourage each other to make a world. One, becoming Earthmaker thereafter, took dirt from his skin (or heart) and placed it on his palm, where a green Greasewood branch grew immediately. Its plant lice oozed gum which he pounded together into a ball. Then he sang as it flattened out and spread. Upon it, he made mountains, located shamans thereon, and sprinkled bird down above as clouds, to go everywhere with this widening world. Below the sky dome, the earth spun so these edges only loosely touched. From this friction, a being (a small bearded man with whitish blond hair) was created. Jumping up and down four times, he called, "I am the child of earth and sky." Earthmaker named him I'itoy. From under a bush in the Northwest, another being sprang up to be called Coyote, foolish but powerful because he was "from the beginning".

The second being of this primordial void became Buzzard, who saw that this world was not yet stable. Together with I'itoy and Coyote, he tried to find a remedy. Finally, two Spider people took rope from their bodies and used it to stitch together the sky dome and earth disk. Earth was too bland. It had shapeless mountains and rivers that all ran to the west. Buzzard gashed it with his wings to align peaks and flows in various ways. Earthmaker threw water into the sky at the north, west, south, and east to create the sun and moon. Then he spat saliva upwards to make stars. Earthmaker also made people from his body, who overpopulated the earth. Lacking natural death, people killed each other to get relief and space until Earthmaker and I'itoy decided to flood the world.

I'itoy created Handsomeman, who slept with all the women so they had babies the next morning. Also pregnant himself, Handsomeman deserted his own child, who cried until its tears flooded the earth. Earthmaker saved himself by going into his wooden wand. Coyote hid inside a reed. Buzzard vanished through the sky. A few men became birds and hung in the sky roof by their beaks. Others rooted themselves as trees.

Afterward, Earthmaker, I'itoy, and Coyote took turns creating people from clay. Coyote's were deformed and thrown across the sea (to Europe!?). Earthmaker's were also misshapen. I'itoy's were normal and became the Hohokam, Maricopa, and Apaches, proving his boasts about having *puwha*. Humans were given access to the *puwha* of animals and other immortals by undertaking a vision quest in a remote locale. There, a being took pity and allowed him (or her) to be its "meeter." Thus, someone with *puwha* from a Coyote was called "coyote meeter".

In his old age, I'itoy angered people by assaulting maidens at a puberty ceremony. They killed him three times, but he kept reviving until killed a fourth time by Buzzard and Sun. Revived again by the four winds after four years, I'itoy went underground to rally the O'odam (Pima, Papago) to invade the Hohokam, though all spoke the same language.[89]

These Invaders continued west, fighting more people who spoke their own language. The Sun became angry, stopped the attack, and forced people to settle.

Northern Papago (later becoming American, Catholic) returned to where they had planted a prayerstick at Archie. They made it their capitol. The hub of the Southerners (becoming Mexican, increasingly Presbyterian) was and is at Quitovaca. Each of them defined boundaries for their respective territories by throwing seed corn into the wind, so that wherever it scattered became their homeland.

Everyone belonged to patri-moieties of either Coyote or Buzzard (also called White/Red Heart, White/Red Ant, Bear/Cougar). Each included two clans whose names were applied to fathers by their own children.

Each of four dialects had an acknowledged narrator of the creation epic. It was recited at the winter solstice in seven long sessions, interspersed with songs, over four days while he fasted from meat, grease, and salt. Summaries could also be provided during winter from November to March, but any mention in summer was taboo because biting animals would take revenge on such sacrilege. Fluency was much admired and language flare was extolled. Special argots were used during warfare or salt pilgrimages.

Each dialect was spoken in several neighboring valleys, each with an array of satellite villages. Within a valley, communities, situated to the north or south, shifted between summer lowland fields and winter upslope springs. The central one was the parent town where a Keeper of the Smoke presided at its Rain House, the community hall. As he grew older, various of his duties were delegated to younger men. These substitutes were named for their remedy as Eyes, Ears, Voice, Legs. Only mature adults could serve as his Memory, Head, or Heart. The Crier awakened a town each morning with its distinctive chant, announced any plans for that day, and, at dusk, called men to council.

Every night, men known to be wise, able, married, and "ripe" met in the Rain House, or, during good weather, in a brush enclosure or open plaza. Hunched on their heels, arms folded, head bent in seriousness; they listened to standardized moral speeches that insisted on the virtues of being industrious while enduring hunger, cold, and thirst. Running was encouraged so men would be warriors, keeping backup bowstrings and arrows at the ready, rallying so women could escape during attacks. War was an onerous duty never to be glorified.

A full adult earned the title of enemy slayer, salt pilgrim, or eagle killer. A "good man" was peaceable, loyal, industrious, generous, modest, spoke only when addressed, and could call on reserves of *puwha*. Bad traits included being selfish, dishonest, treacherous, sexually loose, and impolite.

In council, the Keeper faced the door, with the Crier on his right, unless he needed his Voice near by. His Legs sat behind with the Peg, who fetched embers to light cigarettes. Traditionally, the Keeper held the tobacco supply for the whole valley, passing out a bag each night. More recently, every man brought his own tobacco but only could use it at a signal from the Keeper. Every lecture ended with terms of kinship or friendship. Fine oratory was much prized, particularly "soft words", using standard poetic phrases such as "wooly comrade" for coyote and "shining traveler" for the sun.

Town leadership officers were separated by functions into 1) managing, 2) hunting, 3) sporting, 4) singing, and 5) defense.

1) Overall was the Keeper of the Smoke (also called Wise Speaker, One Ahead, Plaited Basket Keeper). He was only to have good thoughts. Quarreling, anger, or unpleasantness were kept away from him. In return for his prayerful vigilance, people tilled and harvested his fields. As chief, each Keeper held the town *wacha*, the plaited basket filled with its sacred fetishes, which was hidden away in the mountains until

needed.   At the town of Pisinimo, that basket held a carved greenstone frog, sandstone effigy of I'itoy, slate palette, elongated slate and lava pendants, arrowpoints, and three dried deer hearts with six eagle tail feathers stuck in each. Preferred offerings to it were black deer tails, eagle down, and beads.

   2) The hunt leader (_topetam_ = rabbiter) led communal drives for deer and rabbits, choosing the date, time, location, and beaters.

   3) The game leader (called rabbiter for games) arranged intervillage competitions. He properly trained runners, led cheering, argued fouls, supervised relays, appointed referees, and spoke on the virtue of good sportsmanship.

   4) The song leader had a loud voice and good memory to conduct communal music.   Indeed, composing songs was the greatest achievement among Tohono O'odam.

   5) A town war priest planned strategy for the active, younger warriors.

   Headbearers (_mo'opetam_) were professional hunters who lived alone in the uplands except for January and February when they came out of the cold. Male relatives tended fields for them in exchange for venison. A good hunter got twelve deer a year. Most hunted in pairs with a trainee or apprentice. The head of the first deer killed was stuffed to wear with a deerskin tunic, white in front and dark behind. That first meat went to his trainer.

   From the very beginning, shamans stood out as selfish individualists, who were expected to be rich, stingy, and prideful, unlike everyone else. While other leaders might have two wives, they often had four. Under constant suspicion, they were lynched or clubbed if too much harm came to their community. Twins and eagle slayers qualified as immediate shamans, further empowered by later dreams. Each shaman grew four crystals inside his heart, representing the solidified saliva passed from I'itoy onto the head of the first healer placed in the mountains. These crystals enable their own saliva to be effective during cures. Other insignia were a gourd rattle for his right hand, with up to four eagle plumes for his left. A shaman did not begin work professionally until middle age, after curing his own sick relatives at first.

   To gain goodwill, cooperating shamans exorcised their town without pay, sending harm away. Shamans specialized in scrying {* = trance gazing}, rain, war, or love. To demonstrate their _puwha_s, shamans swallowed sticks, ate fire, walked on hot coals, or made things vanish. After menopause, women could become shamans dealing with obstetrics and childhood diseases.

   Droughts and epidemics were blamed on shamans who were believed to have buried fire in the ground to cause plants to wither. On occasion, demands by his _puwha_ forced a shaman into sorcery, allowing him no other option. At their worst, shamans caused death. To kill a patient, venom from a rattler or gila monster was mixed with his own saliva during a fatal cure.

   When villages met for games, each rabbiter linked up with a shaman to benefit his home team and jinx the visitors. Men bet against men, women against women. Kickstick and relay race courses extended along a cleared route for ten to fifteen miles through the desert. Women played shinny with L-shaped sticks.

   Towns hosted elaborate public rituals. Most complex of all was the _Wiigida_ (Vikita, Prayerstick) "to keep the world in order and prevent another flood". In the north (US), it is held every four years in December, but, in the south, every year with Wine Drinking. At Archie, its hereditary officials include a general director, four village directors, head clown, over 30 village clowns, head corn sprinkler, assistant sprinkler, 40 song composers (8 per 5 villages), three men painters (for red, white, or black), a twelve-year-old boy to lead the singers, men aiding the fasting director, a helper for corn dancers, corn meal sprinklers for these dancers, women potters supplying dishes for the fasting director, and many long-haired singers and dancers.

Skipping Dance was a sort of opera with sets, effigies of rainbows, clouds, or water birds, and songs by local composers. Naming Dance paired twenty or thirty names from the hosting villages, with a prompter using marked sticks to make sure these accurately progressed, in a set order, through shamans, keepers, warriors, and elders.

89. Ruth Underhill, A Papago Calendar Record 1938; Social Organization of the Papago Indians 1939; Papago Indian Religion 1946.

8. Plains Culture Area

Ecosystem

The Plains was occupied by both tenders (often herders) and tillers, who blended these economic strategies for millennia.

Initially, it was the home of big game (megafauna) Paleo-Indien hunters over 12,000 years ago. Plains river valleys later sheltered tribes who lived in earthlodge towns. Each lodge looked like a grassy hill, carefully constructed over a massive wooden framework that was covered over by layers of grass, branches, and sod. During the severe winters of the northern Plains, several families stayed dry and warm inside these artificial hillocks. In the south, a warmer climate allowed open dwellings, such as the beehive-shaped, grass-thatched houses of the Wichita. Other Caddoan tribes made houses of wattle and daub or plastered over walls made of reedy canes. These southern villages were often clustered around earth mounds specially made to "raise on high" their temples, where priests tended sacred fires.

With the adoption of the farming trinity, fields became established along rivers. Complex chiefly hierarchies, managing temple mounds and ritual series, became the Caddoan expression of the Mississippian. Particularly large were the chiefdoms of the "real" Caddo in eastern Texas, Arkansas, Louisiana, and Oklahoma. In the north, related Arikaras were the hub of a vast trade network. During summer, these villages were located near fields of corn, beans, squash, sunflowers, and other crops. Between necessary rituals and field care, villagers left for spring, summer, and fall buffalo hunts, with everyone returning for the harvest.

The Plains were a temperate grassland of rolling, hummocky terrain. It shifted from tall grass in the east toward short grass in the west. The characteristic biome was both gramma and needle grass, bison, pronghorn antelope, and smaller grazing or burrowing animals like prairie dogs. The area was especially noted for its extremes of temperature and climate, although these were buffered in the sheltered water courses of the Missouri River drainage and the massive earthlodges.

Foods

While the crop trinity provided plants, the chief attraction was bison (buffalo). By carefully burning off the old grass and hunting to assure herd health, natives were actively involved in managing their local clusters. Despite earlier reports about the characteristics of the whole herd, there were no great, predictable migrations of bison across the plains. Rather, seasonal herd fluctuations included a mating cluster in late summer, a wide scattering in winter and spring, and calving in April to June, followed by coat shedding and summer running before the next mating cluster. This scattering served to shift bison northward in the summer and southward in the winter. Pemmican, a high energy food, was a mixture of pulverized bison meat, suet, and berries.

Labor

Those tribes who lived eastward in earth-lodge winter villages are sometimes placed in a Prairie culture area, in contrast to mobile bison hunting tribes of the Plains. Both, however, were properly Plains because they shared this bison economy and post-contact devotion to the horse (equestrianism). Here, Prairie tribes will be identified as Plains Lodge tribes whose staples were bison hunted by men and maize farmed by women. Plains Tipi (mobile) tribes had bison as their staple.*

PLAINS Peoples

LODGE TRIBES corn + bison	LANGUAGES	TIPI TRIBES bison
	CADDOAN	
Caddo (12 bands, 4 confederacies) Pawnee (4 bands) Arikara Wichita (6 bands) Kichai		
	SIOUIAN	
Mandan-Hidatsa Chiwere (Iowa,Oto,Missouri,HoChunk) Dhegiha (Omaha,Ponca,Osage,Kansa: Upper) 　　　(Quapaw: Lower) Dakota (Santee,E) (4 fires)		-Crow Nakota(Yankton)(2 fires) Lakota(Teton,W)(1 fire) -(Nakoda~Assiniboin)
	ALGIC	
		Blackfeet 　(Pikuni, Kainai, Siksika) Arapaho,Atsina(G-Ventre) Cheyenne-Sutai Plains Ojibwa(Saulteau,Bungi) Plains Cree
	UTO-AZTECAN	
		Shoshoni Numa (11 bands) Comanche (12 bands) Ute Kiowa (5 bands/Plains Apache)
	ATHAPASKAN	
		Plains Apache (Kiłdeen) Sarsi

Bison were enjoyed by ancestors of Lodge tribes, who wintered over in warmer locales eating dried meat and crops prepared during the summer.

Year-round transhumance (scheduled camping) was not feasible on the plains until Spanish horses (escaped or stolen in the 1680 Pueblo Revolt) were traded north by 1750. From surrounding culture areas, ancestors of Tipi tribes moved onto these grasslands, became horse pastoralists, adopted seasonal migrations, and created a technology and social organization congruent with such mobility.

The popular stereotyped image of THE Native American as famous for horses (equestrianism), feather bonnets, and tipis was derived from this recent Plains tradition, lasting only two centuries. It expanded to be romanticized as "The American Indian" and popularized in paintings by Charles Bird King, George Catlin, Karl Bodmer, and others.[90] Hollywood continues the misconception.

The "warbonnet" of eagle feathers, the courage of Plains warriors, and Wild West Shows helped to spread this image. The eagle feathers were earned as war honors, then were assembled together as headgear. The long-tailed feather headdress began with Caddoans like the Pawnee, whose culture emphasized astronomical themes. It represents a comet.[91]

Horses were reintroduced into the Americas by the Spanish thousands of years after indigenous horses, which evolved on these very grasslands millions of years ago, became extinct here. Their ancestors migrated into Asia, then were taken across Europe by saddled warriors like the founders of the Indo-European language stock. The Plains adaptation to the horse was, as bears repeating, only about 200 years old. It was made possible by the breeding success of imported horses. Equestrian technology and skills built on those for native dogs. The Blackfeet called this pre-horse period their "Dog Days", when all the camping gear was carried on a drag (travois) pulled by a large dog. Once the horse arrived, all of this dog technology increased in size, making tipi life much more comfortable.

With the horse, camp dwelling tents known as tipis became larger and more stately. Generally, each was occupied by a married couple and young children. The several families who shared an earthlodge would each occupy a separate tipi while camping and hunting on the Plains. During these communal hunts, for mutual protection, many tipi families banded together.

Outside the Plains, the spread of horses throughout America went with the adoption of styles of Plains skin clothing and feathered decoration, as among the Upper Kootenay of the Plateau and Comanche of the Basin. Indeed, Plains equestrianism stirs the imagination. Its trappings diffused into the Basin, Plateau, California, and Southwest. It gave various tribes a veneer of Plainsization. For the Plains, however, the role and symbolism of the horse was paramount.[92]

Relocations

Inferences based on archaeological evidence indicate that tribes of the Siouian, Caddoan, and Algic families came from a background of unilineal, settled farming from the Great Lakes and Mississippi areas to become Lodge tribes.

Algic tribes with a farming background made up Tipi tribes. They were joined by others of the Uto-Aztecan stock from the Great Basin and by Athapaskans from the Subarctic. Both of these culture areas were devoted to hunting and gathering, to tending.

Genders

The generalized Plains division of labor included men acting as hunters, warriors, and ritualists of camps and villages. Tending tribeswomen served as housekeepers and game butchers. Tilling tribeswomen added farming on the river terraces and crop harvesting to the usual female household tasks.

Plains tribes recognized six functional gender roles. While not every tribe had all six, these do occur in the culture area as a whole. The three female roles ♀ were those of virgin, woman, and manly-hearted; with each having a particular religious, social, and political importance. The role of women as wife typified most females. Among Cheyennes, female virgins ♀♀ held prominent roles in rituals and embodied their family's high status. Their marriage required a substantial exchange of goods. Among Lodge Siouians, honored daughters were tattooed at a bundle rite to assure long life.

The manly-hearted woman ♀♂ had deliberately or accidentally collected war honors by counting "coup" upon or killing an enemy. Often she avenged the killing of a close relative like a brother. At other times, she used whatever was at hand, such as a large hide scraper, to defend her family from enemy attack. Famous warrior women included "Woman Chief" of the Crow; "Yellow Weasel Woman" (renamed "Running Eagle"), "Otter Woman," and "Lone Woman" of the Piegan Blackfoot; and others of the Assiniboin, Gros Ventre, and Teton Lakota.[93]

The three male roles ♂ were those of transgender, man, and contrary. The man role as husband and father is described above. A transgender, often called a berdache, was a man ♂♀ who chose to dress as a woman, actively performing female tasks. While some men transgendered to avoid the warrior role, Hidatsa tell of a Sioux berdache who earned war honors.[94] They commonly functioned as battlefield medics and conferred war name. Their choice was clearly a complex one.

Among the Omaha, Dakota, Assiniboin, and Hidatsa; those who transgendered were considered to be holy. Among the first three tribes, "she" received the Moon as a guardian spirit. Among the Hidatsa, berdaches were gifted by Woman Above and were the most active ceremonialists in the historical period. Women welcomed transgenders into their labor force because they usually did the heavier work.

The contrary ♂♂ was a super-warrior, saying "no" to mean "yes", charging when others retreated, and remaining fearless or reckless in the face of danger. Generally, he was expected to stay away from women in order to keep his *puwha* strong. Among the Lakota, he had Thunder as his guardian.

Successful careers as man, woman, transgender, and contrary were, therefore, largely based on experiences during their "guardian spirit quests". Some manly-hearted women seem to have been spiritually gifted for their role, but others earned the position unintentionally, by rallying to the defense of a warrior or a community. In a few cases, they were taller and larger than most other women. The role of virgin was a temporary one, based on claims to status, discipline, or the attitudes of her family. It was enforced by chastity belts and other devices, such as being laced inside a whole hide each night.

Basic Bonds

Common to the social structures of both Lodge and Tipi tribes was the men's sodality (club, guild). These were age-graded among the Mandan, Hidatsa, Blackfeet, Arapaho, and Gros Ventre. They were peer-equals among the Crow, Sioux, Assiniboin, Cheyenne, Pawnee, and Arikara. While age grades should be expected among the villages and equals among the camps, but this is only a general tendency.

Sodalities (clubs) were most active (and in evidence) during pan-tribal bison hunts because they were then entrusted with the duties of camp police, maintaining order in the encampment. If an individual or family attacked the bison herd before the time set by the council, these police whipped the culprits and destroyed ("shredded") all of their possessions. If, however, those guilty showed proper remorse, then the guild members replaced their destroyed possessions, often a month later.

Villagers emphasized vertical links, smaller to larger, as families, lineages, clans, phratries, moieties, villages, tribes, and confederacies. Matrilineal tribes (Mandan, Hidatsa, etc.) seem to have relied more heavily on female labor and farm products. Patrilineal tribes (Ponca, Ioway, Osage, etc.) seem to have relied more heavily on male cooperation and bison hunting. Among Omahas, matrilineality may have been seasonally more important inside the winter lodges, and patrilineality in summer tipis during annual bison hunts.[95] Along with such seasonal, organizational, and sexual dichotomies, Siouian villages divided into Earth/Sky moieties.

Among these matrilineal farmers, women also had their own clubs dedicated to the healthy growth of plants and people. Among the Mandan, they ranked, low to high, as Gun, River, Grass, and White Bison. Their totems included Snake for the River and Goose for the Grass, since these waterfowl arrived in the spring and left at the harvest. Elsewhere, women had craftwork sigs* devoted to making needed articles, sometimes with great flourish, beauty, and style.

Mobile peoples emphasized horizontal links between families, bands, and tribal congeries. Flexibility and defendable numbers were essential for hunters. The optimal unit became the <u>band</u> because the extended family was too weak, while the tribe was too large to keep it fed. Descent was bilateral, as unilineality was too rigid and brittle. Therefore, bands with less than a hundred members provided necessary flexibility, mobility, and adaptability.

At huge gatherings, tribes coalesced for annual rituals such as the Sun Dance, and for major communal hunts during the same time that the mating cluster drew together the bison herds. Tribal chiefs and hunt police served full time to enforce a coherent unity.

The formal degree of these tribal governments can be directly related to the subsistence background of the tribe. Thus, coming from a farming background, Cheyennes had an elaborate council of forty-four chiefs. It consisted of four tribal chiefs, and forty band chiefs selected to serve for 10 years, from each of 10 camps. Comanche left Wind River Shoshoni (Numics), so it is not surprising that they have maintained a Basin organization of charismatic leaders (sigers) for bands that fluctuated in size and identity over time.

Village ranks, especially for Caddoans, included a small elite core of self-perpetuating families. They were noted for their ritual and economic privileges, their lavish giving, and the careful training of their children to be worthy heirs and leaders.[96]

Mystic bundles could be owned by members of the elite or by distinguished commoners. Its crucial ritual knowledge and ceremonies, however, were held by a priest from such an elite family. According to widespread belief, when the priest started transferring this knowledge to his heir, he began gradually to die. The final information was passed with his last breath. In extreme cases, such transmission was regarded as a type of parricide.

Priests and chiefs were closely linked with life, women, stars, reproduction, crop growth, and perpetuation. In contrast, shamans (sometimes called doctors) were linked with death, men, earth, and decomposition. The fundamental Plains dualism of life and women / death and men makes understandable the often overlooked, if not suppressed, importance of ceremonial sexual intercourse. Among the Hidatsa, old men passed on their power to specific younger men through the medium of sexual intercourse (called "walking with the buffalos") with the wives of these younger men during a private section of a ritual.

Ranks

Among all Plains tribes, but especially the Tipis, ranks became historically identified with the possession of horses. Members of the elite had more burden-bearing horses than others, while active warriors acquired wild horses to tame. Commoners had few if any horses. The poor had none at all, though the wealthy would gain honor by loaning them a nag every so often.

The tribal proportions of horses varied. The Kiowa and Comanche, who were closer to the Spanish sources, had thousands more horses than did northern Plains tribes further away. With more horses, members of the elite could easily acquire more mystic bundles, as well as ritual knowledge, wives, and followers because, according to the native view, these people had greater *puwha* from their immortals.

Somewhat removed from elite ranks but nevertheless indispensable to the labor and defense of each tribe was a general class of "boys". These were men under 40 years of age, considered immature or unmotivated. Leaders relied on these "boys" to act as scouts, workers, and warriors. The great elaboration of Plains sodalities may have existed to help divert, harness, or burn off energies from these boys.

Each war expedition was recruited by a prominent man. He received proper supernatural sanctions to do so from dreams, omens, or visions, and made offerings to a mystic bundle to guarantee success.

Cosmology: *Myth, Ritual*

Mind, pervading Plains universes, was deified as the pivot of several pantheons. Among these was Tirawahat, "expanse of the heavens," of the Pawnee, and Wakan Tanka, "great mystery," for Lakota, who say it was formless yet fourfold (tetradic), unidentifiable yet everywhere.

Lodges usually had creation charters, while Tipis had reform ones, setting things like they are today. The Mandan world was made by Coyote and Lone Man. Together they created men, while Village Old Woman made women and female species. This creation was dramatized in the elaborate, four-day Okeepa Ceremony. In the past, Hidatsa recognized only Coyote as First Creator. By the early 1800s, after severe epidemics, they shared with Mandan a belief in double creators. Pawnee creation included the birth of a daughter to Evening Star and Morning Star and a son to Moon mother and Sun father. When grown, this couple came to earth to become the ancestors of human chiefs.

Blackfeet tell of Old Man Grandfather, who modified the earth as he went south. The Cheyenne world was reformed by Sweet Medicine, who provided the 4 sacred tribal arrows, while Erect Horns gave them the Sun Dance. Great misfortune struck the Cheyenne in 1833 when Pawnees captured their sacred arrows, although Sioux recaptured and returned a pair in 1843.

Today: *Religion*

The endless series of feasts, gift giving, personal bundle openings, shaman's lodge performances, guild events, village bundle displays, and tribal initiations are now much curtailed and handicapped.

The so-called Sun Dance continues, but only by some tribes. This is a blanket name for a wide variety of rites. In the past, the Hidatsa held theirs in honor of the Moon, and the Crow to in publicly plan a revenge raid. Despite the great diversity among these rituals, all called the Sun Dance, they all share a central post within a sacred enclosure, under the care of a set of ritual officials.

Plains tribes were enthusiastic in the Ghost Dances of 1870 and 1890. Tribal delegations used free railroad passes provided in treaties (that were signed in return for land cessions) to visit Jack Wilson (Wovoka) in Nevada. They learned his message of world renewal through accommodation and pacifism.

After a devastating winter and many setbacks in the 1880s, Lakota Sioux reinterpreted his peaceful message into a more forceful one, but in religious not political terms. Overreacting, fearful white officials crushed their fervor at the 1890 massacre at Wounded Knee. Some tribes in the southern Plains like Kiowas still continue, in a quiet way, its songs and beliefs.

Perhaps growing out of an earlier mesquite bean use, the Peyote "cult" or Native American Church, focusing on the sacrament of peyote (a spineless cactus), was inspired by visions and the practices of tribes in northern Mexico in the 1890s. It is still spreading. An early prophet was John Wilson (Nishkantu), a Caddo-Delaware Catholic, who founded the Big Moon way now celebrated only by Quapaw and Osage. The Little Moon way, now the most popular, had Kiowa and Comanche sponsors like Quannah Parker. His Anglo mother (Cynthia Ann Parker) had been captured in a raid.

In the 1970s, many Oklahoma tribes began reviving an earlier Siouian warrior's rite, now call Gourd Dance. It was active during the afternoons at Powwows, an older gathering that draws large numbers of people to its fancy costumes, dancing, and singing.

All Christian denominations occur on the Plains, with many hymns and services using native languages. Among Lakota, the Episcopal church consists of mostly native clergy, due to the efforts of the famous Deloria family. Ella Deloria worked with Franz Boas, recording the ethnography and language of her people.

90. As traced by John Ewers 1965 to account for this popular Indien image.
91. Gene Weltfish, The Lost Universe: The Way of Life of the Pawnee 1971: 457.
92. John Ewers The Horse In Blackfoot Indian Culture 1955.
93. Claude Schaeffer, The Kutenai Female Berdache: Courier, Guide, Prophetess, and Warrior 1965.
94. Alfred Bowers, Hidatsa Social and Ceremonial Organization 1965: 256.
95. Reo Fortune, Omaha Secret Societies 1932: 24.
96. Preston Holder, The Hoe and the Horse on the Plains 1970.

TRIBAL EXAMPLES

Pawnee of Nebraska

Pawnee consisted of four divisions. These were the three South Bands along the Platte River – Chawi or Grand, Pitahawirat or Tappage, Kitkshahki or Republican – and, along the Loup River, the Skiri (Skidi) or Wolves, who occupied about fifteen villages. Within the Plains Caddoan languages, Skiri, Arikara, and South Band Pawnee (which preserved more archaic forms), diverged about the same time. Chawi seems to have been the parent of both Kitkshahki and then Pitahawirat.[97]

Historically, all but two of the Skiri villages belonged to a confederacy that was organized around a hierarchy of mystic bundles. There were several classes of bundles, variously associated with an individual, a village, and the whole confederacy. Every visionary assembled a bundle to represent his partnership. When merited by prestige, warriors could request use of a special war bundle for their expeditions.

A village was defined in terms of its mystic bundle in such a way that the hereditary chief – expected to be wise yet humble, strong yet not aggressive, and generous yet reserved – was supposed to descend from its original owner, a star who decided to live on the earth. The village (totally about 20) was the basic unit. Each had its own ancestral star, chiefly founder, bundle, fields, and cemetery. Lodges of the same town might be scattered among those of other villages because allegiance came through matrilines rather then location, and marriage was limited to other members of the town in order to in-focus the bundle and its *puwha* (*wa•ruksti•*).

Pawnee economy combined bison, hunted by men from tent (tipi) camps, with crops, farmed by women at villages, especially maize (15 varieties), beans (8 varieties), squash (7 varieties), melons, and sunflowers. Seasonal bison hunts took place after the Spring planting and after Fall harvest, with families returning in Summer to their "mudlodge" in town so women could store the dried meat and work their fields. These homes looked like big grass-covered mounds, with long entry ways to keep out cold, that had to be cleaned and fumigated before families moved in for the Nebraska winter. Thick inner layers of poles and outer sod provided insulation. At the village and along the trail, Pawnee women gathered berries, fruits, seeds, nuts, and tubers, particularly prairie turnip, groundnut, sunroot, plums, riverbank grapes, and chokecherries.

When willows sprouted, heightened rituals conducted by men and female work parties ("bees") greeted the farming season. Fields were hilled, planted, hoed, weeded, and harvested. Three ceremonies marked this bounty – Green Corn, Ripe Corn, and Four Pole, when an earthen ring and tiny mound were formed by bundle priests. Crops were processed and dried for storage in enormous cache pits, both inside the lodge for easy access and hidden outside for emergencies. Farming beliefs and rituals centered on maize, which (who) was specifically identified as a symbolic Woman. Therefore, every cornfield was planted with an even number of hillocks to represent her breasts.[98]

In the sea of grass that was the Plains, just as on the ocean, people relied on the stars to guide them at night. One of the Pawnee bundles included a star chart painted on hide that fascinates modern astronomers because it is so accurate for the 1200s sky.

Each bundle safeguarded its village, strongly encouraging ties of internal solidarity and endogamy as well as its own cornfields and burial grounds. Maize was specifically identified as a Woman, therefore, every cornfield was planted with an even number of hillocks to represent her breasts.

The bundles of the Wonderful Skull and of the North Star represented all the Skiri confederated villages. Directly below these in *puwha* were four bundles associated with the semi-cardinal directions, each with a leading chief who held authority over everyone for six months within an overall two year sequence. These were Yellow Tent Bundle of the Northwest, Red Star of the Southwest, Big Black Star of the Northeast, and White Star of the Southeast. Accordingly, North bundles led during the winter, and South ones in summer.

Complementing this sky-based system of priests and bundles were the earth-based shamanic or doctor cults, including the Medicine Lodge that was unique to the Pawnee. The landscape of all Plains tribes was dotted with buttes and hills which were the "holy homes" of the spirits of particular species – such a bison, bear, elk, deer, and antelope. Those blessed by each species formed a separate guild, and presumably recognized a hill as the "holy home" of that particular species. Twice a year, in the spring and the fall, each lodge met to sing and dance.

Named _rahurahwaarukstii'u_ {"holy grounds"}, fourteen of these animal lodges have recorded names, and most have been correlated with specific geographical places that looked in profile much like the earth lodges of ancient Pawnee towns. The insides of both were arranged in the same way, with spirits or humans sitting on the north or south sides of a central fire and an east-facing entryway.

The most famous of these places, shared by other Plains tribes, was Spring Mound or Waconda Spring in north central Kansas, developed into a health spa about 1884 by local whites, who also bottled and sold its water. As an artesian spring atop a low mound, the site became famous for spiritual and medicinal help.

In addition, the Pawnee recognized a special set of animal lodges where spirits of many species gathered and, in special cases, instructed a human in the conduct of an all-encompassing tribal Medicine Lodge. This Medicine (Doctoring) Lodge was unique to each of the four bands, made up of the leading doctors of the other cults. Each Medicine Lodge met in the spring and the summer to sing and dance before holding their major rite in the fall to display their amazing curative _puwha_s. That of the Skiri lasted a month.[99] During each one, offerings of smoke, corn, and meat were given to each of the known animal lodges scattered over the landscape.

Pawnee society was organized around a series of overlapping triads, defining social classes and polity. These were pervaded by symbolism of Man and Woman, reflected in economics, ritual, and cosmology. The classes consisted of the elite "high" born, the ordinary ("good"), and the poor, sometimes with captives beyond the pale (outside the system). Included in the elite were families noted for generations of chiefs, priests, and shamans. At a lesser rank were the families of warriors and other ambitious individuals, lacking pedigree or ancestors of distinction. Chiefs benefited both by ancestry from stars "who" came to earth to found their family, and their own life-long training.

In general, all these triplets reflected a basic one of leader/ executive/ commoner.[100] Society as a whole consisted of hereditary families/ ambitious families/ and ordinary families, including boys – aimless young and old men. Cross-sectioning these threefold segments was the duality of gender reflected in hunting by men and farming by women. Genders had different roles, functions, and responsibilities within the overall whole. For example, while the society was matrilineal, succession to office was generally patrilineal.

In all, this duality expressed a profound belief in the creative conjoining of opposites. It was epitomized in the meaning of sexual union represented as male lightning fertilizing female earth, male fire kindling flames on a female hearth board, and the ubiquity of chiefly _puwha_, which was represented by lances in its coercive aspect and by cobs of Maize Mother in its nurturing mode.

This belief in a Man and Woman creative union was a privilege known only to the elite. It was basic to their store of esoteric knowledge, together with titles and badges, bundle custody, and generosity. On the basis of this belief, some Pawnee recognized that death and destruction were more apparent than real. Time ran in cycles, so life transmuted. Thus, the death of plant crops at harvest allowed people to live, until they too died and returned to the soil to nurture plants.

The Skiri universe was composed of a plethora of metaphoric equations based on the genders. These were particularly represented in mythology and ritual by Morningstar Man and Eveningstar Woman. These links are listed below

MAN	= red	day	light	fire	dry	warfare	sky
Sun	winter	north	east				

WOMAN	= white	night	darkness	rain	wet	farming	earth
Moon	summer	south	west				

97. Roger Grange, An Archaeological View of Pawnee Origins 1979: 136.
98. Gene Weltfish, The Lost Universe 1964: 124, 144. To vivify the crops and the earth, the Morning Star sacrifice of a young enemy girl also took place in the Spring. Douglas Parks, Pawnee 2001 Part 1: 515-547.
99. Douglas Parks and Waldo Wedel, Pawnee Geography, Historical and Sacred 1985.
100. Specifically, these triplets ranged from leaders as chiefs/ priests/ doctors, to subsets of chiefs/ attendants/ members, or leading shamans/ cult shamans/ and ordinary doctors, to domestic roles organized as grandmaternal leader/ senior wives/ junior wives.

Cheyenne "Person"

Cheyennes call themselves "like-hearted people." Like other natives of the Americas, more than just humans were recognized as people. Personhood, therefore, belonged to any conscious and articulate member of the great society of life, to any node in a web of puwha like the belief of the Luiseño of California.

Cheyenne as a Western Algonkian language included the obligatory grammatical distinction between animate / inanimate. But these were not simple living and dead categories. Rocks, for example, might be animate if they were associated with spirits and puwhas, and often indicated a holy place. Similarly, not all humans were people since they might be in some way deficient in proper characteristics. Such were the insane or sinners, as discussed below. Regardless of external appearance or species, a person was conscious of self, the moral order, kinship obligations, speech, understanding, and the virtues of the spirit. In addition, humans had a body, breath, memory, and heart. This allowed them to understand differences and degrees of individuality, provided that each and everyone fully supported the tribal identity and purpose.[101]

A proper human was conceived from three sources. Two were the mother and father, who contributed blood and body to a fetus. The most critical source, however, was the Creator (Ma'heo'o) who provided two "blessings" to each being. The first was a life soul – enabling a fetus to grow and move when fixed into its body. It was diffused throughout the person, and indicated by the heart beat, pulse, breathing, growth, blinking eyelids, and food digestion. Any loss of body parts, particularly amputations, diminished the effectiveness of this life soul.

The second blessing came just after birth when the baby first inhaled omotome – meaning breath, air, speech, articulation, understanding, and puwha. This ability is the means for learning the Cheyenne Way and understanding the important differences that enable any person to survive as a productive member of a community. It enables a person to develop the mahta'sooma, which stores knowledge and experience to become memory in a conscious mind. While humans spend their lives gaining this memory; spirits, known as "listeners," <u>are</u> immortal memory and mind.

Being human was a process of defining this conscience. This was done on the basis of four qualities. These were good or crazy, action or wisdom. Good was anything orderly, controlled, careful, thoughtful, and proper, as taught by Sweet Medicine. He was the man who learned Cheyenne culture from the spirits inside Bear Butte (<u>noaha-vos</u>) in South Dakota. He instituted the Council of Forty-Four Chiefs and the worship of the four Sacred Arrows.

Crazy was anything disordered, impulsive, or brutishly animal-like. Humans have both potentials, but should learn self-control to embrace the good and avoid the crazy. Both good and crazy were, in turn, bisected by the axis of action or wisdom.

For example, men could choose between two role models, that of the active warrior or that of the sage chief or priest. In the circle of life, these four principals have additional associations.

good =	spirituality	white	east
crazy =	sexuality	yellow	west
action =	youth	red	south
wisdom =	elderly	black	north

Ideally, the young should be active, but willing to listen. The old should be wise, and ready to instruct, thereby encouraging one role to develop into the other. Also, greater latitude is tolerated in men than in women. Young men might be crazy and active, but women should always be stable – tempering, quieting, and soothing. Some biological males, known as women-hearted, became berdaches. They strictly subscribed to the good of the female role, spending all their time among women.

The core of every person, the seat of their mind and feelings, was the heart (<u>hestah</u>). This is why the Cheyennes call themselves "like-hearted". While alive, the heart of a person filled up with a life history, spiritual growth, physical identity, and name. It was not done as a distinct individual but as a part of a larger whole.

Nature and nurture also influenced the character of a Cheyenne person. Such conditioners include family characteristics traced through "blood;" the behavior of parents during gestation, observing or violating certain taboos (a hare lip caused by the mother staring at a rabbit, a difficult delivery after blocking a doorway); and influence from those present at the birth. The midwife, the first to touch the child, should be someone of excellent repute.

Born with an "empty mind," a child grew under the care of parents and relatives, particularly grandparents and maternal uncles, who used indirect threats ("boogeymen") and frightening predicaments to coax a child toward good and wisdom. The first twelve years are the most precarious. To help the child, a name will be bestowed at a Give Away. Gifts are presented on behalf of the child to others, especially respected elders who will, in return, send good thoughts for the child's welfare.

Associates of a person will also influence quality. If these are crazy (liars, drunks, or thieves), a person will turn out the same. For this reason, the Keeper of the Sacred Arrows for the Southern (Oklahoma) Cheyenne or of the Sutaio Sacred Hat for the Northern Cheyenne in Montana must be a superior person so that all Cheyenne will benefit. In ancient times, the Arrow Keeper indicated his willingness to suffer for his people by having four strips of flesh removed from his arms, shoulders, back, and legs, along with a circle and crescent cut from his chest.

Especially helpful to a child is contact with a spirit, who transfers *puwha* to assure success. Setbacks to personal development include ill health, injury, or the loss of a good spirit through fright or someone else's ill will. Loneliness was avoided, but inevitable without the support of the community. Only in the case of the "contrary," a super warrior who lived alone and did everything backwards, did the community give support to someone who lived at the margins of being a normal person.

Non-persons, though having human bodies, were those who were insane, murderers, or "thrown way" by their own families for anti-social acts. Cheyennes who murdered other Cheyenne were particularly offensive because their deed flecked the four Sacred Arrows with the blood and stench of their crime. In the past, at death, those guilty of murder, suicide, incest, or promiscuity were cremated to remove their taint from the camp. Then their ghosts took the short fork of the Milky Way into oblivion.

Because Sweet Medicine chose that humans be like plants instead of rocks, they die. Memory leaves the body, followed by breath, removing consciousness. Obsessed with loneliness, that memory might entice a living relative to join it. After four days of searching for the long fork of the Milky Way (the path to Seana, the afterworld in the sky), the memory and breath combined to form a ghost ancestor. After the imposition of US law, if someone was hanged, the noose blocked the escape of breath, preventing the reverse process that enabled the ghost to join other ancestors as a member of the immortal Cheyenne community.

As it left, memory sometimes appeared as a separate shadow image. For this reason, Plains warriors added trade mirrors to their gear, hoping that enemies would see their own images and anticipate death. Remaining with the body, the life soul merged into the bones of the skeleton, which disarticulated on a scaffold burial. In the final phase of this drawn out funeral, the bones were gathered up and buried.

101. Anne S Straus, Northern Cheyenne Ethnopsychology 1975; The Meaning of Death in Northern Cheyenne Culture 1978.

Mandan Okeepa

Along the Upper Missouri River, every Mandan village was a loose cluster of domed, growing-grass-covered earth lodges facing toward an open plaza. A D-shaped Okeepa lodge was on the north side and a fenced shrine, called the ark, was in the center. This shrine was sacred to Lone Man, who made the earth with First Creator (Coyote) and established Mandan culture. A cedar post, painted red, stood at the middle of the shrine to represent Lone Man. It was surrounded by a cottonwood plank palisade, like the one he used to protect Mandans from the Flood, whose highest level was indicated by an encircling willow branch tied near the top edge.

Lone Man made the world to the east of the Missouri River and First Creator made that to the west. Similarly, Mandans were divided into moieties of West = Black = Buffalo / East = Red = Corn. Before over 80% of the Mandans died during an 1837 smallpox epidemic, the East included six matriclans and the West had seven.

Each moiety built, decorated, and painted their appropriate half of the Okeepa lodge. Three east side roof supports rested on cornmeal and were painted red. Three uprights on the west rested on buffalo hair and were painted black.

This lodge represented Dog Den Butte, a "holy home". There Speckled Eagle (*Hoita*) once impounded all the bison, causing great hardship. He released them to join with Lone Man at the first human-sponsored Okeepa. In sum, this rite was a world renewal to celebrate a) the creation of the earth, b) the retreat of the Flood, c) the release of the buffalo, and d) the initiation of boys and men into the tribe. If only one rite were held that year, it was held after families returned from the summer buffalo hunt. If more were held, they were scheduled before and after this outing.

An Okeepa filled four days, each night concerned with both time, an era of tribal history, and space, as a cardinal direction (S E N W). Roles and events depended on owning special bundles, with garments and rights to select the performers who wore them.

Principals in the rite were Lone Man, Hoita, 8 singers (called Blue Herons), 8 buffalo dancers, and the Okeepa Maker. He was a man whose vision to host the rite had been approved by Okeepa officers and the community. For a year after pledging to be host, his family amassed over a hundred gifts of robes, elkskin dresses, cloth, shirts decorated with porcupine quills, leggings, and knives. His matriclan also gave generously. Every villager contributed something as a gift for participants. Before the rite, the Okeepa Maker avoided situations where bison were butchered or their entrails eaten so as not to offend their spirits.

Though Lone Man went everywhere, Hoita remained in the lodge until the last day, as the original spirit stayed in Dog Den Butte to the east. The day before the rite, after residents moved out, the lodge was cleaned, painted, and decorated with fresh willows.

Between fifty and a hundred males pledged to fast, pray, and suffer. They ranged in age from eight to thirty-five, although most were teenagers. Those youngest only fasted for a single day. Older men endured until the last day.

Day 1 Creation ~ South

Before dawn, a crier went through the village announcing the imminent arrival of Lone Man. Chiefs painted their faces black, and gathered at the home of the head chief to wait. With the dawn, the man impersonating Lone Man came from the **south**, painted completely white, wearing a wolfskin robe, jackrabbit fur collar and anklets, and a headdress of porcupine hair, fringed with jackrabbit fur and topped by a stuffed raven. In his left hand was a pipe, and in his right a flat, ashwood club. It was decorated with designs of Moon and Thunderbird on one side, and of the Sun and Morning Star on the other.

Members of the Black Mouth guild, acting as camp police, met Lone Man. After ascertaining his intentions, they took him to the Okeepa lodge where all the men gathered. There, he recounted the origins of the Okeepa, restating his promise to return yearly for the rite when willow leaves were fully grown.

The head chief sent the crier through the town to warn all women and children to remain inside with their pet dogs. Lone Man wandered through the village retelling stories about the creation, impounded buffalo, and flood. At each lodge where a boy or man lived who was about to undergo initiation, Lone Man received knives to take back to the lodge. In return for a knife, Lone Man gave each male a handful of pemmican {greased buffalo flour}.

That evening, the Okeepa Maker took all of his amassed gifts into the back of the lodge, along with bags filled either with pemmican or with meal balls. These were made from ground up corn, beans, squash, and sunflowers. A singer brought in a dry, rolled-up buffalo robe to serve as a drum. During the night, three singers, painted red and wearing eagle feathers and anklets taken out from their bundles, shifted the drum so it moved from west to east. Two men with rattles sat at the ends of the drum. Lone Man sat in front of it, smoking his pipe and eating pemmican. Since the first day was the initial period of Mandan history, trappings were minimal.

Males assembled who were to fast and undergo the initiation ordeal. Each was naked, painted according to personal desires. He carried a shield, quiver, and bow in the left hand, and his father's medicine bundle in the right. Each boy arranged his own place, with a sage-covered bed and a bison skull pillow, according to his moiety and clan membership. His weapons were hung on the adjacent back wall, and the bundle was propped up in front.

An altar, north of the fireplace between the moieties, held four human skulls, four bison skulls, and four sky posts. Each represented one of the four directions divided between the moieties. Knives filled the center of the altar, placed underneath the outfits of the Bull Dancers.

After all was prepared, Lone Man gave his pipe to the Okeepa Maker and directed Hoita to supervise the inside of the lodge. Whenever drummers sang, boys danced in the lodge. By midnight the drum rested in the east and singing ended. Boys "cried" (prayed) all night long.

At daybreak, boys reversed their robes so the hair was outside to assumed the guise of the buffalo impounded by Hoita. Singers took the drum outside, placed it just east of the ark, and sat behind it facing the lodge. Rattlers sat behind them, waiting for the Okeepa Maker. He came out painted yellow and wearing an entire antelope skin as an apron. He placed the pipe and pemmican in front of the drum, then walked to the south side of the ark. A buffalo cow skull had been placed inside the palisade, and a bull skull outside. Standing on the bull cranium, the Okeepa Maker placed his hands and forehead against the planks. He prayed to Lone Man for community wellbeing.

When he finished, the drummers sang as the fasters filed out from the lodge. They danced by moiety on either side of the ark before joining together on the south side. The Okeepa Maker continued his weeping prayer as the fasters took on the roles of buffalo, pawing the ground and hooking horns at each other. Then all the men crowded back into the lodge. Fasters danced four times the first day – at sunrise, pre-noon, mid-afternoon, and pre-sunset. Very young fasters, spared further hardships, often left the lodge after this first day.

At sunset, Lone Man went to the keeper of the sacred turtle drums – rawhide covered frames filled with buffalo hair pellets – which had helped to avert the flood. Lone Man lifted these powerful emblems to predict the success of future bison hunts by their weight – the heavier the drum, the more buffalo there would be.

Women could not enter the lodge. They left needed firewood outside the door. Those females who wanted to fast stood on its entry roof until the third sunset.

Day 2 Ordeal ~ East

The Okeepa, meaning "look-a-likes," was named for the Buffalo Bull Dancers who appeared this day. Before sunrise, green willow branches were delivered to the lodge. Eight large men had been previously selected to embody these bison. Other animal impersonators had also been selected by the owners of appropriate bundles. For example, those with Bird bundles selected the Bird dancers, and those with River bundles appointed the water creatures and snakes, since all rivers were inhabited by Snake spirits.

In all, these dancers included eight Buffalo, two Bald Eagles, two Women (wise, foolish), two Swans, two Snakes, Calumet Eagle, Hawk, two Black Bears, two Grizzly Bears, two Beavers, two Dried Meat Strips, two Nights, two Days, two Wolves, First Creator Coyote, Meadowlark, the Fool (Owl), and many young Antelopes.

For the entire morning, men with proper bundle *puwha* painted and dressed each animal dancer. Bulls wore horned bison head skins and bundled willow branches. Painted on their bodies were stripes and rings of red, black, and white. They were symbols of such strength and potency that their privates were tied up and overcaked with white clay.

At noon, women left food outside the lodge for the dancers, Lone Man, Hoita, and drummers. Inside, the fasters and Okeepa Maker avoided all food and water. The Okeepa Maker led the dancers out of the lodge, left his pipe and pemmican in front of the turtle drum on the **east** side, and resumed his place at the ark to pray.

Pairs of Bulls took up positions at the four directions around the shrine. Dancers went into the plaza eight times that day. The fasters only came out once, after the first Bull dance, because their ordeals now began. Each day, four more dances were added, making a total of 40, the number of days the flood lasted.

Inside, each faster presented himself to men of his father's clan. Using the knife given to Lone Man, these men poked four holes in his chest or shoulders, implanted two wooden skewers, and attached rawhide ropes. These were used to suspend the boy from the roof. Skewers inserted in the legs were attached to bison skulls. Fasters stayed suspended in midair for a time. Then men with poles spun them around until they passed out. Once unconscious they were lowered and left to recover. Upon reviving, they crawled over to a masked man and offered their left little finger for amputation. The loss of this finger was a sign of tribal initiation. Other fingers might also be sacrificed, as women often did when mourning. Some suspensions were timed so that returning Bull dancers could hook the boy with their horns, giving him luck for bison hunting.

That night intended animal dancers came to the lodge so each could receive a special stick conferring authority to dance the next day.

Day 3 Returns ~ North

Called "Everything Returns," this day was devoted to high drama. The entire morning, bundle owners painted and dressed their dancers. Before noon, all filed out of the lodge while the Okeepa Maker went to the ark. Fasters rested and looked **north** from the south edge of the plaza during four dances. Before the fifth, they returned to the lodge for their ordeals to continue.

Every dancer had an assigned location. Bull dancers paired at the four cardinal (N, S, E, W) directions, and then separated to semi-cardinals (NE, N, NW, E, W, SE, S, SW). Day dancers were on the east, and Nights on the west. Bears were on the north. Antelopes, boys painted with yellow bodies and white heads, frolicked all over the plaza.

During the first dance, a figure appeared in the distance. He was painted black with many white and red circles. He had a red sun disk on his chest, and a red moon crescent on his back. This was the Fool, the son of the Sun who had no respect for sacred things. His clothing was a close-fitting buffalo hide cap decorated with a raven feather, cornhusk necklace, buffalo tail, and bison fur anklets. Pure libido, hanging over his bison hair breechclout were a wooden rod and two small pumpkins. He carried an eight foot pole with a red ball of bison fur, representing a human head, tied at one end. A fine thread linked the pole with the rod between his legs so that when he lifted the pole, the rod arose.

Understandably modest, women and children acted terrified of him. Moving in a zigzag, he came toward the ark until the Okeepa Maker confronted him with the *puwha* of Lone Man's pipe. Subdued, this Fool instead acted like a bison bull in rut, approaching the two Woman dancers. The Wise one refused him, but the Foolish one did not. Later, he pretended to mount some of the Bull dancers. While the other animals danced twelve times that day, the Fool only came out four times.

After his fourth appearance, he entered the lodge doorway, with the pole held sideways so it broke. The women then rushed at him, splinted the pole, and drove him **west** out of the village. Cowering on the ground, the rod and pumpkins were removed and given to a woman, who wrapped them like a baby and displayed them from the lodge rooftop.[102] At the river, the Fool dancer washed. Men bound up his cap and necklace into the shape of a doll, and hung it from a pole in front of the lodge as an offering to the Sun. Thus, both women and men received powerful, life-giving effigies from vanquished Fool.

The last dance was led by the two Nights, who, acting as stars, moved very slowly until the first stars appeared in the sky, when everyone returned to the lodge and fasters were released from their vows.

Day 4 Hunting ~ West

Called "Hunting Day," only the four largest and bravest Bull dancers appeared. New willows decorated the inside of the lodge. Special hunters prepared for their roles, using poles and hoops.

The first dance featured only the Okeepa Maker, drummers, rattlers, and four Bulls. During the day, the Bulls danced in honor of each of the clans, thirteen before 1837 and ten afterwards. In all, sixteen dances were held. The Okeepa Maker, along with a few brave fasters, suffered on the last day.

Finally, four special songs were sung. Each turtle drum was lifted to predict the quantity of future bison. In four stages, these drums were moved from east to **west** while the men stamped their feet like a bison herd. Everyone followed Hoita out of the lodge, taking their usual positions. He replaced the Okeepa Maker at the south side of the ark, with the Bulls further south. Four times, the Bulls danced toward Hoita as hunters jabbed them, drawing blood from their legs as a prayer for hunting success.

Then each of the Bulls stood and bellowed to represent, in order, a season and direction: spring = east, autumn = west, winter = north, and summer = south. Finally, gathering around the ark, the Bulls removed their masks and danced at a frenzy with the hunters. The last fasters were led from the lodge by their father's clansmen, who were painted blue on the right side and red on the left. Then, dragging buffalo skulls, the boys ran around the ark, as rapidly as possible, until they passed out. When the last one collapsed, drumming and singing ceased and the hunters threw hoops in the air. When revived, these fasters went into the lodge. Those on the west rubbed their wounds with cornmeal, and those on the east used buffalo marrow. Later they went home to drink broth and eat sparingly, until they could resume taking food.

Meanwhile, Lone Man gave all the knives to the Missouri River, along with a few robes and seven meal balls. In the lodge, gifts were given to all officials, dancers, and participating father's clansmen. Later, the Okeepa Maker and any fasters who had been blessed by visions assembled medicine bundles according to instructions they received at their ordeals.

102. George Catlin's 1967: 83-85 eyewitness description of the 1832 Okeepa has a fascinating sequence, written in Latin, in which ordeals did not begin until after the

Fool was castrated and the woman on the roof called for them to begin. On the night after the Okeepa ended, the same Mandan woman also hosted a "walking with the buffalo" ceremony in which *puwha* was transmitted between men through their wives (Cf Kehoe 1970). Throughout Melanesia and elsewhere, sons did not begin their puberty ordeals until mothers, in public, allowed the tortures that led to initiation and manhood.

Lakota (Sioux) of the Dakotas

Wakan Tanka was the oldest of beings, but it was Rock (_Inyan_), surrounded by Darkness (_Hanhepi_), who began creation because he desired to have _puwha_ over something. His own vitality was in his blue-colored blood. He opened all his veins, allowing this blood to flow out to create a sphere consisting of water and Earth (_Maka_, _Ina_, "Mother"). Rock shriveled up, becoming dense, hard, and _puwhaless_. His blue-blood _puwha_ separated from the water and rose to form the Sky (_Mahpujato_, "blue sky dome"), who then took charge of creation.

Earth and Darkness quarreled. Sky banished Darkness to the underworld, creating Light (_Anpetu_) and an orb (_Wi_, further distinguished as Sun (_Anpetu Wi_) and Moon (_Hanhepi Wi_), who were respectively husband and wife). These made Earth Mother too hot so she pleaded with Sky for the return of Darkness within the sky dome. This was done. To fill the place left in the underworld, humans, intended to be servants of the deities, were created to live there. They were called the Buffalo Nation (_Pte Oyate_). Humans were led by Old Man (_Wazi_) and Elder (_Wakanka_), his wife. Their daughter (_Ite_, Face) was the most beautiful of women. Though a mortal, she married Wind (_Tate_), and had 4 children, the Winds of the primary directions – West, North, East, and South.

Spider (_Iktomi_) appeared, an imp devoted to making others look ridiculous. He schemed to have Sun become enchanted with Face. She then ignored her family responsibilities, even though she was pregnant with a fifth child, _Yumni_. At a feast, Face took the seat of Moon, wife of Sun, and insulted her. In retaliation, Sky made half of Face ugly. As Double Face (_Anuk-Ite_), she became patron of Deer and of women who seduced men to make them crazy, sometimes fatally. Together with Old Man, Elder, and Spider, she was banished to the edge of the Earth. Wind and his children were also stationed at directional points on the Earth, beginning to define space. Each child had a distinct personality. West Wind was cantankerous, North Wind pugnacious, East Wind lazy, but South Wind was the male ideal. Yumni, who remained small, lived with South. Eventually, the other Winds united to battle North Wind and drive him back home, allowing the Earth to flourish.

Spider and Double Face, bored with being alone on the Earth, decided to lure humans up to the surface. They tempted them with meat, saying that it kept them eternally young. Seven men, including First and his family, settled on the Earth and instituted the seven fires that founded the nation. Life on the Earth was hard and these seven starved. Old Man and Elder found them and taught them to hunt bison, using all the body parts to make tools, tipis, and clothing. People prospered until famine came again.

Time had been set in motion by the creation of day and of night when Sky separated Sun and Moon. Their daughter was Falling Star (_Whope_), who became famous as White Buffalo Calf Woman (_Ptehincalasan_), bringer of the Sacred Pipe and the Seven Ceremonies. The epic is rich in complexity.

During famine, a chief sent two men to scout for buffalo. They went westward but found nothing. As they planned their movements for the next day, one of them noticed a speck coming quickly towards them from the west. Soon they knew that it was a woman covered only by her own long hair. It was flowing down on the right side, but tied on the left with a tuft of bison hair. She carried a bundle on her back, and a fan of sage in her left hand. Her face was painted with vertical red stripes. She approached and told the scouts to go back and direct the people to set up a great lodge, with a door facing west, in the center of the camp circle. She said to have sage spread on the honored place at the rear of the lodge, and to arrange a small rack, buffalo skull, and square altar hole in front of it.

As she spoke, one of the men lusted for her. She took the pipe from her bundle and placed the bowl on a buffalo chip with the stem pointing east. Then she laughed and sat down. Just as the impure scout lunged at her, the heavens rumbled, a lightning bolt shot out of the sky, and mist covered the spot. When the fog lifted, only the bones of the man remained. This woman consoled the other brave and gave him the pipe, saying that it would bring many buffalo. The woman left, and the scout returned to camp with both sad and wondrous news.

As promised, Buffalo Calf Woman visited the camp the next day after 4 puffs of smoke appeared under the midday sun. The lodge and a feast were ready for her. Men kept their heads bowed while she approached, was seated, and served. She was dressed in exquisite buckskin with long fringes. She carried the pipe with the bowl in her left hand and the stem in her right, walking in a sunwise spiral. When one man tried to glance at her, his eyes became permanently fogged over.

She came into the lodge, sat in the place of honor, and settled the pipe onto the special rack. The chief rose, addressing her as "sister", and offered her welcome and thanks. She addressed the people, explaining the meaning of the pipe. Its redstone bowl was the Earth. The carved buffalo calf decorating it was the four-legs (animals). The stem was everything that grew on the Earth. The 12 pendant eagle feathers were the two-legs (humans and birds) and wingeds. Next, in turn, she addressed the women, children, men, and chief – urging them all to lead moral lives.

She took up the pipe, lit it with a glowing buffalo chip, and prayed to the 7 directions. She pointed the stem to the Earth, West, North, East, South, Sky, and Center. She passed the pipe to the chief, and instructed him carefully. From him, the pipe passed, left to right, to everyone sitting in the circle. Then the woman took a sacred stone, marked with seven circles, from her bundle. These circles represented the seven sacred ceremonies she would teach the nation.

During the 4 days she remained in camp, she taught the Ghost Spirit Keeping, Sun Dance, Crying for a Vision Quest, Sweatlodge, Menstruation, Making Relatives (Hunka Adoption), and Ball Game. Finally, she asked the chief to send two scouts to the nearest hill to look for buffalo, and had the people prepare for a bison drive in anticipation. The scouts returned, followed by a buffalo herd and an enemy war party. Both were quickly killed to provide a bison feast ending with a victory dance and scalps to decorate the pipe.

Finally, the woman announced her departure. As she walked sunwise out of camp, she appeared, in series, as a red buffalo (emblematic of North), a yellowish-brown one (for East, sunrise), a white one (for South, center), and a black one (for West, sunset). Symbolically, she moved along the sun's path and miraculously disappeared, leaving behind the knowledge of the pipe and ceremonies.

Within their larger world, important Lakota pattern numbers are four and seven, as with the council fires. Foursomes (tetrads) are particularly pervasive. Thus, Wakan Tanka, the ultimate source of *puwha*, sometimes called the Great Mystery, was a profundity permeated by fours, often to a total of 16. The highest aspects of Wakan Tanka are called Rock (*Inyan*), Earth (*Maka*), Sun (*Wi*), and Sky (*Skan*), who instituted the fourfold nature of the world and made roundness important for everything but Rock. Each of these four aspects has a set of equations.

ROCK = south, yellow, hardness, All-Father, authority advocate, arts patron, Bear, and The
    Winged, patron of cleanliness whose voice is thunder and whose glance is lightning.

EARTH = east, green, life, All-Mother, household patron, whirlwind, and Whope, also
    called Beautiful One and White Buffalo Calf Maiden, who is patron of harmony,
    pleasure, and courtship, donor of the Seven Sacred Rites, and instructor in the use of
    tobacco and sweet grass as mediating offerings.

SUN = west, red, fire, highest rank, defender of moral virtues, Moon, and Bison.

SKY = north, blue, mystery, judge of gods and spirits, source of all *puwha* and force,
    Stars, and The Four Winds.

        All other features of life and cosmos are also recognized as being foursomes. Thus, everything has an infancy, childhood, maturity, and old age. Every human has a spirit-personality, a ghost-vitality, a spirit-like essence, and a potency-*puwha*. Plants have roots, stems, leaves, and fruit. Animals move by crawling, flying, four limbs, and two legs. Time consists of day, night, months, and years. Misfortune includes insanity, disorientation, suffering, and accident. Evil itself has four sources in Old Man (*Waziya*), his Elder wife (*Wakanaka*), their double-faced daughter (*Anuk-Ite*), and Cyclone, master of everything noxious.

        While Sky instituted the pattern of the universe, the vitality of gender symbolism was emphasized by the autonomy of Rock as All-Father, who was joined with Earth as All-Mother, and by the union of Sun with his wife Moon to produce Whope, their daughter gave the seven rites.[103]

        Although famous in film as magnificent horsemen, Lakota Sioux had an archaeological past as farmers in Minnesota. Living in towns, they developed this rich cosmology that they took into the Plains, entrusted to holy men (*wichasa wakan*), who were obligated to preserve, transmit, and understand this theology. Significantly, such a man retired when he could no longer remember important information, a reminder of the vital link between memory and *puwha*.

        The Dakotan Sioux homeland was the Mille Lacs region. It was won and occupied by Ojibwa, in Minnesota, where the Eastern (Santee, Dakota) Sioux remain. Over centuries, three language communities emerged, each identified by a consonant shift as the D, N, and L dialects. These are neatly illustrated by the tribal names themselves. Thus, the Dakota were to the east, the Lakota (Teton) to the west, and the Nakota (Yankton) in between, with Nakoda (Assiniboin, Stonys) spliting off to become enemies.

        As a whole, Sioux spoke of themselves as the Seven Council Fires. These were founded by their ancestors who came up from the underworld, and included 4 of the Santee, 2 of the Yankton, and 1 of the Teton, who recently had the largest population. The council of seven fires was said to have existed when all of them lived together in their Minnesota homeland. This may have been more legendary than literal before the middle and western divisions moved away after a series of 1700s defeats by Cree and Ojibwa using French guns.

        As the largest Siouian group, the Lakotas were segmented into Burnt Thighs (*Brule*), Those Who Plant By the Stream (*Minneconjous*), Two Kettles (*Ohoenonpas*), Those Who Camp At The Entrance (*Hunkpapas*), Blackfeet (*Sihasapas*), Without Bows (*Itazipchos*, Sans Arcs in French), and Those Who Scatter One's Own Seed (*Oglalas*).

        Each of these bands occupied a series of seasonal camps while engaged in their annual round of bison hunting. Political authority rested in esteemed members called the *nachas*, led by the *nacha ominichia* (Big Bellies or Buffalo Headdress Wearers). They formed a fixed council of distinguished leaders and elders. From among the other Nachas, they appointed a set number of tribal officers called *wichasa itacans*.

These in turn selected the actual camp leaders, called the Shirt Wearers in honor of their official garment, painted blue and yellow or red and green, and fringed with scalplocks. When all Lakotas camped together for the summer hunt, four men were named *wichasa ytatpikas* to act as Shirt Wearers for the entire camp. Hair was a symbol of life, both for the Lakota and many other people in the world. They traditionally took scalps, therefore, to tap into the vitality of the enemy, and also as a proof of prowess, badge of honor, and sign of victory.

The enforcers of this authority were the *akicitas*, the various warrior clubs. These included White Horse Owners (*Ska Yukas*), Tall Ones (*Miwatanis*), and Kit Foxes (*Tukolas*). Each one had a set of officers consisting of two pipe bearers, two drummers, four lance owners, two rattlers, and two whippers. For the duration of the tribal camp and bison hunt, one sodality was selected by the council to serve as the camp police, and enforce decisions made for the good of all.

Their primary responsibility was to keep the camp quiet and the herd calm. No one was to startle or attack bison before the start of the planned hunt. People who did so were severely punished with a beating. Their possessions were also destroyed because they threatened the well being of the community. If they were properly contrite, however, the police compensated them by replacing any damage done to their goods or prestige.

The basic unit of Lakota society was the *tiyospaye* a kindred of 30-50 members, tracing kinship to a common leader. It cooperated for hunting, warfare, chores, the care of old and young, and the burial of the dead. Regardless of the event, all activities were done according to gender patterns.

A virtuous man, at all times, showed bravery, fortitude, generosity, and wisdom. A woman extolled bravery, generosity, truthfulness, industry, fidelity, and many healthy progeny. Genders were regarded as separate and antagonistic. In the extreme, women regarded men as dangerous predators, while men considered women to be drains on vitality, best treated like foes to be vanquished.

Blending the gender distinction, to some extent, were the *winkte* (transgenders) {* = individuals who took on the dress and role of the other sex}. Often, these were boys who had been overprotected as children, and who received a vision from Double or Deer Woman, legitimating their life change. Male berdache were acknowledged to do the best tanning and quill work, indicating how strongly they identified with their female status. They were expected to live at the edge of the camp with widows, orphans, and other outcasts. A special ability of such Lakota, moreover, was the bestowal of "winkte names" upon boys, a sure guarantee of their continued health.

At death, ordinary people were buried in shallow graves at the crest of a hill. The body of a camp leader was placed upon a scaffold and sealed inside a tipi. During winter, bodies were often placed in trees. The most noble of deaths was that of a warrior killed in battle. Some had their bodies left unattended because it was considered "good to remain unburied in enemy territory."[104]

Significantly, Lakota speech used female forms as generic ones, indicating that Woman was inclusive and Man exclusive. The greatest gifts were given by women, particularly White Buffalo Calf Woman. In the underworld, people were called *Pte Oyate*, the Buffalo Nation. In the language, *pte* refers to a buffalo cow, as *tatanka* refers to a bison bull. Thus, Woman is inclusive and generic. In the creation saga, the men have specific names, while the women usually have generic ones. For example, the wife of Old Man is called Elder without reference to her gender.

The ultimate expression unifying life and the genders was Wakan Tanka, described as unidentifiable yet everywhere, incomprehensible yet worthy of the most serious reflection, and formless yet fourfold. Represented by the ball that all seek during a game, "It" is enlightened wisdom, intelligence, and preordained memory, deified as Mind.

103. Royal Hassrick The Sioux 1964; Joseph Brown and Black Elk The Sacred Pipe 1971.
104. Royal Hassrick The Sioux 1964: 293.

Blackfeet *(Nitsitapix "real people") Nation*

Living in the far northern Plains on the Canadian and US border, these three Algic tribes are, south to north, the Pikuni ("scabby robes," Canadian Peigan, American Piegan), Kai-nai ("many chiefs," Bloods), and Siksika (American Blackfeet, Canadian Blackfoot). Once a confederacy, today they are known as the Blackfeet nation.[105] They were allied with Sarcee (Athapaskan Tsuu T'ina). Their alliance with the Atsina (Algic Gros Ventre) soured and they enemies after 1861.

Their homeland was created by *Napi* (Old Man) from a speck of earth brought up from under the sea by Muskrat as earth diver. Above them, in the sky, lived the holy family of Sun, his wife Moon, and his son Morning Star. These lands belonged to the entire tribe, though occupation and use was by bands (nodal kindreds named for some collectively distinguishing characteristic). These units came and went according to the success of their leaders, both a civil chief and a war captain. One Blood band, Followers of the Buffalo, was so successful that every few years excess members split off to become other bands known as Many Fat Horses, All Tall Members, or Knife Owners. Less fortunate, Bear People scattered after their leaders died in an 1872 battle.

A chief served as judge, with police duties carried out by warrior clubs (guilds). These were male age grades, such that each took up five year intervals from ages 15 to 60. Among the Canadian Blackfoot, youngest to oldest, they were Mosquitos, Bees, Grouse, Crows, All Brave Dogs, Bad Horns, Raven Bearers, Dogs, and Bulls.[106] When bands came together to form a tribal camp, those age grades between 20-30 often served a camp police during bison hunts.[107] As noted, they wrecked the home of anyone who dared to attack a herd before the time that had been decided by council and consensus.

This far north, their short grass plains was deeply cut into by coulees and streams. Long bitterly cold winters and brief hot summers, moving bison herds, and limited sources of drinkable water made any of the sparsely located tree groves into ideal camp sites. Fish were never eaten, tabooed as food except during dire starvation. Waterfowl and their eggs were enjoyed. Women dug roots and picked berries through the fall. A young man went along as lookout and guardian. When blizzards, droughts, or prairie fires trapped people in one place, famine loomed. Ever on the move, any preserved and stored food only served as emergency rations for a short while.

During the "dog days" before the horse, tipis were short and compact, easier to set up on a four pole foundation and transport on drags called travois. Women had laborious care of household, children, unruly dogs, and guests. Everything (tipi covers, bedding, utensils, containers) was provided by bison, made from hide, bone, horn, sinews, hooves, and innards. Skulls, horns, choice cuts, and other portions served religious purposes. At the first spring thunderstorm, medicine bundles were unwrapped and honored at feasts.

A boy quested in secluded, sometimes dangerous, locales such as peaks, cliffs, or burial grounds. He built a rock shelter, lay down beside a pipe, and prayerfully fasted for four days. Sometimes help came without great effort. As a boy, the famous leader Red Crow was bow-hunting gophers when he fell asleep. He dreamed that a Gopher promised to keep him safe in battle if he would only go away and leave those gophers alone. Thereafter, during 33 battles, he wore a blade of grass in his hair as a talisman and escaped unharmed.

Important men had dreams to assemble powerful objects, including a pipe, into a bundle that benefited his band, age grade, or tribe. Each could be transferred, inherited, or sold to continue its protection for the new owner. Each member of the same age grade had a bundle of appropriate paints and clothing. Unlike most other Plains tribes, Blackfeet had a women-only guild called _Motoki_ (Sorority). It was devoted to thanking and appeasing bison. It was adopted from the Mandan in 1832, along with the Ancient Pipe for men.

Most venerable of all was the Beaver bundle, which was given to a man in what became Glacier Park, Montana. He had been overkilling animals and birds so his wife was kidnapped to the bottom of a lake. There, she was dressed in finery to lead a return procession of Beaver, Sun, and Moon to her former home. The husband was promised this bundle if he would practice conservation. One by one, the pelts and skins decorating the inside of his lodge walls were taken down, celebrated with songs and dances, and added to the growing bundle. Then red ocher face paint and sweetgrass braids completed its contents.

Absorbing the powerful rays of the Sun, in daylight, bundles hung from tripods set in front of their owner's tipis. At night, the wife of the owner hung it above their bed to keep their thoughts good. Wealthy families set up a double tipi made of 30 hides with two doors, and two hearths. It was visited only by warriors who had gained dual war honors such as killing two enemies with one shot.

Ancient bison kills involved three techniques, 1) cliff jumps about 70 feet high to kill the animal without damaging the meat, 2) surrounds by hunters wearing animal skin disguises to shoot arrows into animals at the edge of a herd, and 3) impounds into a corral of posts set up below a hillside that was made too slippery for escape by a frozen plastering of dung. When the horse and gun arrived in the northern Plains about 1760, hunts were conducted on horseback to selectively cull the herds.[108]

After wintering as separate stretched-out clusters of kindred camps along a sheltered waterway, an entire tribe gathered in July, while grass was still lush, for their major ritual of the Sun Dance (Okan, "pole"). Each of these annual rites was pledged by a pure woman – a girl or faithful wife giving thanks for the safe return of a male relative from danger, disease, or some near death experience. All of her kin rallied to provide help and gifts like horses, blankets, clothing, and fabric goods for her to give away. She purchased the _Natoas_ {* = Sun dance bundle} of a previous pledger, along with her practical advice.

The ripening of saskatoon (sarvice) berries, needed for sacramental meals, set the time for the rite, which was held at a progression of locations. Chiefs and warriors selected a place with protected horse grazing near many bison. People came together to visit, gamble, and race horses. The Motoki set up a central lodge made of travois and tipi covers, where they lived for four days and then gave away many gifts.

Since, by then, their large horse herds had eaten the nearby grass, the camp moved five miles away. There, the age grades held dances to consecrate the space. Then the pledger moved her tipi inside the circle and leaned evergreen boughs against it. This act signaled the start of her fast. The former pledger showed her how to thin slice and dry-smoke buffalo tongues. For these four days, she avoided water in any form, instead wiping and drying with a muskrat skin towel.

Every morning, the circle moved. The first day, just north of the circle, a huge sweatlodge was framed by arching a hundred willows sticks. It was painted half black for night and half red for day. When fifty stones were hot, the pledgers sat outside while their husbands went inside to purify. That year's pledger painted a bison skull with designs of the Sun, Moon, Morning Star, and Sun Dogs to rest at the base of the center pole. Each day at the new camp, the sweatlodge was set up in a different direction until they reached the main site of the rite.

That morning, a warrior grade left to scout a likely forked tree for use as the center pole and took it by mock combat. It was carried to the camp center. The outer walls of the lodge were set up before the pledger came to bless the pole prior to setting it upright. When it stood free, enthusiastic shouts and gun shots marked this relinking with the sky. Radiating roof poles connecting the walls to the pole were covered over with a roofing of moist, green boughs, renewing their faith in the Sun. Boys and girls went together to gather these boughs, released from strict rules of modesty and reserve.

The pledger's fast ended with the completion of this lodge at sunset, when she feasted and gifted everyone. The quality and amount of goods lining the route between her tipi and the lodge indicated family wealth and rank. All that night, four warriors sang inside a bower set within the lodge. In the morning, weather dancers performed in two facing rows, then warrior grades danced.

About noon, men who had pledged to suffer had wooden skewers put through their chest and attached to the pole by thongs. Those pierced over the back shoulder blades had a heavy shield or bison skull attached. These vows were in gratitude for the recovery of a loved one, or an answered prayer to the Sun. They ended when the skewers pulled out.

During recent centuries, Blackfeet had to defend their lands often. Two Montana Piegans were the only fatalities of the Lewis and Clark expedition. Indeed, this nation was hard pressed on several fronts. During summers after horses became widespread, massive hunts were conducted by tribes from the Plateau such as the Sahaptian Numipi (Nez Perce), Salishan Columbia, and Kootenay. Metis were making pemmican and Americans were slaughtering to take only bison robes for Eastern sale, wasting all the meat.

Some of the hides were sold as fur coats, but most became belts to run machines in New England factories. To supply this same trade, Blackfeet men needed several wives since preparing the hides was always a female duty. Epidemics repeatedly killed over half the nation in 1819, 1837, 1864, and 1869.

Blackfeet signed a treaty with Americans in 1855, though the promised huge Montana reservation has been much reduced. In 1870, US Lt Eugene Baker massacred almost 200 Piegans, with survivors fleeing to Canada. There, devastation caused by American whiskey traders known as "wolfers" had to be checked by the founding of the Royal Canadian Mounted Police in 1874. In 1877, Treaty 7 set up Alberta reserves for Peigans, Siksika, and Bloods, which remains the largest in Canada. Today, in the United States, Montana Blackfeet are best known as the makers of a fine grade of pencil, a far cry from their warrior past, but well expressive of Algic woodworking tradition.

105. Hugh Dempsey, The Blackfoot Indians, Chapter 17, <u>Native Peoples</u>: The Canadian Experience 1995: 381-413.
106. Clark Wissler, Ceremonial Bundles of the Blackfoot Indians, AMNH 7 (2) 1912; Societies and Dance Associations of the Blackfoot Indians AMNH 11 (4) 1913: 369; Sun Dance of the Blackfoot Indians AMNH 16 (3): 1918.
107. Walter McClintock 1935 The Blackfoot Beaver Bundle, Southwest Museum Leaflet 2 & 3 1937 Blackfoot Warrior Societies, Southwest Museum Leaflet 8.
108. John Ewers, <u>The Blackfeet</u> ~ Raiders on the Northwestern Plains 1958; The Horse In Blackfoot Indian Culture 1955.

9. Lakes Culture Area

Ecosystem

Glaciated except in the Driftless Region of southern Wisconsin, the Great Lakes region formed a squat triangle ▽ whose lower tip was the juncture of the Ohio and Mississippi Rivers. Its mixed forests and prairie grasslands were home to many large mammals. The forests included broadleafs like oak, hickory, birch, or maple to the south and conifers in the north. Land residents were once numerous moose, deer, caribou, bear, and buffalo. Lake trout, whitefish, and sturgeon swam in lakes, ponds, and rivers.

Residents were speakers of Siouian, Iroquoian, and, mainly, Central Algonkian languages. From Sault Ste Marie, Ojibwa expanded well beyond its western limits. At Kathio about 1745 a decisive battle between Ojibwa and Dakota drove these Eastern Siouians southward. This victory established Ojibwa Algonkians around Mille Lacs and northern Minnesota.

LAKES

Central Algonkian
  Ojibwa(Chippewa)-Ottawa-Potawatomi
  Menomini
  Sauk-Fox-Kickapoo-(Mascouten ?)
  Shawnee
  Miami-Illinois

Siouian
  Ho-Chunk (Hochungara, Winnebago)

Iroquoian
  Huron (Wendat ~ Wyandot)
  Erie
  Neutral
  Petun (Tobacco)

Foods

Fishing, especially during whitefish runs, dominated the summer. Winter involved deer hunting. Spring saw the tapping of maple syrup. A busy fall was devoted to wild ricing, berrying, and nutting. Speared sturgeon fed large numbers. In sheltered locales, corn, beans, squash, and other crops were farmed. Bison hunts on the Illinois prairies were arranged around crop weedings and harvest.

Carefully tended, the unique local food was wild rice (<u>manoomin</u> in Algic). It is an environmentally-sensitive or indicator species. Its roots anchor into the alluvial mud of slow moving, mineral rich flows. Though not a true rice, these seeds were an important wet grass cereal. Plots were owned by usage, with families in canoes taking time for the bending, knocking, drying, parching, hulling, winnowing, and storing their harvest. These stages are explained below.

Just before their plot was ripe, a couple in a canoe made claim to the plot as they made open rows by bundling and binding up stalks by the handful, using colored twine or distinctive knots to distinguish their work. When fully ripe, a canoe was again poled from the bow through these open rows. A woman in the stern rhythmically beat stout sticks against the sheaves to knock grain into the canoe. Some always fell into the water to reseed. In barren sections, a few seeds were placed inside mud balls to sink and root. The harvest was then dried, parched, tramped upon in a skin lined pit to loosen hulls, winnowed to blow chaff away, and then stored in dry caches until cooked for soups and side dishes.

Maple syrup was tapped from owned groves, called sugarbush. It was used as seasoning in many foods. Some was stored in duck bills given to children as a sweet treat. The processing of maple sugar, however, was probably learned much later from Europeans for sale in the world market.

Labor

Both genders worked in tandem during fish runs. Otherwise men hunted and women gathered. Men also mined aboriginally, digging out copper and galena (iron ore) from the Minnesota Mesabi iron range and Illinois sources along the Mississippi. These entered the intertribal trade in exchange for shells, obsidian, and other goods. Today, this tradition continues as nearby Santee have a legal right to work the blood red layer at Pipestone National Monument, and to sell their carvings. Women from leading families had especially strong roles. Ohio tribes like Miami (Meearmear) and Shawnee had both peace and war matrons paralleling those of men.

Basic Bonds

Leadership involved the full complement of chief/captain roles, along with shamans and bundle priests. As just noted, elite women served as both civil or war matrons. At least one Potawatomi woman chief signed a US treaty.

Clans were divided into ranked lineages based on their ownership of elite bundles. These were matrilineal for Iroquoians, or patrilineal for Siouians and Algonkians. Menomini had 19 patri-clans in 7 phratries, Potawatomi had 40 clans in 6 phratries (Water, Bird, Buffalo, Wolf, Bear, Man) within Black/White moieties. Kickapoo once organized their clans into moieties of Dark Hoofed (Bear, Buffalo, Eagle, Man) / Light Others (Raccoon, Water, Berry, Tree). These have become mere groupings named for these animals, passed on to a child by the person who also provided his or her personal name. They are no longer unilineal.

Siouians and others emphasized Sky/Earth moieties, though neighboring Ho-Chunk and Menomini reversed their primary peace/war attributes. For Ho-Chunk, the Sky half was led by a tribal chief of the Thunder clan, while that for Earth was a captain, called the police, of the Bear Clan. For Menomini, the civil chief of the Bear clan led the Earth half, as the war captain of the Thunder clan headed the Sky.

For Sauk, Fox, and Potawatomi, the Light Kiishkooha / Dark Ashkasha moieties alternated membership by birth order. Each child was assigned to one or the other in sequence of birth. For example, Fox gave the firstborn to the moiety opposite that of the father, the second born to the father's own, and so on for all the siblings. Only the Tiwa of the Southwest also have such a tradition of alternating moieties.

Cosmology: *Myth, Ritual*

Elaborate accounts of Lakes creation involve a high god and immortals who made the earth. They slowed its dangerous spinning by positioning giant serpents as earth anchors, and then populated it with plants, animals, and humans.

For Ojibwa, Nanibozo (Manabush) served as trickster, marplot, and reformer. His miraculous birth as the human Hare was foretold in a dream to a grandmother, living alone with her grand daughter. The old woman warned the girl never to sit facing west. When, finally, she did so, she was immediately impregnated by the four winds. She died giving birth to four beings. These were Nanibozo, deer, chickadee, and Sun.

Wandering the world in misadventures, Nanibozo adopted a young Wolf who hunted assiduously. All the animals became alarmed by his overkilling success, and pleaded that action be taken. Warned never to cross over water, Wolf finally did so. He was drowned by the Underwater Longtails, who looked like horned, serpentine lynx. Plunged into grief, Nanibozo took revenge by pretending to be a stump on the beach where these spirits came to sun themselves on cloudless days. They only emerged when the sky was clear because they were locked in mortal combat with the Thunderers, bird-like beings who came in clouds and blasted them to death with lightning bolts.

Warned in advance, Nanibozo shot the shadows of the two leaders, who became gravely ill. He hid out until he met an old Frog-Toad woman. She was out gathering bark fiber to complete a web strung all over the earth as an alarm to trip him up and reveal his where-abouts. Learning that she was the doctor who was slowly curing the wounded Longtails, he tricked her into telling how to copy her actions. Then he killed her, flaying off her skin to wear. Going into the underwater lodge, he found the two patients, and, on the sly, drove the arrows deeper inside to kill them. As he fled, he grabbed the door covering, which was the skin of his Wolf nephew.

In revenge, the earth was flooded. Nanibozo hid within a mountain burrow and so managed to escape. Finally, a truce was declared between the Longtails and Nanibozo. Wolf was revived to become leader of the ghostland afterworld. Humans benefited from the full series of Earth, Sky, and Ghost grades and degrees that came to comprise the Midewiwin (shaman's academy).

The prehistoric Feast of the Dead or "Kettle" had been the major ritual expression. Every decade, graves were opened, their bones cleaned and bundled inside rich furs, and living kin gathered for a night-long dance. The next day, these bundles were reburied in a huge common grave known as an ossuary (bone pit). With the lapsing of this Feast, the Midewiwin gained in importance as a unifying force. Its ranking members became known as Mide priests.

Boys and some girls were sent on vision quests to guarantee future success. They often fasting in "nests" constructed high in trees. Those with similar or the same immortal partner often joined together to feast as a namesake sig. Clan and tribal bundles, however, had formal ceremonies led by priests for their spring unwrapping, as well as each time they were used for curing, planting, hunting, or other purpose – such as the tattooing of clan designs.

More informally, shamans conducted cures or made predictions from a "shaking tent". For this latter rite, a shaman would enter a thin, tall, conical tent to commune with various spirits. These were Turtle, Owl, spark-like human souls, and others. As these spirits entered the tent, it began to shake violently. Sometimes, the shaman was taken on a tour of the world by several spirits, while one immortal stayed to guard the tent. On his return, the shaman was able to answer questions put to him by interested members of the audience who were sitting outside of the tent.

Across the northern states, in the Plateau, Plains, and Great Lakes, the shaking tent has been widely reported for the Ojibwa, Cree, Montagnais, Naskapi, Cheyenne, Colville, Blackfeet, and Gros Ventre (Atsina). Since almost all these tribes belong to the Algic stock, the shaking tent probably originated with them. Moreover, the ritual has clear parallels among Siberian shamans, suggesting an even earlier and more global source among proto-Mongoloid peoples.

As noted, an important guild, spread from Ojibwa, was the Midewiwin. Its most elaborate form consists of a Life grade with 4 Earth and 4 Sky degrees. Each one was indicated by the same kind of pouch made from whole skin of a species specific to that membership. These were mammals for the Earth ones and birds for the Sky. Overall, the rite emphasizes death and rebirth symbolism, particularly the "shooting" of initiates with a marine shell (a cowry called a _megis_). After the actual biological death of a member, he or she was taken into the Ghost grade and someone was then adopted to take that vacancy in the Life series.

After epidemics and dislocations, most Ojibwa abandoned their localized patriclan villages and their Feast of the Dead reburial rite. Some consolidated into multi-clan villages after 1670. They fostered tribal cohesion by reforming the Midewiwin about 1700 at La Pointe, Wisconsin, where their tribal sacred fire burned. This resynthesis provided a survival strategy which has enabled Ojibwa to reorganize themselves in response to pressures from the fur trade. The degrees then diffused to other tribes of the Great Lakes and eastern Plains.

Today

With the demise of the Great Lakes fishery, natives have resorted to federal courts to assert their aboriginal and treaty rights. They are braving a nasty, racist backlash in Wisconsin and Minnesota that unfairly "blames the victim." These "fish wars" have even led to the brief sale of "Treaty Beer" to gain funds to use against native rights. Native jokes in the upper Midwest make the best of a bad situation.

Menomini have long had a successful lumber mill at Neopit. Its general success, compared to other tribes but not to their Anglo neighbors, led to their forced "termination" (legal abandonment) by the federal government from 1961 to 1973. This bill to callously get the US government "out of the Indien business" was passed in 1954, an exact century after a treaty with the Menomini was signed to safeguard this very land.

TRIBAL EXAMPLES

Huron of Ontario

Like most natives in the Northeast, the Huron lived in round-top longhouses formed by bent saplings and shingled with slabs of bark. A central hallway was dotted with fires, and mat walls divided up cubicles along each side. Bunks built along the walls served as seats and beds. Storage places were located underneath, above on shelves, and in cache pits dug into the floor. Many plant foods were hung from the rafters to dry in the warm smoke.

Mothers and daughters owned and shared the same longhouse. Each married couple occupied a side compartment, sharing a fire with the family across the aisle. While everyone could snack from the boiling clay pots during the day; at meal times, the senior matron of each household dished out the food. They made sure that men ate before women as a gesture of respect to the protectors of her family.

Brothers or uncles (MB, mother's brothers) of this senior woman led the clan members resident in that village. Leadership in each of these clan segments {* = lineages} rested with a particular household. The eldest, able-bodied woman was the clan matron, coordinating domestic and economic needs. She chose, from among her close male relatives, two men to lead their clan. Most of the time, the active clan official was a civil chief – a wise and calm man of wide respect and ability. During hostilities, however, the war chief (captain) of the clan took charge to plan strategy and defense. After the European invasion, such captains assumed more and more control of clan and town affairs because conditions remained unsettled for so long.

Married men lived in the households of their wives. Marriages were often brittle because a man retained primary responsibility to his own matriclan (that of his own mother and sisters), rather than to that of his wife or wives. All the children of sisters belonged to the same clan. Their brothers had the primary responsibility for their teaching, training, and assuming roles in society. Closer to him than his own children by his wife, these niblings {* = nieces and nephews of US kinship, children of siblings} were under his tutelage to become proper adults, well informed about their clan heritage and affairs. Yet men were often away for long periods – trading, raiding, and visiting. Therefore, closely related women formed a basic unit, jointly raising crops and rearing children.

Hurons were divided into eight matriclans (Turtle, Wolf, Bear, Beaver, Deer, Hawk, Porcupine, Snake). Every village had most of these clans because each was exogamous – members had to bring in spouses from outside the community. When conducting ceremonies, these clans were grouped into three phratries called Turtles, Wolves, or Deer. These clans and phratries were shared among a confederacy of four tribes, two of which joined in 1590 and 1610 for mutual protection after devastation from epidemics and intertribal warfare.

Various curing guilds and interclan councils, requiring the cooperation of unrelated neighbors, helped to fuse the town into a cohesive community. Such sharing became even more important after the arrival of the French and trade goods in the 1600s. Iron tools were slower to dull than stone tools, making life easier. These new exotic goods also encouraged Hurons to elaborate their rituals, particularly their Feast of the Dead

(Kettle). Participation defined membership in a town and affirmed clanship. There was no higher level regional organization like that developed by the Iroquois League.

Every decade or so, a Huron village would gather to express this unity during a rite known as "The Kettle", presumably because the excavated bowl filled with bones was intended ritually to "cook" the dead for final release of their souls. When the nearby fields were depleted of nutrients and local firewood was scarce, a village relocated. While these fields had a useful life of 4-6 years, Hurons were able to plant them for almost a decade by adding wood ashes and carefully weeding the crops.

Before moving, as a last act at the old village, most of the dead were removed from their scaffolds or graves to be placed together into a common ossuary (bone pit). If any flesh remained, kinswomen lovingly cleaned it off as a final gesture of affection. Many gifts and offerings also went into the pit at this joyous pre-planned celebration. In contrast, the original funerals had been done in grief and haste.

At each actual death and initial burial, mourning had been impromptu. The closest relatives remained unkempt and literally prostrate with grief, laying silently with their faces pressed to the earth for ten days. Public mourning by close kin continued for a year. Years later, a renewed emotional outburst occurred at the Kettle.

In all, this final rite was the culmination of a long process of death and mourning. Not everyone was treated same, neither during life nor after death. While most people were typically buried on a high scaffold before remaining bones were eventually buried, there were exceptions. Babies were buried in pathways with the hope that their spirit would be reborn into a passing woman. The bones of captives and witches {* = antisocial members} were merely thrown out into midden piles.

Individuals who drowned or froze to death had to be treated in a special way because they had offended underwater spirits. The body was taken to the town cemetery and cut up. The flesh and entrails were burned and the bones buried. Anyone who died a violent death was buried under a small earthen mound with a bark hut set on top. This was their final resting place since the bones of any such person would not be added to the ossuary. He or she was believed to be disruptive or, at least, unquiet. They would be disturbing to the harmony of the other village dead. In the afterworld, suicides and slain warriors lived apart.

The Kettle released the second soul of a Huron from the village environs. This allowed it to rejoin a prior soul that had already gone to the afterworld. There, everyone lived much as before but with less hardship. Some of these lingering souls went there via the Milky Way. Others went along the south shore of a bay, visiting a rock where spirits got paint and encountering an immortal who removed their brains and memory. This route passed over a deep ravine where the unlucky could fall in and drown. Because this journey was so arduous, souls of the very old and the very young never left. Instead, they stayed at abandoned villages and planted ghost crops in the depleted fields.

Eventually, during the international competition caused by the fur trade, particularly the Beaver Wars after these animals were locally exterminated, a huge force of Iroquois devastated the Huron towns in 1649. The survivors scattered. Their descendants include the Hurons living at Lorette near Quebec and Wyandots living in Ontario, Michigan, and Oklahoma.

HoChungara (Winnebago) of the Great Lakes

Among nations of the Midwest, the mythic traditions of the Ho-chunk (called Winnebago by Algonkians) are particularly well known. Their homeland was Wisconsin, although half later found refuge in Nebraska. There, Paul Radin undertook 1908-13 research, followed by a lifetime of friendship and writing. Hochungara distinguish two types of literature. _Waikan_ {* = what is sacred, mythic} is set in the fixed past and noted for happy endings. _Worak_ {* = what is recounted, experienced, historic} occurs in a time that is subject to memory, often with tragic outcomes.

A sacred epic describes the creation by Earthmaker, once known only by initiates of the Medicine or Mystic Lodge. This is a guild of shamans like the Mide of the Ojibwa. Interestingly, the story of how Rabbit (Hare) founded the Medicine Lodge is regarded as historical, not sacred, because it directly relates to humans, like the origin accounts for the various clans.

Through amazing circumstances, Jasper Blowsnake described this epic of the mystic lodge, whose ritual initiation of new members enacted this creation of the world. It was later retold during memorials for deceased members. Blowsnake gave his account only with the greatest reluctance. He felt compelled by a series of startling events. By 1908, the peyote religion, brought to the Ho-chunk by John Rave, had achieved a core of strong converts. It included men who had formerly been members of the medicine lodge. In their zeal to convert others, three old men were convinced to give Radin an account of Ho-chunk creation, though they had to leave Nebraska before doing so to avoid revenge from local spirits.

Thus, in the top floor of a small hotel in Sioux City, Iowa, precisely at midnight, these men began the saga. They finished it five hours later. By the next afternoon, every Ho-chunk knew what had happened and many pressed for a public reading of the text. Previously, only elite members of the lodge knew its details. Agreement was quickly reached. The native text was read to a stunned audience. Much anger focused on the old men, but John Rave gave them firm support until Radin left for New York at the end of the summer, taking along the untranslated text.

The following year more converts were made, including Jasper Blowsnake, who was regarded as the most knowledgeable member of the mystic lodge. As a test of his change of faith, peyote leaders urged Jasper to dictate the fullest account and he agreed to recite the Ho-chunk words of the rite. He warned, though, that someone would die from this forced telling. Radin wrote the text in longhand (this was before tape recorders), working six hours a day for two months.

As the recitation ended, Radin received a telegram that his own father was gravely ill, dying a few days later. More grievously, Radin was distressed that while he had a native text of unusual significance, never to be repeated, he lacked a proper translation because Jasper blamed himself for the death of Radin's father.

Later, in Washington, DC, Radin gained a literal translation of the rite from a visiting Ho-chunk. But that speaker was not a member of the lodge and could not understand the many esoteric, poetic, and metaphoric usages.

After great effort, Radin returned to the Nebraska Ho-chunk, but Jasper avoided Paul until he took ill and had to remain at the home of a friend. There, upon reflection, he decided that telling the medicine rite to Paul Radin was indeed "his mission in life".

For the first month, Jasper corrected the prior dictation. The translation itself took six hours a day for another two and a half months. Lodge members remained bitter at Jasper for half a year, but the peyote believers continually extolled his courage for performing a dangerous and heroic act.

Four other mythic cycles were added later. After creation by Earthmaker, various protagonists engaged in complex activities to make the world as it is today. Radin saw these different cycles – named for the Trickster, Hare, Red Horn, and Twins – as a temporal series defining the psychological growth of the individual and tribe. Each of the four, in turn, was progressively gaining and giving virtues of character to those who came after.

Trickster lived during a primordial, unformed cosmos of vague beings. Many of his traits were (or foreshadowed) human ones, but his total being was never specified. From the beginning, although he is a chief, all of his actions were contrary to modern ideals. Some of his adventures were prophetic, others were parodies, yet all contributed to an increasing orderliness in the world.

Hare (or Rabbit), born of a spirit father and human mother, was raised by his grandmother, the Earth. In his cycle, humans made their initial appearance and gained advantages as he matured and learned about parts of his body through a series of misadventures. Through his actions, few of them laudatory, various customs and institutions began. These included the use of tobacco, slain bear thanking rituals, and menstruation observances, along with the special creation of the medicine rite.

Red Horn was heroic, living in a well-differentiated world with a wide range of defined characters – including humans, monsters, and giants. A majestic figure, his death was avenged by his sons, who revived him, then rid the earth of giants. They received war bundles from Thunderbirds, a great benefit for human beings, who now came into their own during this cycle.

Twins (Flesh and Stump) behaved as bravado juveniles, with a promise of new beginnings. Their contrasting temperaments caused trouble, until they learned a final lesson from Earthmaker that curbed their unbridled enthusiasms. After killing one of the four animals (Snakes) holding up the earth, they were terrorized by a giant Turkey to learn fear. Thus, the twins benefited from prior characters to mature as full individuals. Since they had at least one adventure with Red Horn, they were doubly tied into the Hochungara mythic past.

By the end of all these cycles, this world included four underworlds led, from bottom to top, by Turtle, Trickster, Earthmaker, and Rabbit. The sky was supported by four island weights as anchors ("island quiet makers"), located at its corners. One was near Effigy Mounds National Park, along the Iowa shore of the Mississippi. There, in addition to a collapsed Longtail mural on a cliff face and piled earthen mounds shaped like lines and dots, a row of heaped hummocks in the shape or bears and birds march up the hillside. At the Gottschall Cave in southern Wisconsin, some of their images were painted on the walls of this shrine, in continuous use for 1700 years after AD 350.

Ojibwa (Anishanabe)

Both Cree and Ojibwa represent Algic populations expanding outward from Sault Ste Marie, the fishery at the intersection of Lakes Huron, Michigan, and Superior.[109] Cree has two main dialects, divided by Hudson's Bay. East Cree has three subdialects of Eastern, Innu (Naskapi), and Montagnais; while West Cree has six (indicated by different sounds, known as reflexes, of the Proto-Algonkian letter "l"). These are Attikamek (using r in place of l), Moose (l), East and West Swampy (n for l), Woods (dh for l), and Plains (y for l), including Mitchif with its nouns and consonants derived from French.

Ojibwa's eight major dialects, from the St Lawrence to Lake Winnipeg, are Algonquin, Eastern, Central, Ottawa, Southwestern, Northwestern, Severn, and Saulteaux. Each represents both a distinct population, and, in the case of Ottawa, greater prestige because of its use in intertribal trade and diplomacy.

Eventually four (or five) Ojibwa adaptations resulted. These are known as Southeastern (Ontario peninsula, Lower Michigan), Southwestern (Chippewa, along southern Lake Superior in Minnesota, Wisconsin, Michigan Upper Peninsula), Northern (across Ontario, Manitoba), and Saulteaux (from the Sault), though those who moved far to the West became Bungi (or Plains Ojibwa).

The prehistoric economy shifted by season from winter hunting camps, to spring maple syruping, to summer fishing towns.[110] Women "owned" maple tree groves known as sugarbush that were tapped for sap. Ancestors moving south added farming of corn, beans, and squash. Chippewa added wild ricing and bison hunting learned from Dakota and other Siouians they drove further west.[111] About 1650, in the aftermath of the defeat and dispersal of the Huron by the Iroquois, Ojibwa began gathering at summer towns where clans mingled and mixed. In 1736, a Dakota massacre of French traders at Lake of the Woods mobilized Ojibwa to push westward.

Northern Ojibwa moved away from farming, ricing, and sugaring areas, abandoned clans and Midewiwin (below), and concentrated on fish and small game. Birchbark remained important around the Great Lake for canoes, houses, bins, and artworks. These last include cut out patterns and doily-like designs made in bark panels that are folded and punctured by women with their teeth.[112]

Saulteaux movement along the Berens River of Manitoba, carefully traced through genealogical charts, shows occupation by animal name dodems, many including several patrilines (each indicated by a different capitol letter). At the outlet into Lake Winnipeg, these "clans" are Bullhead, Kingfisher (A B), Moose C, Pelican (A B C D E), and Sturgeon A; midway at Little Grand Rapids are Duck, Kingfisher (A B D), Moose B, Pelican (B C D), and Sturgeon A. Inland at Pikangikum are Loon, Moose B, Pelican D, and Sturgeon (A B). One Moose A patriline of sigers who became trading and then elected chiefs included Yellow Legs, Bear, Jacob Berens, and William (Billy) Berens, the source for much of this understanding.[113]

William Warren,[114] a Minnesota Ojibwa elected to the state legislature, suggested segmentation into five idealized phratries of 1) Fish = Catfish, Merman, Sturgeon, Pike, Whitefish, Sucker; 2) Crane = Crane, Eagle; 3) Loon = Loon, Goose, Cormorant; 4) Bear = Bear, and 5) Marten = Marten, Moose, Deer. Of particular note, all are associated with water and thereby strongly suggest origins as patriclans owning fisheries along Lake Superior. As Ojibwa dispersed, these names, each a dodem,[115] served as labels among far-flung kin.[116]

140

Of these fisheries, the most important was that at Sault Ste Marie. Men positioned their canoes below the rapids, probing with long dip nets to bag five or so whitefish until they had a full load. Then they put in to shore for women and families to unload, slice up, and dry these fish for winter meals and extensive trade.

Nearby, moose, deer, woodland caribou, and beaver were also abundant.[117] A new lodge was built each winter on the family's "claimed" hunting tract. Large bones from successes were hung from a special tree, and the camp was kept as clean as possible to "please" the immortal bosses who provided hunting luck. Only one married couple occupied this house, though the husband was often absent "running trap lines" and hunting. Boys slept on his side, girls on that of the wife, divided by gender but united by shared workload. These seasonal activities drew attention to one's birth in summer or in winter, which was believed to confer abilities to control appropriate weather. These were personal traits, not formal moieties.

Large mammal populations collapsed by the 1820s, forcing Ojibwa to rely on smaller animals and develop a less communal society. For example, during the winter of 1670-71, hunters on Manitoulin Island killed 2400 moose by using only snares.[118] In the century after 1680, armed by the French and advancing with fur trading posts, patriclans gave way to kindreds. These were nonetheless identified by labels and logos referring to these same "aquatic" animal dodems. As these animals dwindled, a cult of Wabano magicians specializing in handling fire and boiling pots tried to bring them back, but to no avail. Two hundred years later, moose and caribou were making only a modest comeback.

While a Kettle held every three years had once provided a focus for community sentiments, after 1700, the Midewiwin, reformed at Chequemegon (La Point, Wisconsin), took its place. It involved and involves a progressive series of initiations, each adding detail, meaning, and powerful access to universal forces. Overall, members are divided into Life grades with Earth and Sky degrees. A final Death grade was entered by the ghost when a living replacement was initiated. Sometimes, these events were rehearsed by moving peg figures upon diagrams traced in the sand. Creation epics were told with greater thoroughness at each higher degree, along with curing techniques and medicines.[119] Senior leaders had birchbark scrolls depicting immortal patrons, places, passages, and serial procedures. Mide membership indicated rank among leading families. An intertribal Great Lakes network came to include Menomini, Winnebago, Ottawa, Potawatomi, Sauk, Fox, and Kickapoo.

Boys and some girls were sent out before puberty on vision quests. They often waited on small scaffolds, called "nests," set high up in trees. The immortal who "gifted" a successful child remained with him or her until death approached, as long as "it" was treated with respect and regard. These beings belonged to the same moral and emotional world as other than human persons, and were treated as such.[120] Dreams also influence creativity since "Women 'dream' beadwork patterns, songs, decorations for a dress, complicated dance patterns; men dream traditional tales, or tales about culture heros, or have visions of the architecture of the after-world."[121]

The safest communication with immortals occurs through a membrane that provided minimal separation. These include stretched surfaces, such as a skin drum head, a film of grease in a scrying bowl, hair oil to promote good thoughts, hollow rattles, and thin bones like shoulder blades cast into a fire and retrieved to predict upcoming events.[122] The use of such oracles served to distribute responsibility for success or failure throughout the entire group, not just the hunter alone. At its most dramatic, though in reverse from

Tillers Lakes

most domestic situations, the wall of a shaking tent kept immortals inside with the shaman, while the interested human audience remained outside.

Ojibwa kin terms applied only to relatives by birth. Cross-cousin marriage was the preferred pattern, linking distant kin of another hunting household and animal dodem. Kin terms distinguish generalized classes of siblings from spouses. These were treated respectively with reserve or familiarity, mostly as defined by gender. Siblings maintain a distancing formality that extends to all known sisters or brothers. Cross cousins of opposite genders could, did, and do joke, play, and generally act to indicate they were "intended" for each other in marriage. The span across generation and age between grandparents and grandchildren was expressed by great warmth tinged with awe for a long, productive life.[123]

Some time in the 1870s, Tailfeather Woman, a Dakota, fled from a battle with American soldiers in which her four sons were slain. Hiding among the lily pads in a pond for four days, she had a vision to construct a drum suspended from four arched legs, to compose special songs, and to transfer these drums among tribes, often former enemies, to create peace. These Dream Drums have since spread among the Woodlands and Plains.[124]

Ojibwa survived and even thrived in the aftermath of European dispossession and disease. They spread themselves thinly over much of northern North America. Using their diverse skills as fishers, hunters, and wild harvesters, they maintained loose ties through shared dodems and periodic gatherings. Under the auspices of leading families, key meetings occurred at Midewiwin initiations, which also served a wide variety of social, political, and religious purposes. There, marriages, councils, and cures also took place.

109. Helen Hornbeck Tanner, Atlas of Great Lakes Indian History 1987; The Ojibwas, A Critical Bibliography 1976.

110. Robert Brightman, Grateful Prey ~ Rock Cree Human-Animal Relationships 1993.

111. Thomas Vennum, Wild Rice and the Ojibway People 1988.

112. Ruth Landes, The Ojibwa Woman 1938.

113. William "Billy" Berens's research work with Irving Hallowell have made these Ojibwa world famous in academia, and a grandson with an earned PhD in history continues the tradition. As Jacob advised Billy, "Do not think you know everything. You will see lots of new things and you will find a place in your mind for them all." Jennifer SH Brown, "A Place in Your Mind for them All." Chief William Berens, Being and Becoming Indian 1989: 204-225.

114. William Warren, History of the Ojibways ~ Based on Traditions and Oral Statements 1885: 44-50.

115. This Ojibwa concept of "dodem" became popularized as the totem by Henry Schoolcraft (1793-1864), US Indien agent at the Sault married into a local family. After his wife Jane Johnson died, leaving two children, he married Mary, a Southern woman whose racial intolerance approached bigotry. He published several collections of Ojibwa or Iroquois stories, which inspired Henry Wadsworth Longfellow to mix and match them under the name of the Iroquois Hiawatha. He undertook the first federally- sponsored research to provide a summary on Native Americans, producing six massive, disorganized volumes. See Henry Rowe Schoolcraft and the Ethnologist as Historian and Moralist, Robert Bieder, Science Encounters the Indian, 1820-1880, The Early Years of American Ethnology 1986 Chapter 5: 146-193.

116. Edward S Rogers, Southeastern Chippewa, Smithsonian Handbook of North American Indians, <u>Northeast</u>, Volume 15: 760-771.

117. Charles Bishop, <u>The Northern Ojibwa and the Fur Trade</u> 1974.

118. W Vernon Kinietz, Chippewa, <u>The Indians of the Western Great Lakes, 1615-1760</u> 1940: 317-329. In 1836, by land cession from Ojibwa and Ottawa, Sir Francis Bond Head, Lt Governor of Canada, established Manitoulin Island as a reserve for all natives of Upper Canada.

119. Frances Densmore, <u>Chippewa Music</u> I 1910, II 1913; <u>Chippewa Customs</u> 1929.

120. William Jones, <u>Ojibwa Texts</u>, Truman Michelson, ed, Volume 7, Parts 1 & 2 1917 & 1919.

121. Ruth Landes, <u>Ojibwa Woman</u> 1938: 9.

122. Adrian Tanner, <u>Bringing Home Animals</u> 1979: 130-135.

123. A Irving Hallowell, <u>The Ojibwa of Berens River</u> 1992; RW Dunning, <u>Social and Economic Change among the Northern Ojibwa</u> 1959; Victor Lytwyn, The Fur Trade of the Little North 1986.

124. Thomas Vennum, <u>The Ojibwa Dance Drum</u>,~ Its History and Construction 1982.

Metis -- A New People

Since the 1850s, Metis have made up a quarter (1/4) of First Nations people in Canada. They emerged from particular trading conditions in the Great Lakes and Plains, where large distances separated supplies from consumers. Though transracial children were long a product of French reliance on natives, distinct Metis only emerged with their occupation of the interior. Initially, French offspring had to choose to be French or native because the coastal factory system made neighbors of both natives and newcomers. Then Samuel Champlain established trade factories up the St Lawrence after 1608. This trade developed into a link between Hurons and Montreal after 1641, using <u>courer de bois</u> {* = "woods runners, rangers", more often rascals, roustabouts, and rowdies} who lived much of their time among native communities to save expenses.[125]

After <u>engages Canadien</u> (contract workers) were allowed to retire on interior lands instead of under the watchful eyes of Montreal, they supplied forts by itinerant peddling (<u>en derouine</u>) in groups led by a literate clerk (<u>commis</u>). He served as a middleman-broker between hunters and traders. Side pork and corn had formerly supplied Montreal fur brigades, dominated by the Northwest Company by the 1780s. These foods were replaced by more portable and available wild rice taken from the Great Lakes into the Plains. Like Ojibwa dodem (totems), each York boat brigade was named for a locale and an animal, such as Badgers (<u>Blaireau</u>) of Saskatchewan, or Bulls (<u>Taureaux</u>) of Red River.

Retired traders chose to stay in the Plains as bison hunters and horsemen.[126] They hunted with a determination, killing all they could while acting as their own masters. Their greed was highly offensive to most natives. Producing large families, most sons became hunters except for a few who were educated to become clerks. Daughters were married to allies. These families survived the British take over, but not American settlement, which destroyed the very basis of their livelihood.

The main Metis settlement, modern downtown Winnipeg, grew up at the joining of the Assiniboine and Red rivers, divided into riverine long lots in French style. Each started at the river bank and went straight back into the uplands, providing ownership of several terrains and their resources. Just north was Kildonan, founded by 1812 Protestant

Highland Scot crofters sent as settlers by Thomas Douglas, Earl of Selkirk. At nearby St Peters lived Swampy Cree and Saulteaux Ojibwa. Northwest Company agents agitated Metis against Selkirkers for taking up land. This led to the Battle of Seven Oaks (9 June 1816), when British-educated Metis leader Cuthbert Grant killed over 20 Scots, including the colony governor Robert Semple.

During the final, cut-throat fur trade competition, the Hudson's Bay Company (HBC) hired commercial efficiency managers in 1810. These advisors forced the 1821 merger with the Northwest Company. Monsieur Grant was paid 300 pounds a year and styled "Warden of the Plains" by the HBC to appease Metis.

In springtime, Metis planted root crops and barley, then left for a buffalo hunt. Their transport was called Red River carts with huge screeching wheels. All headed for the rendezvous at Pembina, where they elected hunt sigers. They voted on 10 _capitaines_, who each selected 10 guides called _soldats_. The foremost captain, often Gabriel Dumont, nominal overall head, was known as _le President_ or war chief. Each day was in the charge of one of the captains and one of the guides, who, at dawn, raised the hunt flag over his own cart. The daily captain positioned his guides, riding in pairs, around the rows of advancing carts. If these scouts saw a herd, they rode away from each other. If sighting enemies, they rode at each other. Then the cart flag was lowered. This act passed authority to the president, who quickly organized the group and gave the command of "_allez_".

When taking bison, shooting from horseback, each hunter tossed a bit of clothing upon his kill before riding on to the next one. Lead balls were held in his mouth, and powder was added on the run. The gun charge was set by ramming the gunstock against the saddle or thigh. After 1860, repeating rifles made kills of 20 bison routine. Slaughter took a heavy toll. The last hunt was 1874, when bison were doomed.

When a foray ended, each hunter butchered his own prey. His wife and daughters sliced, dried, and pounded it. This trade used standard bison hide sacks, each filled with 90 pounds of pemmican {* = a high energy food of dried meat flour, melted fat, and berries}. These were sent to Norway House on Lake Winnipeg to provision York boat brigades.

The summer hunt returned in time to harvest crops, which had been tended by the old and infirm who stayed behind. Each fall the Metis Council of Assiniboia set the date for haying on open prairie lands, a necessity for those with large herds and families.

In 1844, Norman Kittson, a Canadian linked to the Marion Metis family, opened a post of the American Fur Company at Pembina. It eventually attracted many younger Metis men freeing themselves from Grant. In 1849, HBC sued four Metis (particularly Guillaume Sayer incriminated by his own son) for trading furs in violation of the monopoly of their company charter. While Louis Riel (father, pere) and 300 armed Metis surround the courthouse, the men were convicted but pardoned as a general lesson. Legal victory meant nothing until commercial punishments were applied, particularly after Metis developed strong ties with St Paul (Minnesota) to trade winter bison hides as robes and warmers.

In 1869, HBC transferred Assiniboia to Canada but Louis Riel (son, fils) blocked the arrival of the Lt Governor designate William McDougall. The 1870 Manitoba Act (regarded as a treaty by Riel) was supposed to protect the corporate survival of Metis communities. But individualism won out. Personal opportunity found favor over corporate privilege. Many Metis fled to Dakota Territory, then Montana, as did Riel. He was asked back in **1885** by his people to lead a last effort at Batoche to keep the promised safeguards for corporate, communal Metis. He failed and was hanged.[127] By then his earlier Catholic seminary experience had inspired a mysticism that has further distanced him from Protestant Canada.

Metis reserves were created between 1870-1900 in the Prairie Provinces. Many families were forced to eke out a living near no-man's "road allowances" along railroad right of ways and crown lands. During the 1929 Depression, Metis politicized their stuggle to stay alive. A 1934 Royal Commission resulted in the 1938 Metis Betterment Act, creating 8 colonies in northern Alberta. Today, Metis political groups are active in Ontario, Manitoba, Saskatchewan, Northwest Territories, and Alberta, following the lead of the 1981 Metis National Council. Defeat of the 1992 Charlottetown Accord dashed a Metis Nation Accord, though efforts continue for justice for Canada's "New People." Their national flag is blue with a white ∞ infinity sign.

125. John Foster, The Plains Metis, Chapter 18, <u>Native Peoples</u>: The Canadian Experience 1995: 414-443.

126. Donald Purich, <u>The Metis</u> 1988.

127. Punishment, however, fell heaviest on natives, who had their annuities curtailed, along with treaty guarantees, to force their compliance to the will of Ottawa. In punishment for the Frog Lake massacre, eight men, Plains Cree and Assiniboin, were hanged at Battleford on 27 November 1885, see Blair Stonechild and Bill Waiser, <u>Loyal till Death</u> ~ Indians and the North-West Rebellion 1997.

10. East Culture Area

Ecosystem

The East had a temperate deciduous forest of white oak, maple, white-tailed deer, and turkey. These trees were stratified into horizontal woodland zones with animals living in habitats at different heights. Glaciation left sections of the area poorly drained. Deer thrived around these marshes and ponds.

The East was mostly populated by speakers of the Algonkian (Algic) stock. Interspersed were clusters of Iroquoian speakers, such as the Five Nations of New York and the Cherokee of the Carolinas. Algonkian tenders north and west of the St. Lawrence River were hunters. As just noted, those living along the Great Lakes fished, hunted, and gathered wild rice. They had clans traced through fathers, while the Subarctic Algonkians had kindreds.

In recent centuries, ancestral Algonkians departed from Minnesota for the northern Plains to become the Cheyenne, Blackfeet, and Arapaho. They left behind their towns and clans for a life of tending bison herds. More remotely related to Algics were Ritwan languages in northern California like Yurok and Wiyot.

Foods

In this mixed economy, staple foods were deer hunted by men and maize farmed by women. Male subsistence contributions predominated during the winter and the spring runs of fish. Female contributions dominated the fall, the time of natural and field harvests. At European contact, women tended maize, beans, and squash. There is archaeological evidence for the earlier native domestication of sunflowers, Jerusalem artichoke, amaranth, and other local foods. Female labor was viewed as more constant and demanding in contrast to the more sporadic and removed exertions of men.

Abundant wild foods were gathered from hardwood forests, hills, rivers, beaches, ponds, and marshes. The ever-increasing population later adopted maize, beans, and squash about a thousand years ago. People moved to likely farmlands, becoming the Algic, Iroquoian, and Gulf speaking tribes of the historic period. Women assumed farming chores, while men continued to hunt, mostly deer, during the fall and winter. In the spring, both men and women gathered along rivers and streams to catch and cure fish for storage. In the Northeast, periodic fish runs assured abundance, while the Southeast, mobilizing large labor parties, used plant extracts (poisons) to kill or stun fish in empounded waters to take sufficient quantities. Along the coast, huge refuse piles, called shellfish middens, indicate that camps along beaches were used for millennia.

Basic Bonds

Evidence from the Delaware (Lenape) and Creek (Muskoke) suggests that each village once "belonged" to a single matriclan with an ancient bond with that location and a large membership. Its members held all important offices and invited members of other matriclans to live there as spouses or friends. After contact, people from these separate clan villages joined into multi-clan towns that were nominally under the leadership of the head of the most numerous clan.

EAST Peoples

Algic	Macro-Siouian
	Iroquoian / Siouian
Northeast	
Pennacook	Erie
Massachusetts	Huron (Wendat, Wyandot)
Wampanoag	Neutral
Narragansett	Tobacco
Niantic	Iroquois
Podunk	Mohawk
Montauk	Oneida
Wappinger	Onondaga
Mohegan-Pequot	Cayuga
Mahican	Seneca
Delaware	Tuscarora (post 1712)
Unami	Susquehanna-Conestoga
Monsey	
Nanticoke	() represents a tribal synonym or alternate name
-	- represents linguistic closeness

Algic / Gulf	Macro-Siouian
	Iroquoian / Siouian

	Southeast	
Powhatan		Cherokee
Pamlico		Tuscarora (pre 1712)
	/ Muskogean	Nottaway
	Choctaw-Chickasaw	Meherrin
	Koasati-Alabama	/ Tutelo
	Hitchiti-Mikasuki	Catawba
	Creek-Seminole	Biloxi
	Atakapan	Ofo
	Tunican	Saponi
	Natchezan	
	Timucuan	Isolate
	Chitimachan	Yuchi
Calusa ?		

In the harsher climate of the Northeast, winters were spent living communally in longhouses. These bark-covered homes were occupied by related women. Each had family cubicles along either side of a central hallway dotted by fires. These female-linked residents formed a matrilineage, which in turn belonged to a matri-clan. Various aspects of nature served as clan totems. Wolf, Bear, Turtle, Snipe, and Snake were fairly common names. Often the totem of the clan was painted over the doorways at each end of the longhouse.

Male responsibilities for child rearing and education fell to the mother's brother, rather than to the father. The former was a member of the same matriclan as the children. Their own father was not. He belonged to his own mother's clan and was responsible for educating and disciplining his own sister's children.

After winter was over, families circulated through a series of long established resorts (camps) across their territories. During the rest of the year, people lived in wigwams (bark-covered, domed houses), sometimes in tents, set in hunting and gathering areas. Periodically, they would return to the towns of longhouses and fields in order to tend the crops and to harvest them.

Members of Southeast matri-clans and towns lived in square compounds with buildings at the four sides. Each cluster was occupied by a married couple. The separate buildings each had particular functions, like cooking, storage, greeting, and sleeping in this warmer climate.

Each village appears to have been linked, in terms of diffuse tribal identity, with other villages. Larger communities shared a water course, dialect, rituals, and span of endogamous marriages. Therefore, a tribe was composed of interacting matrilineages, clans, and villages that were probably centered upon a focal town. There, a tribal leader was selected from a special clan, and supervised important annual rituals. The basis of tribal identity, therefore, was religious and not political. Members of a tribe defined themselves by performing the same ceremony, rather than adhering to the same leaders. The community was based on communion, not only alliances.

In proto-historic times, many Eastern tribes also belonged to larger confederacies sharing a common allegiance to a primary or "capitol" town where a sacred fire burned and a chieftain coordinated major ritual events. These confederacies seem to have arisen in self-defense against chiefdoms. With population collapse from epidemics and massive slaving, chiefdom survivors themselves founded confederacies.

At these tribal and confederacy levels, matriclans were subsumed into phratries and moieties. For example, those matriclans named for birds, clouds, and types of weather were logically classified as a Sky phratry. Those named for plants, animals, trees, etc., might compose a Land phratry. Other appropriate aquatic clans might belong to a Water phratry. Common Eastern moieties were Peace/War and White/Red, best reported for the Creek and Iroquois.

Leadership

This complex social structure included mutually articulated patterns of leadership and rank. Congruent with matrilineality, positions of leadership passed from men in the category of "mother's brother" to heirs in the category of "sister's sons" or an uncle to a nephew related through the mother. Eastern matriclans and towns had both civil and war leaders. Civil or Peace leaders were expected to be older, wiser, more concerned with rituals and matters internal to his constituency. His duties have more feminine associations. War captains were expected to be younger, fiercer, and more concerned with external diplomacy, in more masculine ways.

During periods of warfare, the civil official surrendered authority to the war leader. When hostilities ceased, civil leadership resumed responsibility to negotiate the terms of peace and to exchange tokens of trust, such as wampum belts. In the historic period, war leaders were sometimes killed by their own people for presuming to initiate peace negotiations.

In colonial times, however, the almost constant state of warfare with European settlers and tribal enemies gave warriors unprecedented authority and might. Some Cherokee went so far as to secede from their traditional villages and the advice of senior civil leaders. They founded their own villages and established their own system of ranking. For example, by January of 1777, a faction of young Cherokee warriors, collectively called the Chicamaugas, had founded several new settlements under the nominal leadership of Dragging-Canoe. He was the warlike son of the old and influential leader called Little Carpenter.[128] The famous League of the Iroquois was itself seriously threatened by the growing unruliness of its younger warriors. However, these imbalances between the civil and the military spheres were caused by the destabilizing European presence, not traditional conditions.

Ranks

In addition to this alternating civil and war leadership, other prominent ranks were held by shamans, the owners of bundles (power packs) with associated rituals, and clan matrons. These shamans frequently belonged to ritual consortia (guilds) that were dedicated to specific tasks, such as curing, plant germination, animal wellbeing, sorcery, and so forth. The False Faces (carved wooden masks) are the best known of perhaps a dozen Iroquois sodalities.[129] Creeks recognized several classes of shamans. These were knowing prophets, fasting doctors, sucking doctoresses, weather controllers, and sorcerers, among others.

Mystic bundles are not well reported for the East, but they had important functions among Iroquois, Delaware, Cherokee, and Seminole. In each case, they and their associated knowledge and rituals were held by men of high status and transmitted through members of prestigious families. Among Delawares (Lenapes), important persons kept medicine, love, and witchcraft bundles. Their important families transmitted bundles associated with Doll, Bear, Otter, and other tribal rites.

Although men hold positions of authority in matrilineal societies, they did and do so by virtue of connecting links through women as mothers and sisters. In several Eastern tribes some women held formal positions of authority in their own right. These include a Iroquois clan matron and Shawnee war matron (captainess). The matron was and is the senior most knowledgeable and active clanswoman. With the death of the holder of one of the fifty name-titles that compose the _royaner_ {* = federal chiefs of the Iroquois League}, the matron, in consultation with other clanswomen, selects the clansman who will succeed to the name-title. This successor is then installed by the other Federal chiefs at a Requickening.

If the successor proves incompetent in office, he will be warned by his clan matron three times. The first time she goes to him alone and admonishes him. The second time she goes together with the clan warrior, and both give warning. The third time she and the warrior give a final harangue before the warrior symbolically "de-horn" him. Iroquois royaner are likened to buck deer and wear special caps decorated with horns and feathers as insignia of tribe and position. With their assumption of a name-title, they are said to receive their "horns of office." Prehistorically, we know from Moundbuilder graves, each chief actually had such an antler headdress, sometime mounted on a copper base.

Among the Creek, elderly and gray-haired men who had led distinguished, unblemished lives were called Revered or Beloved Men. They were also called "the brains of the Busk" because they were the recognized custodians of knowledge, especially with regard to the supreme event in Creek life and culture □ The Busk Green Corn Rite.

Moreover, Creeks and Cherokees also recognized a small and select number of virtuous females who were known as Beloved, Pretty, or War Women (_giga'_). Cherokee may have once had a Beloved Woman as matron for each of their seven matricians. The pro-white exploits of Nancy Ward (1740?-1822), the last and youngest Cherokee Beloved Woman, are famous.

As elsewhere in Native America, the tribe respected and admired those special persons who successfully envisioned guardian spirit partners. Visionaries were eligible for positions of prominence. These were usually men, although some "gifted" women were reported. Those people without proper visions, access to positions of authority, powerful relations, ability, or acceptable moral reputation occupied a commoner or lesser status. As distinct from visionaries who fulfilled the ideal state, Delawares say that those without a gift of _puwha_ were "empty". They nonetheless led happy and productive lives. At the tribal or village margins were the very poor, the disabled, the incompetent, and war captives who had not been successfully integrated into a normal family.

Early missionary accounts, such as those by Moravian John Heckewelder for the Delaware, make clear that there were elite families who consistently intermarried, were generous to the least fortunate, managed larger and more populous households, and either held or were closely related to positions of importance.

Cosmology: _Myth, Ritual_

In the north, when winter blizzards kept everyone close to home, stories were the primary form of both instruction and entertainment. While everyone was together, the full-length versions of legends could be told without interruption. These stories explained the workings of the universe and human foibles. They gave moral lessons without directly confronting the guilty.

Each tribe or nation identified itself in terms of a unifying ritual. Throughout the East, this was often a Green Corn Ceremony. It was and is held in the fall just before harvest when the crop was in the milk stage. Still alive and able to appreciate this ceremony of thanksgiving, the corn ears were then picked for eating and storage.[130] Iroquois (among others) held thanksgiving rites throughout the year for each food as it became available, in addition to celebrations of life leaps and funerals.

The Iroquois Midwinter Ceremony formerly included the sacrifice of white dogs as a gesture of devotion to the Creator. Now, through 1800 reforms, it is a centerpiece of the Good Word (*Gaiwiyo*) of the remarkable prophet known by his Seneca (Turtle clan *royaner*) name-title of Handsome Lake.

Another elaborate world renewal rite was the Big House Rite of the Delawares (Lenape), which has lapsed since the 1940s. For tribes like the Huron of the Great Lakes, who lived at the border of the northern limit for farming, the national ritual was the Kettle.

Indeed, archaeological evidence indicated many Great Lakes and Coastal tribes had a mortuary complex with such a "Kettle" Feast of the Dead. It was held every decade or so, when burials were dug up so their bones could be carefully cleaned, individually wrapped to rattle during a night-long dance, and then communally buried with valuable grave goods in an ossuary. For Southeastern province tribes, the bodies of deceased leaders were dried and kept by priesthoods in temples built upon earth mounds. Ordinary people had their bones picked clean for special burial after a long series of mortuary rituals.

In Iroquoian creation epics, deities dwell in the sky as "man beings" and as "man-woman (female) beings." When one of these man-woman fell from the sky, the earth was quickly created on the back of a turtle so that she would have somewhere to "land". Pregnant, she bore twin boys. The good son was called Sapling. He was born naturally and made helpful and beneficial things on the earth. The bad son was called Flint. He chose to be born through his mother's armpit, killing her. He went on to make the harmful and malevolent things in the world. Thus, when Sapling made butterflies, gourds, and rolling meadows; Flint made mosquitos, poison ivy, and earthquakes.

Most Eastern tribes recognized a supreme Creator linked with human life and thought. Delawares call him "The One Who Created Us By His Thoughts". Creeks refer to "Breath Holder." The Delaware world was created on the back of a turtle before a man and a woman sprang from a tysic cedar tree to become ancestral parents.

Although Eastern epics are creational, water usually is already present as a primordial preceding substance. The Creek and Yuchi shared a belief in the "earth diver" who helped create land from a lump of mud he "fished up" from the sea bottom.

Today

The East bore much of the brunt of first European contact, avarice, and manipulation. This was particularly evidenced in epidemics, slaving, beaver fur trade, and international conflicts. For this reason, strategies and reorganizations worked out by Eastern tribes and confederacies are worthy of special attention. Other culture areas resorted to them as the Frontier moved westward.

The Iroquois were revitalized by the "Good Message" preached by Handsome Lake. The Delaware kept moving west under the combined pressure of European encroachment, as well as their own belief in a supernatural punishment called *kʷulakan*, which was brought on by interpersonal hostility. However, the Unami Delaware were able to preserve the main outlines of their culture by revising their thanksgiving and Green Corn Dance into the 12 day long Big House Rite (Gamwing), last fully held in 1924, with attempts during World War II.

The Creek "opened up" their society to accept refugee peoples and whole towns into their White moiety. Similarly, Iroquois accepted other tribes as Props of their confederacy. By this process, both the Creek and the Iroquois maintained a reasonably steady population size during times of trouble. Some Southeastern tribes, especially the so-called Five Civilized Tribes (Creek, Choctaw, Cherokee, Chickasaw, Seminole) had members who built huge plantations by the labor of African slaves. Their descendants are listed on tribal rolls as "freedmen", though sometimes with contentious political status. Choctaws now use for "church" the word (*iksa*) they once used for "clan". Caddos use their word for "mound" for rural Oklahoma churches.

In many cases, new tribes were created from the remnants of former ones, such as the Mohegan from the Pequot after a 1640 war. A splinter group of Creeks became the Seminoles ("ferals") of Florida during the early 1800's.

Another radical strategy was represented by tribes from present Massachusetts, Connecticut and the Hudson River. They adopted Christianity and European styles as "Red Puritans" in Praying Towns. Some of their descendants, together with some Oneida Iroquois, continue to live in the vicinity of Green Bay, Wisconsin, driven far from their homelands despite their best efforts to blend in with the English.

Some Iroquois, Mississippi Choctaw, and a scattering of tri-racial remnant groups continue to occupy their homelands in the East. While all these tribal societies have been deeply affected by Americanization, several of them are reintegrating their cultures. During Colonial times, even wampum was transformed from being a pledge of trust and good faith to a kind of money or currency.

128. Fred Gearing, <u>Priests and Warriors</u> 1962: 103.
129. Frank Speck, <u>The Iroquois</u> 1945: 86.
130. John Witthoft, Green Corn Ceremonialism in the Eastern Woodlands 1949.

TRIBAL EXAMPLES

Mississippians

The Ho-chunks (Winnebagos) split from those Chiwere Siouian ancestors who were among the effigy mound builders. They were at the northern limit of the Mississippian tradition of chiefdoms and cult of the dead. Others, like Osage and Caddo, were mainstays. Indeed, in the aftermath of the Mississippian collapse, other confederacies, such as those of the Huron, Iroquois, Choctaw, and Creek, formed along its eastern border.

Across the Americas, a major reason for earth moving was the construction of such mounds. Best known as the sites for Adena burials and Mississippian temples, other monuments include Anasazi Pueblo passage markers, Tsimshian fort emplacements, and shaped effigies throughout the upper Midwest. These latter were often in the shapes of bears, birds, and other creatures that served as the namesakes of moieties and clans. Regardless of intent, form was always a significant consideration. The difference between Adena conicals and Mississippian sloping blocks probably represented beliefs about configurations of their worlds. Moreover, throughout the East, mounds were believed to be open inside, inhabited by spirits and the dead. Artificially constructed, mounds were the built up equivalent of a "holy home" inside hollow (and hallowed) hills, where a particular infrahuman species lived or gathered, as best known for the Pawnee animal lodges.[131]

All these mounds served as centering tysics for dispersed populations. Indeed, since the dead were the only permanent residents of a district, burial mounds provided deeds of claim passed through ancestral bloodlines.

Nor is this belief unique only to the Americas. In Celtic folklore, best known from Ireland, similar hallowed hills, called Shidhe, remain the dwelling places of fairies. These beings are a version of a prior godly race called the Tuatha De Danann. If a human got inside, he or she was thoroughly enchanted and lost all track of ordinary time. Those few who emerged described the insides, in a manner appropriate to their culture, as ornate palaces. Like American mounds, the Shidhe were the focus of periodic rituals, particularly during the four times each year when the "magic mounds" were "open" because the barrier between mortals and immortals was thin. On Samain (Nov 1, which became All Souls for Christians, the day after Halloween), all parts of the world renewed their connections, and, long ago, the Irish high king at Tara symbolically married the earth goddess to assure the prosperity of the country. On Beltine (May 1, May Day, Beltaine), cattle were driven between two fires to ward off disease. On Imbolc (Feb 1, now St Bridget's Day), ewe's milk was honored to mark spring renewal. On Lugnasad (Aug 1, harvest), games and festivals honored Lug of the Long Arm.[132] After conversion by Saint Patrick, the Irish Catholic Church redirected these events to saints and built churches and shrines atop these same holy places.

With the collapse of Mississippian chiefdoms, radical changes had to be devised. Previously, the heads of clans probably met inside temples atop mounds. After severe depopulation, beginning with Spanish-introduced diseases by Hernando de Soto, a communal labor force became difficult to muster. Mounds could no longer be built according to ritual demands, few leading families survived to direct the work and worship, and the labor force was now weak and sparse.

Ritual came down from the heights and into the town. The open plaza replaced the mound. Instead of ranked seats in the temple, men sat according to their clans in sunshades on the four sides of a town square. A sacred fire burned in the center, a symbol of the intense purity of the town. In large multi-clan towns, these four seating areas were built like stepped bleachers, with clan elders and town leaders sitting on the bottom row. Sometimes, covered walkways and arbors looked like a stadium built around the plaza. Designs for each clan were painted over the front of its section. Town treasures were kept in a small room at the back of the west arbor where the town chief sat.

Ceremonies honoring the ancestral elite were lost, while rites marking the agricultural year became more important. Four times during the summer, everyone gathered to celebrate the ripening crop. The Green Corn (Busk) ceremony was held just before the harvest, marking the New Year. Everyone gathered to fast, pray, and dance while the corn was still alive in their fields. The last rite was held in the fall (around Halloween) with masked dancers to consecrate the economic shift from farming to hunting. During winter, some towns used a huge domed rotunda (hothouse) for indoor meetings and ceremonies, until these 44became too difficult to maintain.

131. Vernon Knight, Symbolism of Mississippian Mounds, Powhatan's Mantle 1989.

152

132. Katharine Scherman, The Flowering of Ireland, Saints, Scholars, and Kings 1981; Alwyn Rees and Brinley Rees, Celtic Heritage, Ancient Tradition in Ireland and Wales 1978.

Osage of Missouri

Our best example of a living Mississippian priesthood, though historically living on the Plains, is the Osage. They were studied by Francis La Flesche, himself an Omaha and a native speaker of this related Siouian language.[133] Largely spared devastations from epidemics until the 1880s, when their population was almost 4000, Osage preserved priesthoods of clans, of pipes, and of the whole tribe. They likely derived from those of mound centers like nearby Cahokia, the ancient mound-rich city near modern St Louis.

Concentrating on clan and tribal initiation rituals, which both prayed for blessings from the Creator (*Wakonda*) and explained the universe in stages, La Flesche totaled 170 such rites. Clan priest initiations generally lasted four days, most of the time spent alerting all the universe for the finale. After pledging to be inducted and submitting to the "penalty verses", a candidate had seven years to gather the necessary gifts and food. For the consecration of a high priest for each of the two great bundles, the rite was very rapidly, lasting only one day because the unseen *puwha* of the universe hung in the balance.

In addition to this pan-tribal pair, the other rites (168 total), concerned with the visible world, ordained members of clan priesthoods. Each of the 24 clans had seven degrees, culminating in the ultimate Sayings of the Ancients. The embodiment of each clan and priesthood was its sacred bundle. That of a clan, called a "hawk", held a hawk skin, woven mat bag, deerskin bag, buffalo hair bag, buffalo hide rope, eagle leg, scalp, and buffalo hide strap.

For Osage, rituals were equated with books since they preserved and transmitted knowledge through a complex interaction of words, actions, and objects. They were intended to puzzle the serious, intrigue the curious, and impress the literal minded. Each ritual combined songs (*wathon*), actions (*we'gaxe*), and recitations (*wi'gie*), which repeated many of the same poetic verses. The main image, however, often symbolic animals, varied according to that specific clan and degree. A vital identifying phrase specified "I am a person who has made of an X his body" to indicate the clan's life symbol (below) through which they approach the Creator. Examples of X vary from the immensities of the Sun, Water, and Stars to the names of animals, plants, objects, weather conditions, colors, and abstractions.

Each initiation involved a set of officials who served formal or functional roles.[134] Typically, these were the candidate and his wife, a sponsor, an assisting sponsor, priests of all 24 clans sitting at fixed positions, a sacred warrior who had earned all 13 possible military honors, a messenger, widows of former priests, and singers. The candidate and sponsor had formal claims to that clan and degree. The assisting sponsor was the expert, like a skilled clerk, who knew the involved ritual in all of its intricacy and precision. Songs were particularly important to bring the universe "to life", with special verses extolling their human ancestors's ability to think – to search with the mind and thereby learn (termed *wathi'gethon*) "to bring things to pass." Songs and recitations were context sensitive, describing a body from head to feet to indicate birth and new beginnings, or from feet to head to indicate growth and maturity.

As all of life, the original Osage came from the sky (called father) to the earth (called mother). There, they met one clan who had always been there and so became known as the Isolated Earth. Between the sky and the underworld was and is the "snare of life" (ho-e-ga), owned by a sacred spider,[135] stretching along the surface of the earth and holding everything together between birth and death. On this snare, the clans were divided between Sky or Earth moieties. Earth is further separated into Land and Water clans.

Symbolic oppositions between these moieties (Sky / Earth = land & water ~ hcižo / hąka) include considerations of gender.

Sky =	left	six	morning star	male	father
Earth =	right	seven	evening star	female	mother

Someone of the Land slept on the right side, or, if Sky, slept with head to the left.

East =	sun	birth	life	red	male
West =	moon	death	destruction	black	female

For the whole tribe, living among Upland Foresters, the great bundle keeper was Gentle Ponka clan and that of the great medicine bundle belonged to Gentle Sky. Each clan had a sacred bundle whose contents provided various tokens for identifying it. All of the sacred objects ("life symbols") of the clans were called waxo'be. Moreover, two clans, Men of Mystery and Buffalo Bulls, were the symbolic keepers of all the clan bundles. The Elder Water clan was the nominal keeper of the peace pipes, symbolizing unity, with their own great bundle priests (wawathon). Among secondary sacra were war standards, rattles, war clubs, sacred bows and arrows, charcoal, and more. These included, though known only to the adept, unconsecrated symbols called "those carried to excite enthusiasm" (wazhawa athinbikshe) and therefore not real.[136]

After uniting the moieties on earth, Osage priests decided to reorganize their society three times. Each one was phrased as a "move to a new country." First came an internal reordering in three phases that were begun by Water people of the Earth division. The Isolated Earth priests became responsible for a symbolic "house" where all Osage children were named. The Land (particularly Bear and Puma) priests were given charge of the "house" where war ceremonies were held. War or hunt leadership was assigned to the Bear, Water, Sky, and Isolated Earth clan priests.

Prompt action, however, was impossible because of excessive ceremonialism, so another reordering improved military tactics, though each expedition was still led by a priest. This second "move to a new country" allowed various clans, as needed, to organize three types of war parties. These were composed of men from all the clans, from a few clans from one moiety, or from a single clan.

The third "move" instituted the civil government by two chiefs, titled gahi'ge, from the Ponka clan of the Earth and the Sky clan of the Sky. To distinguish these clans as the source of chiefs, they added "gentle" to their name because that was a defining characteristic of such leaders. Each man held vigil until a spirit revealed to him the contents of a great bundle, for either medicines (symbolized by the cormorant, and by man and woman roots) or for long life (symbolized by the pelican, and tattoos). The other great bundle priests had the pipes, particularly one with a human face carved into the black pipebowl. Hanging from its stem were seven shell beads for the Earth and six copper beads for the Sky. Such emphasis on shell and copper is distinctly Mississippian.

154

While clan houses were arranged in order around the edges of the town, the two houses of these tribal chiefs were set directly across the central path, east to west, of the sun. While each house had a door facing north or south across this open plaza, these chiefly homes had a door on both the east and west ends.

The goal of this complex religion is an unbroken line of descendants stretching far into the future. A crucial belief was and is that nothing in the universe ever moved backwards. Today, having deliberately "unloaded" those arduous religious burdens, Osage now rely on their ilõõška dance and Big Moon peyote rites of the Native American Church.

133. Garrick Bailey, The Osage and the Invisible World ~ From the Works of Francis La Flesche 1995.
134. Garrick Bailey, The Osage and the Invisible World 1995: 76.
135. Garrick Bailey, The Osage and the Invisible World 1995: 241, line 13.
136. Garrick Bailey, The Osage and the Invisible World 1995: 47.
Caddos of the Trans-Mississippi South

The Caddos were one of the great unsung chiefdoms of North America. They are better known from their complex archaeological mounds and towns than through their decimated ethnographic past. Settled along interior rivers draining into the middle Gulf coast, Caddos, speaking related languages, composed four historic confederacies and other allied tribes.

These confederacies were the Kadohadacho along the Red River, mostly in modern Arkansas; the Hasinai in eastern Texas; and the Natchitoches in Louisiana. At the northeastern frontier near enemy Osages, the Cahinnio along the upper Ouachita lived in a compact town before their remnants joined the Kadohadacho.[137]

In addition to local diversity, overall Caddo complexity included features shared with the Southeast, Plains, Southwest, and Mexico. According to a recent Origin Saga, most of the nation emerged from Caddo Lake, along the border between present Oklahoma and Louisiana near the center of their overall population distribution.

Kadohadacho traced themselves to a cave in a hill called Chakanina ("crying place") where an elderly couple came up from the underworld. The old man carried fire, a pipe, and a drum. The old woman had corn and pumpkin seeds. Other people and animals followed them out until Wolf closed off this passage, amidst the crying of those who were left behind.

Among Hasinai, Moon, their culture hero acting on behalf of a supreme being called *Ayo-Caddi-Aymay* {"father chief above"}, appeared on earth after his mother was killed by a giant horned snake. His grandmother and virgin aunt found a drop of her blood inside an acorn cap. They kept it secluded as it developed into a tiny boy the size of a finger. The next day, fully grown, he killed the monster, established earthly patterns, and then went into the sky with the two kinswomen.

Most Caddos lived in scattered farmsteads along a river. Each cluster of houses was controlled by the senior woman of an extended family. As intensive farmers, each house expected to have a two year supply of stored crops on hand, in case of war or famine.

Each major community had a central temple, built atop a flat earthen pyramid, serving as the focus of seasonal and farming rites conducted by their officials. Periodically rekindled afresh, flames from this new sacred fire were used to relite all household hearths within that community.

In keeping with their high population density and wide distribution, which may have numbered a quarter of a million, leaders were graded into an administrative hierarchy. It consisted of patrilineal offices that combined political, social, and religious responsibilities.

At the top of a confederacy was a high priest, whose title was written as <u>shinesi</u> by the Spanish, but it was probably *tsah neeshee*, Mr Moon. Districts and communities were headed by a <u>caddi</u> or tribal chief, who supervised a staff. This consisted of various offices called the <u>canaha</u> or subchief, <u>chaya</u> or lieutenant, and *tamma* or aide. The shinesi lived in a four-sided compound with his own home on one side, a meeting room across the patio, and, on the other two sides, guest rooms for visitors. Near the temple were two small buildings sacred to the <u>kokoniki</u>, twin boys who were messenger oracles between the deity and the shinesi. At least once a year, more often in times of stress, the shinesi, surrounded by other officials, consulted with these twins in a darkened temple and, using another voice, announced what had to be done to embrace or avert some impending situation.

Like the Pawnee, also Caddoan speakers, the liturgical role of the priestly chiefs was balanced by that of doctors or shamans. Some of them were organized into guilds or cults empowered by the same spirit to treat specific illnesses. Unfortunately, these guilds have sometimes been mistaken for clans, unknown among all Caddoans.

Caddo prestige was based on their impressive rituals, mound complex, and trade network involving salt, fine pottery, Osage orange bow wood, and black velvety hides. Most recently, Caddo worship of Moon provided the basis for much of the symbolism for the use of peyote by the Native American Church.[138]

137. George Sabo, The Caddos, <u>Paths of Our Children</u> 1992; WW Newcomb, The Caddo Confederacies, <u>The Indians of Texas</u> 1961.
138. See Jay Miller, Changing Moons: A History of Caddo Religion 1996.

Calusa of South Florida

Along the southwest coast of Florida, the Calusa ("fierce people"), a dense population of 10,000 fishers and harvesters (who tended but never farmed), lived among chiefdoms that were similar to those better known and longer lived along the North Pacific Coast. On both Gulf and Atlantic coasts, staple foods were fish and shellfish, supplemented with deer, raccoons, birds, reptiles, plants, and roots.

Neighbors to the north along the Gulf were the Tokobaga, inland were the Mayaimi, and along the Atlantic were the Ais, Jeaga, and Tequesta. After these nations, including the Alachua and Timucua, were devastated by Spanish missions, foreign diseases, and massive British slave raids, Florida was resettled by Creek renegades who became known as Seminoles.

The Calusa capitol was called Calos (Mound Key, Esteros Bay), with 50 subject towns. Each was governed by a chief of appropriate rank. A high priest, often the brother of the paramount chief, supervised the sacred fire, temple, and rituals. A war captain, sometimes a brother-in-law of the chiefly family, defended the land and led warriors into battle.

The high chief, who sat on a special stool, wore a gold headband and beaded leg bands.[139] Like ancient Egypt, the Calusa high chief married a full sister as his first wife. In formal greeting, he was approached on the knees, with the hands up. His authority rested on the ownership of prime fisheries, nets, stored foods, trading contacts, and secret esoteric information.[140]

By his decree, public works – storerooms, canals and mounds for temples or burials – were constructed, mostly with religious intent. Canals provided access, sometimes in canoe processions, to mounds dedicated to a trinity of gods. Indeed, Chief Carlos resisted conversion to Catholicism because, as he explained, knowledge of this triune divinity was a secret of his own royal line. The highest one was the creator, the second the culture hero who fixed most social rules, and the third was concerned with male activities such as war, demanding human sacrifice in order to consume the eyes. Masks, such as those later found submerged at Key Marco, were worn during a major rite, probably in the fall, when a procession came down from the temple to bless the land.

Death was accompanied by elaborate treatment of the body in charnel houses, ossuaries, and final burial mounds. Carved sculptures of turtles, barracudas, and other animals, perhaps related to possible clans or spirit patrons, guarded these cemeteries.

As a huge, densely settled population, Calusa were highly vulnerable to European diseases. Many succumbed during recurrent epidemics. After Spain ceded Florida to the British in the 1750s, survivors retreated as Catholics to the Caribbean, where they blended into those mixed populations.

139. This office continued for six known generations, passing from the founder to his brother, Senequne, to his son, Carlos (died 1567), to his father's sister's son Felipe, then finally to another cousin, Pedro. These bands were constrictions inticating probity, like the belts worn by Yup'ik.

140. Randolph Widmer, The Evolution of the Calusa 1988.

Iroquois Confederacy of New York

Crystallized as a league governed by the holders of 50 name-titles, called *royaner*, Iroquois culture was integrated by gender symbolism. This was noted by J. N. B. Hewitt, both a Tuscarora and anthropologist. This unifying principal of exclusive Man and inclusive Woman was evoked by immortals known as either "man beings" and "man-woman (female)" beings. In other words, unlike most other cultures, Woman was the generic and Man was the specific for Iroquoians.

The League of the Iroquois was founded by the legendary Deganawidah, assisted by *Hiyawenthah* ("comber," Hiawatha) and the Peace Queen (*Jigonsahsay*), probably after a 1250 or 1350 eclipse. His message called for an end to fighting among various Iroquoian-speaking tribes and their union into a confederated league. The first tribe to convert was the Mohawk, with Oneida, Cayuga, and Seneca following soon after. Onondaga held out, however, because of the obstinacy of their leader *Tododaho* ("ensnared, tangled"). His name referred to the snakes which slithered over his head and twisted body. Tododaho was won over after Hiyawenthah agreed to let his name become the first one among royaner peers in the league. The names of these 50 converted leaders became the titles passed down within the matrilineages of specific clans and tribes. As with Hurons, each clan included both a civil and a war leader.

In addition to these alternating executive and military leaders, the other prominent position based in kinship was that of the clan matron. She was in charge of the distributing the food at each meal, establishing her authority at "gut level". Shamans owned bundles with associated rituals. These belonged to any of a dozen guilds dedicated to specific rituals for curing, plant germination, and animal wellbeing. The masked False Faces are still the best known of all.[141] On the dark side were guilds devoted to sorcery.

Although men hold the matrilineal positions of authority, they do so by virtue of connecting links through women as brothers or sons. The Iroquois clan matron was and is the most senior, best informed, and most active clanswoman. With the death of the holder of one of the fifty royaner name-titles, its matron, in consultation with the other clanswomen, selects the clansman who will succeed to that name-title. This successor is then installed by fellow royaners at a poetic and elaborate Condolence and Requickening Ceremony. If he proves incompetent in office, he will be warned by his clan matron two times and dehorned on the third visit, as noted before.

Name-titles are not evenly distributed but vary by tribe. For Mohawk, the Turtle matriclan holds three names, which include those of Deganawidah and Hiyawenthah, and both the Wolf and the Bear matriclans also have three names. Oneida Wolf, Bear, and Turtle matriclans each also hold three hereditary name-titles. Onondaga hold fourteen name-titles distributed among seven of their nine matriclans, with the name of _Tododaho_ descending through the Bear clan. Cayuga hold ten royaner names, which are distributed among six of their ten matriclans. Seneca, although the most populous tribe, had eight name-titles which are the hereditary property of four of their nine matriclans, in addition to two titles associated with senior men who act as war strategists for the entire league.

These differences in the number and distribution of name-titles did not effect the deliberations of the league since each tribe cast only one vote and all binding decisions had to be unanimous.

Since its founding, other tribes have been admitted to the league, but in the category of "props, braces, or supports" rather than as full-fledged members. In historic times, these have included splinter Delawares, Mahicans, Tutelos, and other Native American refugees to Canada. The usual procedure was for the Iroquois to offer prop status to a local enemy three times. After a last refusal, they attacked and conquered them, forcing them into the league.

After 1712, Iroquoian-speaking Tuscarora (below) fled from British attacks in the Carolinas and found refuge in New York. They received full rank (about 1722), in, thereafter, a league of Six Nations. But they did not gain or add any federal name-titles, which remained fixed at 50 within the original Five Nations.

Mohawk Turtle names of Deganawidah and possibly Hiyawenthah are never actually held by humans. The rationale is that no mere mortal could emulate these legendary founders. Instead, an open-ended class of Merit or Pine Tree Chiefs give homage to Deganawidah. These were ordinary men who "stood tall" to earn respect and deference on the basis of their own character, exploits, and initiative. A Pine Tree Chief earns this position – open to all men, regardless of clan, social standing, or birth right – by general consensus of his outstanding abilities.

Colonial delegates, such as Ben Franklin, at the Albany Convention of 1754, mingled with royaners. It has been suggested that their fixed number of positions may have influenced the form of the United States Senate, while the variable number of Merit Chiefs is like that of the House of Representatives. Any link, though, is much debated because prior European models better explain the US system.

Iroquois imagined their league as like one of their own bark-covered longhouses. Mohawks were the Keepers of the Eastern Door, Onondaga were Keepers of the Council

Fire, and Seneca were the Keepers of the Western Door. As these associations indicate, this imaginary longhouse ran east and west with the Mohawk River as its central axis.

The chiefs of the confederacy met (and meet) in either of two patterns, depending upon the purpose. For the Requickening address of condolence for a deceased royaner and the installation of his heir, the league met as two sides. Mohawk, Onondaga, and Seneca represented the superior, Father, or Man's side; while Oneida and Cayuga were the inferior, Son, or Woman's side.

For deliberations and negotiations, the league met in the fall as a triplex with Onondaga royaner under _Tododaho_ overseeing the deliberations among Mohawk-Seneca or Oneida-Cayuga. An item of business was brought up by Mohawk _royaners_ to those of the Onondaga, who discussed it and passed it to Seneca, who then passed it "across the fire" to Oneida, followed by Cayuga, who, after 1722, deferred to the Tuscarora at the end.

Each tribe casts a single vote based on the consensus of all its federal chiefs. The entire league must reach a unanimous decision. Deliberations extended for days until the Mohawk had the last word on that subject. One and only one topic was considered at a time, skillfully focusing royaners on their task at hand.

Women were not allowed inside the council house, but they were not without influence. During deliberations, they provided meals, which they left outside the door. These once including such delicacies as beaver tail. Iroquois women had a high status, in any and all contexts.

The crops of women matched the venison of men, the kinship system recognized both woman and man, and social relations involved sedentary women and absent men. The tribal moieties, together with the confederacy itself, emphasized the mutuality of woman and man linked through mothers. The Iroquois were comprehensively engendered because their universe was pervasively human and saturated with the quality of human intelligence, or Mind. In speeches, Iroquois insist on reminding each other that "we are all of one mind." Indeed, as a political body, the royaner were believed to have "one head, one heart, one mind, one blood, and one dish of food."[142]

Iroquois Thanksgiving rites, analogous to the Green Corn ceremony throughout the East, occurred throughout the year as each new food matured, starting with wild strawberries. In addition, life crisis and mourning rituals were held as needed. The climax of the year was the Midwinter ceremony, which formerly involved the sacrifice of a white dog to the Creator. It now represents an aspect of the revitalization undertaken by the remarkable prophet, known by his Seneca Turtle clan title of Handsome Lake, whose "Good Word or Message" was learned from a visionary encounter with angels and God in 1799. He also had a letter of support from Thomas Jefferson, when he was president.

Today, whether Catholic, Anglican, Longhouse, or other, Iroquois maintain a strong voice in the political and religious life of the US and Canada. Their sense of time remains defined by the three epics of their past, the making of the world by Earth Grasper, the founding of the League or fifty royaner, and the Good Word of Handsome Lake.

141. See Frank Speck, The Iroquois 1945: 86.
142. John N.B. Hewitt, A Constitutional League of Peace in the Stone Age of America: The League of the Iroquois and its Constitution 1920:542.

Tuscarora[143]

Tuscarora, possibly meaning 'hemp gatherers', were a confederacy of three tribes along the upper Roanoke, Neuse, Tar, and Pamlico Rivers (modern North Carolina). Component tribes were Submerged Pine Tree People (*Katenu'aka*), *Akawenytsh'aka* (adopted allies of another language ?), and Tuscaroras proper (*Skarur*Error!).[144]

Their language is Iroquoian, one of three branches (Five Nations, Huron-Petun, Tuscarora) of the Northern branch, as distinct from the Southern one represented by Cherokee and others. Descent is matrilineal, with primary clan lineages providing both civil and war chiefs, appointed by clan matrons. About eight clans (Bear, Wolf, Turtle, Deer, Eel, Snipe, maybe Beaver) formed about five phratries. Vague memories suggest that moieties (halves) once figured in rituals, divided as First (Bear, Eel, Turtle, Beaver) and Second (Wolf, Snipe, Deer). Clan names are descriptive of attributes not of entire species, so Bears are called "broken off tails people", Snipes (Plovers) are "clean sand people", Beavers are "stream people", and Turtles are "climbing the mountain people".

After 1711-13 wars with the Carolina British colonies, survivors found refuge among the Iroquois in New York. After late September 1722, they were admitted to the League of the Iroquois as the sixth nation, though without access to any of the fifty federal chief titles. Their chiefs are, however, mourned by League Rites of Condolence and raised up by the Requickening Address. After the Revolution, they mostly fled into Ontario, though others stayed around Buffalo.

Since many of their words for features of this government are borrowed from other Northern Iroquoian languages, their polity in North Carolina was probably less complex, with peace and war leaders for each clan and town. In North Carolina, Tuscarora national *puwha* and protection came from a pair, presumably male and female, of ostrich-like beings called Uhstruuri' who provided them with an oracle fetish that spoke through its human keepers. Over time, however, these custodians neglected its proper feeding and care. The Creator took this oracle away and the Tuscarora consequently suffered their defeat by the British. Later, in New York State, another Uhstruuri' came to their aid, warned of enemy attacks, and provided successful defenses until foreign enemies worked magic to take away its power. Its body rotted with such a terrible stench that it had to be buried alive, and the Tuscarora thereafter again lost their spiritual protection.[145]

Chiefly titles in New York are Spear Trailer (*Sakwarishra*), Small Voice (*Ni'hawenyna'a*), and Grasps the Multitude (*Hotio'kwawa'k*Error!) of the Turtles; *Nakaienyt*Error!, Bearcub (*Utakwa't*Error!*'a*), and Forepaw on Chest (*Lonenytchanen'nak*Error!) of Bears; *Naio'kawe'a* and Bent (*Neiotcha'kdony*) of Wolves; Tree Holding (*Karonydawa'k*Error!) and T*hanadak'hwa* of Snipes; and Teaching Along (*Kari'kenytia'*), Hide Anointing (*Ni'hno'ka'wa*), and Twenty Canoes (*Naka'henwa'sheny*) of Beavers. Many titles but not all are duplicated in Ontario. About fifty years ago, the New York Chief's Council ordered their tribal role to be sealed so that no Canadians can officially be added to this reservation.

In the Carolinas, each chief was advised by a council of 40 or so elders. Farming settlements took the form of dispersed neighborhoods set among their fields and palisaded towns. Their houses were bark-shingled domes. Ridge-topped tents were used in hunting camps. Inside benches (described as hurtles) along the walls provided seats and beds. Farming was the major occupation of women, with men doing some hunting. A special figure, well dressed and draped with wampum to be the abode of a famous warrior's spirit, was set up in a field. It was consulted by leaders and elders using a covert language, but it was avoided by young men under threat of misery if they did not work hard.[146] Bodies were coated with blackened grease on most days, though red was used for ceremonies.

Their large population was fed by a double planting of maize and by fall game drives, setting fire to canebreaks to force out animals. Fish were taken in abundance by the use of poisons placed upstream. Tobacco was grown for smoking in clay pipes. Weapons, wooden bowls, spoons, and woven mats were made in winter.

Women chiefs sponsored public feasts with dances, along with gambling games. Like other Iroquois, the wooden bowl with plum seed dice provided fun and mid-winter prophesies. Life leaps were marked by celebrations of birth, namings, puberty (particularly the boy's ordeal called *huskanaw* among nearby Powhatans), successes, and death (in the *quiocosin* mortuary house). Earthen mounds were placed over deceased leaders. In New York, major events became a summer picnic and midwinter feast, where hunters competed as married or single teams to provide the most game for the meat pies.[147]

Described in North Carolina as mild, kind, peaceable, ingenious, and industrious, Tuscarora hardships began when 1660s British settlers denied they had any rights to their own soil and sold many of their kidnapped children into slavery. According to tradition, in North Carolina, about 24 large villages could raise about 6,000 warriors, but depopulation by 1710 left about 6 towns with about 2,000 fighters. Pennsylvania, responding to pressure from local tribes, banned slaves from Carolina after 25 March 1706.

In response, on 8 June 1710, through Conestoga and Shawnee intermediaries, Tuscaroras petitioned redress from Pennsylvania, presenting 8 wampum belts. Each belt expressed, in set order, the particular interests of matrons and mothers, children, young men, old men, entire tribe, chiefs, safety, and an official path to gain redress. But this was not to be, though by passing these belts on to the Iroquois Confederacy, Conestogas soon opened the way to a haven for Tuscaroras in New York. In 1763, the last Susquehanna Conestoga survivors were massacred by the Paxton Boys near Harrisburg.

Keen prehistoric traders of copper, salt, and herbs, and later rum runners who sold by the mouthful, Tuscaroras were defeated and dispersed in two wars with North Carolina British colonists, aided by South Carolina and a reluctant Virginia. Three years of strife, bad crops, and other hardships left the colony demoralized and ripe for Tuscarora attack.

The first began in September of 1711 when John Lawson, surveyor general, was captured, condemned, and killed by Tuscaroras,[148] before 130 of his Swiss and Palatine settlers were killed on the Pamlico and Trent Rivers on 22 September. Lawson knew Tuscaroras well, as indicated in his history of North Carolina, written in 1708 and published in 1709. He admits they treated the English much better than deserved, since "with all our religion and education, we possess more moral deformities and vices than these people do." Ironically, his own ethnographic report accurately descried the manner of his own torture and death.

From South Carolina, Col John Barnwell drove Tuscaroras into palisaded Narhantes Fort above Newbern. He attacked on 30 January 1712 and forced a peace treaty. Two thousand bushels of corn were destroyed in 374 houses. His own allies cooked and ate pieces of the slain. Angered that he was not more lauded for this victory, Barnwell, despite very fresh peace terms, sold captives into slavery.

This started the second war that ended at the 20-23 March attack on Chief Hencock's capitol of Catechna by Col James Moore of the South Carolina militia and 900 native allies. Many of these warriors were Catawbas who were, in turn, betrayed into their own 1714-15 defeat. Again, all prisoners were sold into slavery, though 500 families

(1,500 people) fled to safety among the Iroquois. A few hid out in their homeland under self-serving chiefs – Tom Blount, then Withmell Tuffdick by 1778, and Samuel Smith, who died in 1802. Many Tuscaroras went north carrying the bones and bodies of their ancestors on their backs. By late 1722, sponsored by the Oneida, Tuscaroras joined the League of the Iroquois to make it Six Nations. About 130 pro-British Tuscaroras led by Sagwarithra joined other Six Nations when they were given asylum on the Grand River in Ontario (British Canada).

First settled in New York at one castle (palisaded town) between the Oneida and Onondaga, Oneidas sold this land from underneath them by the Treaty of Fort Herkimer in 1785. They scattered into three towns in western New York until their understandable anti-British sentiments brought most of them to the American side in the Revolution. Attacked and scattered by Iroquois loyalists, Tuscaroras gathered again on a stream, lined by butternut and walnut trees, near Niagara on lands claimed by Seneca after Wenro-Neutrals devastation. This abode became the Tuscarora's three-square-mile reservation on 15 September 1797.

About 1802 South Carolina appeased them with $13,722 - funds used to purchase 4,249 acres to make the Niagara lands almost ten square acres. By 1804 Tuscarora survivors in the south joined those in New York, but times were not happy. During the War of 1812, British burned out this village. Resistance to Protestant missionaries resulted in 70 converts being driven from Niagara to Six Nations about 1820. Continued strife led Christians to burn the New York Longhouse, used for socials and ceremonies. It was never rebuilt.

From 1828-31, North Carolina sold off remaining Tuscarora land claims for $3,250, with any leases ending in 1916. In 1836, remaining New York Iroquois were forced to cede remaining lands in a much disputed treaty, renegotiated in 1842. Seeking a haven, in 1846, 200 Iroquois (with 40 Tuscarora) went to Kansas. There, a third died before survivors struggled back. Among the New York Tuscarora, men committed themselves to farming according to the *Gaiwiiyo* (Good Word) teachings of Handsome Lake, and their community prospered.

In 1957, however, New York Power Authority decided to flood a fifth of the Niagara reservation for a storage reservoir. A fierce legal battle ensued until the US Supreme Court gave the go-ahead for the flooding in 1960. Ever since, Tuscarora have been politicized, and are now widely regarded as key founders of the 1970s Red Power movement.

Most Tuscaroras are now Christians, but some in Canada attend Good Word Longhouses, particularly with Oneida, where the yearly farming rituals timed by growing crops, harvest, thanksgiving, and New Year are still celebrated.[149]

143. Much of this information was provided by John Napoleon Brinton Hewitt (1869-1937), whose mother was Tuscarora and father a Scots physician. He learned Greek and Latin from his father, and Tuscarora from school mates after he was eleven years old. Intending medical school, he was working as a street car conductor in Northern New Jersey when Erminie Smith hired him in 1880 to help with her collection of Iroquois tales. When she died, he was hired to finish her work by the Bureau of American Ethnology in 1886, collecting data for fifty years. Among his triumphs was proving that Cherokee was a language of the Iroquoian stock. Though he left 12,000 pages of notes, he published little because he was a perfectionist, fond of referring to

"anthropologists and other suspicious characters."

Other Tuscarora authors include Elias Johnson, <u>Legends, Traditions and Laws of the Iroquois, or Six Nations, and History of the Tuscarora Indians</u> 1881; Ted Williams, <u>The Reservation</u> 1976; and Clinton Richard, <u>Fighting Tuscarora</u> 1973.

144. Northern Iroquoian speakers refer to *puwha* as *-aktę'~ -uktę'*, though *orenda* is better known in publications.

145. Blair A Rudes and Dorothy Crouse, The Tuscarora Legacy of JNB Hewitt 1987 II: 553-568, Text 33, The Prophetic Bird.

146. John Lawson, <u>A *New* Voyage to Carolina</u> 1967: 177.

147. These feasts in all their competition and hilarity are described by Ted Williams 1976: 51-56, 141-180.

148. Lawson was tried once and acquitted, then retried and condemned after he argued with Coree accusers and chiefs Cor Tom and Hencock. His body was festooned with splinters that were then ignited, as he had described in his own published ethnography. His greatest crime was deliberately settling Europeans on lands still claimed and used by Tuscarora, without any warning at all.

149. Basic Tuscarora references include Barbara Graymont 1969, The Tuscarora New Year Festival, <u>New York History</u> 50 (2): 143-163; JNB Hewitt 1910 Tuscarora, Handbook of American Indians North of Mexico, Frederick Hodge, ed. Bureau of American Ethnology, Bulletin 30, Volume 2: 842-853; Elias Johnson 1881 <u>Legends, Traditions and Laws of the Iroquois, or Six Nations, and History of the Tuscarora Indians</u>, Lockport, NY: Union Printing and Publishing; Frank Johnson 1968 <u>The Tuscaroras</u>: Mythology, Medicine, and Culture (2 Volumes); David Landy 1958 Tuscarora Tribalism and National Identity, Ethnohistory 5 (2): 250-84; John Lawson 1967 A <u>New</u> Voyage to Carolina, Hugh Talmage Lefler, ed; Clinton Richard 1973 <u>Fighting Tuscarora</u>: The Autobiography of Chief Clinton Richard, Barbara Graymont, ed; Blair Rudes and Dorothy Crouse 1987 <u>The Tuscarora Legacy of JNB Hewitt</u> (2 Volumes); Bruce Trigger 1978 Smithsonian Handbook of North American Indians, Northeast, Volume 15; AFC Wallace 1952 The Modal Personality Structure of the Tuscarora Indians, as Revealed by the Rorschach Test, 2012 <u>Tuscarora ~ A History</u>; Ted Williams 1976 <u>The Reservation</u>.

Mikmaq (*Elnu* to themselves) of Northeastern Canada

Long resident along the North Atlantic coast, Mikmaq lived from the sea, the source of ninety percent of their foods.[150] During summers, many lived on the coast near shellfish beds, others worked their way up a river, taking flounder and smelt near the mouth, birds midway along, and alewives (fish) and eels inland. Coastal traps and weirs, opening and closing with tide changes, assured a constant supply of fresh fish. During severe, coast-battering, winter storms, all Mikmaq moved into the woods. The men hunted and women made "moose butter" by smashing and boiling these bones to skim off the oil.

Huge, hollowed out, hardwood kettles were permanently stored at these locales to mark these homes. Canoes with a peak in the middle of each side carried people to and fro.[151] Such watercraft were said to be inspired by the form of a bird breastbone (sternum).[152] Houses were bark covered and oval, with two separate doors, one for girls and one for everyone else. During a traditional lifetime, there were two outstanding events. One was a year or two of bride service by the boy to his future inlaws before the marriage could take place. The second was a expected funeral feast hosted by a man just before his own demise.

Of the seven major gifts of Mikmaq culture, women provided five. These were fire, eel spear, snowshoes, moose hair weaving, and corn. Men added dyes and specialized arrows shot by a bow. While Mikmaqs did not grow corn, they did plant tobacco.[153]

Villages, districts, and the whole nation each had logos depicting a totem animal.[154] Most activities were directed by sigers. Councils governed by chiefs, of local, district, and national levels, met periodically, particularly to reassign hunting tracts among deserving families. A chief (_sagmaw_) stayed attractive to followers by placing a special flower inside his hat. A captain (_keptin_) had charge of warfare.

Though its antiquity is much debated, the national council has long met during the annual Catholic festival in honor of Saint Anne, the mother of Mary, on July 26. It uses the ancient and widespread image of an imaginary person, represented by a high chief at Cape Breton Island, facing the mainland. Three districts were to his left (mostly Nova Scotia) and three to his right (mostly New Brunswick). An important chief and shaman named Membertou living on the Bay of Fundy was baptized in 1610 and is regarded as an ancestral high chief. His most famous quote recalled a time before Europeans came, when his own people were as numerous as the hairs on his head. Since he also had a beard, there must have been many of them.

Mikmaqs were also the youngest members of the international Wabanaki confederacy. With the Maliseet, Passamaquoddy, and Penobscot, they met every three years at the Mohawk mission of Kanawake with an Odawa presiding. Its insignia included dog feasts, wampum belts, long stem pipes, and burying weapons ("the hatchet") at concluding peace ceremonies. Probably confederated after Iroquois and British ascendancy, they formally revived in 1978, as further response to Canadian injustices.[155]

Rituals were addressed to _mntu_ (manitu, immortal) to celebrate first foods, life leaps, and, most recently, Catholic saints. While other tribes used a spokesman to express the views of women, the most distinguished woman present could herself address a Mikmaq gathering.

Their most distinctive belief, however, involved trans-species beings that moved between outer shapes. Thus, old moose, caribou, and bear entered the sea to revive by becoming whales, while old whales came onto the land to take one of these three outer forms. Similarly, beavers interchanged with black ducks, as squirrels did with snakes.[156]

Near the once codfish-filled Grand Banks of Newfoundland, Mikmaqs bore the brunt of hundreds of years of both the wet and dry fishery. (Their Beothuk, the original red Indien, neighbors did not survive at all.) The wet was less disruptive since the ships salted their catch on board to take back to European ports. For the dry one, however, the catch was taken to the coast, sliced, and sun-dried. These locales were often at major native fishing places, where forced alcohol and prostitution took a heavy toll. From Basques, Portuguese, and others, Mikmaqs quickly adopted sailing shallops (sloops), becoming renowned as master seamen.

Indeed, a continuing Mikmaq reputation as travelers is based on several chiefs and families who visited (or were taken to) Europe from the 1500s onward. Eventually, the major defenses of Port Royal, Louisbourg, and Halifax were built on their lands. When the English took over, Acadian French (Cajuns) were banished from there to Louisiana by 1760, and United Empire Loyalists fleeing the US victory in the Revolution took over remaining prime locales.

During recent centuries, Mikmaqs survived by working as market hunters for the fur trade, as ethnic soldiers for the French, as stoop labor in Maine potato and blueberry fields, as high steel fitters, and as factory hires in New England, particularly the Boston area. During the 1800s they specialized in porpoise hunting to extract oil needed for beacons in Atlantic lighthouses.

When a Jesuit noticed children drawing pictures to remember their lessons, he devised a cumbersome set of pictographs to convey Catholic prayers and to send diplomatic messages based in this Eastern Algonkian language. These Mikmaq rubic mnemonics were never widely used.

Most notably, Mikmaq, through early intermarriage with French seigneurs who had been "given" enormous tracts of their homeland by the French King, as well as resident natives and imported settlers, helped to begin the distinctive and vital Metis population of Canada.

150. Virginia Miller, The Micmac: A Maritime Woodland Group, Chapter 15, Native Peoples: The Canadian Experience 1995: 345-374.

151. These arched gunwales (gunnals) were the vessel form of the Beothuk, whose extinction involved hired Mikmaqs, cf Edwin Tappan Adney and Howard Chapelle, The Bark Canoes and Skin Boasts of North America 1964: 94-98.

152. Wilson and Ruth Wallis, The Micmac Indians of Eastern Canada 1955: 330.

153. Wallis, The Micmac 1955: 246.

154. Philip Bock, Micmac, Handbook of North American Indians, Northeast 15 1978: 109-122.

155. Harald Prins, The Mi'kmaqs 1996: 119-120.

156. Parry Island Ojibwa believe that sturgeon turn into bears when berries ripen (Jenness 1935: 80 #2).

IV. *SIMILARITIES:*
Native America

The Americas are a very special place because humans have developed here in ways unknown to the rest of the world. They were responding to local and regional climates, habitats, terrains, and fellow beings, of all types.

Yet, like humanity, natives shared basic concepts and relationships from which to build in varied ways. While these ancient human+land interactions are most susceptible to archaeological research, they continue to color and mold contemporary relations with the landscape. They survive, sometimes subtly, in language use, rituals, and behaviors. Indeed, Americanists have worked long and hard to amass just such information about Native America, particularly in terms of more obvious details of technology and food economy. Yet, because few speak native languages or correctly record them, they have dealt mostly with such surface tangibles, avoiding the crucial but unseen concepts which underlie these outward manifestations.

Any of these obvious features have, of course, been given form, substance, and coherence by the over-all importance of engendering. It projects Mind-Man-Woman into the conditioning of enjoyment, content, and context for all events. Regardless of specific details, in order for any aspect of the concrete world to have meaningful significance, it must be engaged by gender. It must be filtered through existing concepts, and given import within a culturally defined worldview. Wrongfully called looking toward the past, it is actually using the past to make sense of the future. Nylon nets and motor boats now do the work of handwoven nettle twine and canoes, but fishers still begin and end by properly thanking the fish for providing food.

Hence, then as now, Native America was profoundly anthropocentric. Most often these human genders have attributes such that Mind is enclosive, Man is inclusive, and Woman is exclusive. Yuchi, Keres, and Kootenay provide telling counter examples. Similarly, in the universal tension between exclusive Human (own) Culture and inclusive (other) Nature, the overarching Mind is also their ultimate enclosive mediator.

Often women symbolize Nature because their own physiological cycles of menstruation and gestation is recognized to coincide with phases of the moon and rhythms of the tides, and thus closer to or more integrated into Nature than men.

While the enormously complex symbolism of menstrual blood and pubic hair in Native America has been slighted, suffice it to say that female puberty rites and monthly seclusion were widespread. They reenforced a belief that menstrual blood was extremely dangerous, to men if not also to the rest of the world. It, along with corpse bones and ghost powder, is used in powerful sorcery and counter-magic in awesome rites dealing with cosmic order. Tohono O'odam Papago warn that contact with a menstruant will cause deer to avoid hunters, all-powerful crystals (insignia of a shaman) to rot, and tobacco plants to shrivel up.[157] Yet from this alternative, more natural *puwha* came life.

Overall, depending on local conditions, recognized gender emanations conform to variable axial tensions. These echos are used to articulate distinct cultures. While over a dozen tensions have been recorded for all human cultures, the human metaphor is what most informs other echos in the Americas. After all, it was and is humans who make these recognitions. Even the spirits, still the original owners of America, have human form in their own holy homes with their out species cloaks removed.

Thus, while all cultures, at some level, regard the same anthropocentric echo as universal, each expresses differently. Its ideas are projected onto local images and objects, as concrete manifestations of an underlying concept. In much the same way, items in a medicine bundle serve to harness and represent abstract cosmic forces. Thus Crow Rock Bundles include a pair that over time produces pebbles. Similarly, neighboring cultures often reverse the inclusive/exclusive polarities of genders. This was done by Iroquois and Delaware of the Northeast, or Tewa and Keres Pueblos of New Mexico. All of these factors add to the incredible dazzle of details for which Americanists are both famous and infamous.

What must never be lost sight of, then, is that the Americas reflect only a portion of the human condition. To better understand humans, natives must be understood both in terms of themselves and by comparison with other peoples and cultures. Indeed, in other modalities, gender was and is equally important in the culture of India. There, the Hindu meditation mantra "OM" is believe to represent unity because the "O" is considered in some sects to be open and feminine, while the "M" is closed and masculine. Moreover, only men should recite this mantra.

Similar engendered associations and restrictions were also vital to upholding life in the Americas. Mercifully lacking nation states, each culture, allowing for its political organization from band to chiefdom, was free to express itself as time, place, neighbors, and spirits allowed.

Just before 1900, the American government began to come to terms with a national "inferiority complex". It concerned the lack of "US history" when compared with Europe and Asia. As a young nation state, Americans lacked "both an ancient history and a cultural tradition rich in art, architecture, or literature."[158] Its response was a "scenic nationalism" that regarded majestic landscapes as compensation for these deficiencies. As "earth monuments" to American greatness and as future inspirations, the Yosemite Valley of California and Yellowstone in Wyoming were set aside as National Parks. They were viewed as rivaling in grandeur the ancient monuments of Europe (and Asia). In deciding to set these extremely rugged and remote places apart, the government also marked them as worthless for economic exploitation.

The irony in all this legislation, of course, was its immigrant white-only mindset. Certainly, in Cahokia, Chaco Canyon, Abbott Farm, the Mandan Okeepa, Pawnee animal lodges, Blue Lake, and Big Horn Medicine Wheel, as well as countless other sacred shrines across the continent, Native America matched in time depth and effort the impressive cultural and religious feats of Europe (and of Asia). Yet, because they seemed so "naturally" a part of the landscape, as well as having been produced by "other, alien" ancestors, settlers refused to see them as monuments to comprehensive human history, art, or civilization. If recognized at all, regard was distorted by misconceptions about non-native races of Mound Builders or other preposterous originators, who now linger on only in the Book of Mormon. By settler consensus, the goal of European colonization was "to get the land subdued and the wilde nature out of it," that is, remove every and any thing indigenous, including these ancient human beings and their works.[159]

Yet what makes America distinctive in the world community was and is its native inhabitants and their works. They settled here first and they learned to know the land better than anyone who came later. After all, these invaders have destroyed much more than they ever learned. Indeed, what distinguishes United States law from that of other nation states is the existence of legally binding treaties with tribes now on reservations. What sets apart the regional style of the Southwest is its native character, still strong after half a millennia of pressures by Spanish and other Europeans.

More than their monuments, Indiens also deserve to be known for their brilliant ideas. These arose as solutions for very human concerns and problems. Many are expressed particularly well in their rituals. A key feature of these public events was that there was literally something for everyone, as the Okeepa makes all too clear. The more practical and pragmatic members were satisfied by being involved in doing something, while those usually oblivious could be attracted by the dazzle of costumes, aromas, and feats of appearing or disappearing. Some spectators could be entertained by watching their relatives and friends take on new personas. Those more mystical could look beyond the obvious to be inspired by glimpses of divinity. Because these rituals involved so much of the exterior, and were often held outdoors, they could be widely seen and experienced. Always, for some, their consequences included much that was interior.

Today, tribes, regardless of their origins, survive because they know and appreciate such virtues of tradition and community. Something older and venerable guides present communal actions according to past understandings. Though land was taken away and religions oppressed, natives maintain their position of moral superiority because they knew how to defer to age-old practices, and to use them in new, creative, and exciting ways. That is what tradition is about – keeping together a close, caring, and continuing community linked from the past into the future.

If America is to survive, it too must learn similarly to delight in diversity, to honor landforms, and to defer to the elders, and, most especially, never again to deny or doubt other realities. As a first step, the thousands of years of native civilizations in the Americas must receive their due. Hero Twins, Hare, Raven, and Coyote deserve to be as well known as St. Paul of Tarsus because all worked to make a better world.

After all, to paraphrase Shakespeare, "The measure of all things is human" in multiple versions and incarnations, whether biological, spatial, metaphorical, spiritual, or immortal.

157. Ruth Underhill, <u>Social Organization of the Papago Indians</u> 1939: 163.
158. Richard White, <u>"It's Your Misfortune and None of My Own"</u> ~ A New History of the American West 1991: 410.
159. Walter Crockett, a settler on Whidbey Island in Puget Sound, wrote these incisive words 15 October 1853, See Richard White, <u>Land Use, Environment, and Social Change</u> ~ The Shaping of Island County, Washington 1980: 35.

Endnotes

Endnotes

ABBREVIATIONS USED FOR SERIALS

AAq American Antiquarian
AA American Antiquity
AA-M Memoirs Of the Society for American Archaeology
AAA American Anthropologist
AAA-M Memoirs of the American Anthropological Association
ABC Anthropology in British Columbia
AE American Ethnologist
AES-M Memoirs of the American Ethnological Society
  -P Proceedings of the American Ethnological Society
AL Anthropological Linguistics
AMNH-AP Anthropological Papers of the American Museum of Natural History
An Anthropos
APS-P Proceedings of the American Philosophical Society
  -T Transactions of the American Philosophical Society
AR Anthropological Records
BAAS Reports of the British Academy for the Advancement of Science
BAE-AP Anthropological Papers of the Bureau of American Ethnology
  -AR Annual Report of the Bureau of American Ethnology
  -B Bulletins of the Bureau of American Ethnology
CA Current Anthropology
CUCA Columbia University Contributions to Anthropology
E Ethnology
EH Ethnohistory
En Ethnos
FMNH-AS Anthropological Series of the Field Museum Of Natural History
ICA Selected Papers of the Annual International Congress of Americanists
IJAL International Journal of American Linguistics
IURC Publications of the Indiana University Research Center In Anthropology,
  Folklore, and Linguistics
JAF Journal of American Folklore
JAR(SWJA) Journal of Anthropological Research, formerly SWJA
M Man
MAI-INM Museum of the American Indian, Heye Foundation, Indian Notes and
  Monographs
MS Mercury Series, National Museum of Canada
NARN Northwest Anthropological Research Notes (now JONA)
PA Plains Anthropologist
PP Papers of the Peabody Museum of Harvard University
SMC Smithsonian Miscellaneous Collections
SWJA Southwestern Journal of Anthropology, now JAR
UA-P Anthropological Papers of the University of Alaska
UA-AP Anthropological Papers of the University of Arizona
UC-PAE University of California Publications in American Archaeology and Ethnology
UNM-AP Anthropological Papers of the University of New Mexico
UM-AP Anthropological Papers of the Museum of Anthropology of the University of

Michigan
UW-AP Anthropological Papers of the University of Washington
VFPA Viking Fund Publications in Anthropology
YUPA Yale University Publications in Anthropology

BIBLIOGRAPHY

Adair, James 1930 History of the American Indians. New York: Promontory Press. 508pp. [1775].

Allen, Grover 1920 Dogs of the American Aborigines. Museum of Comparative Zoology of Harvard, Bulletin 63: 429-517.

Anonymous 1930 Index to Volumes 1 to 40 of the Journal of American Folklore. JAF-M 14: 1-106.

Asher, Brad 1995 A Shaman-killing Case on Puget Sound, 1873-1874. American Law and Salish Culture. Pacific Northwest Quarterly 86 (1): 17-24. Winter 1994/95.

Bailey, Garrick A, ed. 1995 The Osage and the Invisible World. From the works of Francis La Flesche. Norman: University of Oklahoma Press.

Balikci, Asen 1970 The Netsilik Eskimo. New York: Natural History Press. 264pp.

Ballard, W. L. 1975 Aspects of Yuchi Morpho-phonology: 163-187 in Crawford, ed.
1978 The Yuchi Green Corn Ceremonial: Form and Meaning. University of California, Los Angeles, American Indian Studies Center.

Barnett, Homer 1953 Innovation: The Basis of Cultural Change. New York: McGraw-Hill.

Barry, Barry 1972 The Beginning of the West: Annals of the Kansas Gateway to the American West, 1540-1854. Topeka: Kansas State Historical Society.

Basso, Keith 1996 Wisdom Sits In Places. Landscape and Language among the Western Apache. Albuquerque: University of New Mexico Press.

Bauxar, J. Joseph 1957 Yuchi Ethno-Archaeology. EH 4 (3): 279-301; 4 (4): 369-464.

Bean, Lowell John 1974 Mukat's People: The Cahuilla Indians of Southern California. Berkeley: University of California Press. 201pp.

Bean, Lowell, and Florence Shipek 1978 Luiseño. California. Robert Heizer, ed. Handbook of North American Indians 8: 550-563.

Benedict, Ruth Fulton 1923 The Concept of the Guardian Spirit in North America. AAA-M 29: 1-97.
1960 Patterns of Culture. New York: Mentor Books. 254pp. [1934].

Berger, Peter and Thomas Luckman 1966 The Social Construction of Reality: A Treatise in the Sociology of Knowledge. Garden City: Doubleday. 219pp.

Berlin, Isiah 1953 The Hedgehog and the Fox: An Essay on Tolstoy's View of History. London: Weidenfeld and Nicolson. 86pp.

Bharati, Agehananda 1965 The Tantric Tradition. London: Rider and Co. 350pp.

Bicchieri, Marco 1972 Hunters and Gatherers Today: A Socio-Economic Study of Eleven Such Cultures in the Twentieth Century. New York: Holt, Rinehart, and Winston. 494pp.

Bidney, David 1967 Theoretical Anthropology. New York: Schocken Books. 528pp. [1953].

Black, Lydia 1988 The Story of Russian America. Crossroads of Continents ~ Cultures of Siberia and Alaska: 70-82. William Fitzhugh and Aron Crowell, eds. Smithsonian

Institution Press.

Black Hawk 1964 Black Hawk: An Autobiography. Urbana: University of Illinois Press.

Blodgett, Harold 1935 Samson Occom. Dartmouth: Manuscript Series 3: 1-230.

Boas, Franz 1916 Tsimshian Mythology. BAE-AR 31: 29-1037.

    1918 Kutenai Tales. BAE-B 59: 1-387.

    1935 Kwakiutl Mythology,,,

Boas, Franz and others 1915 Anthropology in North America. New York: G.E. Stechert and Co. 378pp.

    1916 Phonetic Transcription of Indian Languages: Report of Committee of American Anthropological Association. SMC 66 (6): 1-15.

Bonneyea, Biren 1933 General Index to Annual Reports 1-48 of the Bureau of American Ethnology. BAE-AR 48.

Bourke, John 1891 Scatological Rites of All Nations. A Dissertation upon the Employment of Excrementitious Remedial Agents in Religion, Therapeutics, Divination, Witchcraft, Love-Philters, etc., in all Parts of the Globe. Washington: W.H. Lowdermilk and Co. 496pp.

Bowers, Alfred 1950 Mandan Social and Ceremonial Organization. University of Chicago Press. 407pp.

    1965 Hidatsa Social and Ceremonial Organization. BAE-B 194: 1- 528.

Brasser, Ted 1974 Riding On The Frontier's Crest: Mahican Indian Culture and Culture Change. MS 13: 1-91.

Brinton, Daniel 1896 Left-Handedness In North American Aborginal Art. AAA 09 (5): 175-181.

    1901 The American Race. Philadelphia: David McKay. 392pp.

Brown, Joseph Epes and Black Elk 1971 The Sacred Pipe: Black Elk's Account of the Seven Rites of the Oglala Sioux. London: Penguin Books. 144pp. [1953]

Brown, Paula and Georgeda Buchbinder, eds. 1976 Man and Woman in the New Guinea Highlands. AAA-SP 8: 1–108.

Buckley, Thomas, and Alma Gottlieb 1988 Blood Magic. The Anthropology of Menstruation. University of California Press.

Buckstaff, Ralph 1927 Stars and Constellations of a Pawnee Sky Map. AAA 29: 279-285.

Bunzel, Ruth 1932 Introduction to Zuni Ceremonialism. BAE-AR 47: 469-544.

Burt, Jesse and Robert Ferguson. 1973 Indians of the Southeast: Then and Now. Nashville: Abingdon Press. 304pp.

Calloway, Colin G. 1987 Crown and Calumet. British-Indian Relations, 1783-1815. Norman: University of Oklahoma Press. 345pp.

Calloway, Colin G., ed. 1988 New Directions in American Indian History. Norman: University of Oklahoma Press. 262pp.

Carpenter, Edmund 1973 Eskimo Realities. New York: Holt, Rinehart, and Winston. 224pp.

Catlin, George 1976 O-KEE-PA. A Religious Ceremony and Other Customs of the Mandans. Lincoln: University of Nebraska Press. [1867].

Chafe, Wallace 1962 Estimates Regarding the Present Speakers of North American Indian Languages. IJAL 28 (3): 162-171.

    1965 Corrected Estimates. IJAL 31 (4): 345-346

Chamberlain, Alexander 1892 Report on the Kootenay Indians of South-Eastern British Columbia: 549-615. Report of the British Association for the Advancement of Science

Meeting in Edinburgh.

Chamberlin, Ralph 1908 Animal Names and Anatomical Terms of the Gosiute Indians. Proceedings of the Academy of Natural Sciences of Philadelphia.

1911 The Ethno-botany of the Gosiute Indians of Utah. AAA-M 2 (5): 331-405.

1913 Place and Personal Names of the Gosiute Indians of Utah. APS-P 52 (208): 1-20.

Chamberlin, Von Del 1982 When Stars Came Down to Earth. Ballena Press.

Cobb, John 1917 Pacific Salmon Fisheries. Department of Commerce: Bureau of Fisheries, Document 839: 1-255.

Cohen, Felix 1942 Handbook of Federal Indian Law. Albuquerque: University of New Mexico Press. 662pp.

Cole, Douglas 1973 The Origins of Canadian Anthropology, 1850-1910. Journal of Canadian Studies 8: 33-45.

Collier, John 1963 Indians of the Americas. New York: Mentor Books. 191pp. [1947].

Crocker, Christopher 1973 Ritual and the Development of Social Structure: Liminality and Inversion: 47-86. The Roots of Ritual. James Shaughnessy, ed. Grand Rapids, Michigan: Wm. B. Eerdmans Publishing Co. 251pp.

Crosby, Alfred 1972 The Columbian Exchange: Biological and Cultural Consequences of 1492. Westport, Connecticut: Greenwood Publishing Co. Contributions in American Studies 2: 1-268.

Crawford, James 1973 Yuchi Phonology. IJAL 39: 173-79.

1975 Studies in Southeastern Indian Languages. University of Georgia Press.

ms A Yuchi Conversation.

Crowe, Keith J 1991 A History of the Original People of Northern Canada. Montreal: McGill-Queen's University Press.

Culin, Stewart 1903 Games of the North American Indians. BAE-AR 24.

Curtis, Edward 1924+ The North American Indian. Norwood: Plimpton Press. 20 volumes.

Damas, David, ed. 1984 Arctic. Handbook of North American Indians 5: 511-513.

Davis, Edward 1920 The Papago Ceremony of the Vikita. MAI-INM 3 (4): 157-177.

d'Azevedo, Warren, ed. 1967 The Current Status of Anthropological Research in the Great Basin: 1966. Reno: Desert Research Institute. 379pp.

1986 Great Basin. Handbook of North American Indians 11. 852pp.

De Peyster, Arent 1908 Collections of the State Historical Society of Wisconsin 18: 387-388.

Deloria, Ella Cara Waterlily. Lincoln: University of Nebraska Press. 244pp.

Densmore, Frances 1953 The Belief of the Indian in a Connection Between Song and the Supernatural. BAE-B 151 (37): 217-223.

Dent, Frederick 1979 Federal and State Reservations and Indian Trust Areas. US Department of Commerce. 604pp.

Dewdney, Selwyn 1975 The Sacred Scrolls of the Southern Ojibway. Toronto: University of Toronto Press for Glenbow-Alberta Insititute. 199pp.

Douglas, Mary 1970 Purity and Danger: An Analysis of Concepts of Pollution and Taboo. London: Pelican Books. 220pp.

Driver, Harold, John Cooper, Paul Kirchoff, Dorothy Rainier Libby, William Massey, and Leslie Spier 1953 Indian Tribes of North America. IJAL 19 (3): 1-30.

Driver, Harold and James Coffin 1975 Classification and Development of North American

174

Indian Cultures: A Statistical Analysis of the Driver-Massey Sample. APS-T 65 (3): 1-120.

Drucker, Philip 1965 Cultures of the North Pacific Coast. Scranton: Chandler Publishing Co. 243pp.

Dubois, Cora 1939 The 1870 Ghost Dance. AR 3 (1): 1-151.

Duff, Wilson 1964a The Indian History of British Columbia. The Impact of the White Man. ABC-M 5: 1-117.

1964b Contributions of Marius Barbeau to West Coast Ethnology. Anthropologica 6 (1): 63-96.

Dwyer, Daisy Hilse 1978 Images and Self-Images, Male and Female In Morocco. New York: Columbia University Press. 194pp.

Dyen, Isidore and David Aberle 1974 Lexical Reconstruction: The Case of the Proto-Athapaskan Kinship System. London: Cambridge University Press. 498pp.

Eddy, John 1977 Medicine Wheels and Plains Indian Astronomy: 147-169. Native American Astronomy. Anthony Aveni, ed. Austin: University of Texas Press.

Eggan, Fred 1966 The American Indian: Perspectives for the Study of Social Change. Chicago: Aldine Publishing Co. 193pp.

Eggan, Fred, ed. 1967 Social Anthropology of North American Tribes. Chicago: University of Chicago Press. 574pp. [1937].

Elliott, Henry 1976 Biographical Sketches of Authors on Russian America and Alaska. Anchorage Historical and Fine Arts Museum, Occasional Paper 2. 52pp.

Elmendorf, William 1960 The Structure of Twana Culture, With Comparative Notes on the Structure of Yurok Culture by A.L. Kroeber. Pullman: Washington State University Research Studies 28 (3): 1-576.

Emmons, George Thornton 1991 The Tlingit Indians. Frderica de Laguna, ed. NY: UWP for American Museum of Natural History, Anthropological Paper 70.

1911 The Tahltan Indiens. University of Pennsylvania Museum, Anthropological Papers 4 (1): 1-182.

Epstein, Lawrence 1975 Blood and Thunder: Theories of Causation in Tibet. The Tibetan Society Bulletin 9: 40-45.

Ewers, John 1955 The Horse In Blackfoot Indian Culture, With Comparative Material from other Western Tribes. BAE-B 159: 1-374.

1965 The Emergence of the Plains Indian as the Symbol of the North American Indian. Report of the Smithsonian Institute (1964): 531-544.

Farrell, Brenda 1995 Do You See What I Mean?. Plains Indian Sign Talk and the Embodiment of Action. Austin: University of Texas Press.

Fenton, William 1950a Problems Arising from the Historic Northeastern Position of the Iroquois. Essays in the Historical Anthropology of North America (In Honor of John Swanton). SMC 100: 159-251.

1950b The Role Call of Iroquois Chiefs: A Study of a Mneumonic Cane from the Six Nations Reserve. SMC 111 (15): 1-73.

1987 The False Faces of the Iroquois. Norman: University of Oklahoma Press.

Fenton, William and John Gulick 1961 Symposium on Cherokee and Iroquois Culture. BAE-B 180: 1-275.

Fernandez, James 1974 The Mission of Metaphor in Expressive Culture. CA 15 (2): 119-145.

Fienup-Riordan, Ann 1990 Eskimo Essays. Yup'ik Lives and How We see Them. The Real

People and the Children of Thunder: 71-93. Rutgers University Press.

1991 <u>The Real People and the Children of Thunder</u>. The Yup'ik Eskimo Encounter with Moravian Missionaries John and Edith Kilbuck. University of Oklahoma Press.

1994 <u>Boundaries and Passages</u>. Rule and Ritual in Yup'ik Eskimo Oral Tradition. Norman: University of Oklahoma Press.

Fitting, James, ed. 1973 <u>The Development of North American Archaeology</u>. Garden City: Anchor Books. 309pp.

Flint, Richard Foster 1971 <u>Glacial and Quaternary Geology</u>. New York: John Wiley and Sons. 892pp.

Fogelson, Raymond and Richard Adams, eds. 1977 <u>The Anthropology of Power</u>: Ethnographic Studies from Asia, Oceania, and the New World. New York: Academic Press. 42pp.

Forde, Daryll 1931 Ethnography of the Yuma Indians. UCPAE 28: 83-277.

Fortune, Reo 1932 Omaha Secret Societies. CUCA 14. 193pp.

Foster, George 1944 A Summary of Yuki Culture. AR 5 (3): 154-244.

Foster, Laurence 1935 Negro-Indian Relationships in the Southeast. University of Pennsylvania: Theses (Ph.D.) in Anthropology. 86pp.

Fowler, Catherine 1970 <u>Great Basin Anthropology</u> ... A Bibliography. Reno: Desert Research Insit, Social Science and Humanities Publication 5: 1-418.

Franklin, Fay, ed. 1981 <u>History's Timeline</u>. New York: Crescent Books.

Freeman, John and Murphy Smith 1966 A Guide to the Manuscripts Relating to the American Indian in the Library of the American Philosophical Society. APS-M 65.

Frachtenberg, Leo 1920 Eschatology of the Quileute Indians. AAA 22 (4): 333-340.

1921 The Ceremonial Societies of the Quileute Indians. AAA 23 (3): 320-352.

Gardiner, Howard 1974 <u>The Quest for Mind</u>. New York: Vintage Books. 283pp.

Gearing, Fred 1962 Priests and Warriors: Social Structure of Cherokee Politics in the 18th Century. AAA-M 93, AAA 65 (5), II.

Gifford, Edward 1937 Coast Yuki Myths. JAF 50 (196): 115-172.

1939 The Coast Yuki. An 34, 292-375.

Gilberg, Rolf 1975 Changes in the Life of the Polar Eskimos Resulting from a Canadian Immigration into the Thule District, Northern Greenland, in the 1860s. <u>Folk</u> 16-17: 159-70.

Goddard, Ives 1975 Algonquian, Wiyot, and Yurok: Proving A Distant Genetic Relationship: 249-262. <u>Linguistics and Anthropology</u>: In Honor of C. F. Voegelin. M. Dale Kinkade, Kenneth Hale, and Oswald Werner, eds. Lisse: The Peter de Ridder Press. 720pp.

Goldschmidt, Walter 1951 Ethics and the Structure of Society: An Ethnological Contribution to the Sociology of Knowledge. AAA 53 (4, Part 1): 506-524.

Golla, Susan 1975 Skidi Pawnee Religion: A Structural Analysis. George Washington University: MA Thesis. 95pp.

Goldman, Irving 1975 <u>The Mouth of Heaven</u>: An Introduction to Kwakiutl Religious Thought. New York: John Wiley and Sons. 265pp.

Graburn, Nelson and Stephen Strong 1973 <u>Circumpolar Peoples</u>: An Anthropological Perspective. Pacific Palisades, Ca: Goodyear Publishing Co. 236pp.

Graymont, Barbara 1969 The Tuscarora New Year Festival. New York History 50 (2): 143-163.

Graymont, Barbara, ed. 1973 Clinton Richard, Fighting Tuscarora: The Autobiography of

Chief Clinton Richard.

Grange, Roger 1979 An Archeological View of Pawnee Origins. Towards Plains Caddoan Origins: A Symposium. Nebraska History 60 (2): 134-160.

Grayson, Donald 1977 Pleistocene Avifaunas and the Overkill Hypothesis. Science 195: 691-693.

Greenberg, Joseph 1966 Language Universals. The Hague: Mouton and Co. 89pp.
    1975 Research on Language Universals. Annual Review of Anthropology 4: 75-94. (G 9553).

Griaule, Marcel 1975 Conversations with Ogotemmeli: An Introduction to Dogon Religious Ideas. Oxford: University Press. 230pp.

Griffin, Naomi 1930 The Roles of Men and Women in Eskimo Culture. Chicago: University Press. 113pp.

Griffin, James 1952 Archaeology of the Eastern United States. Chicago: University Press. 392pp.

Grun, Bernard 1979 The Timetables of History. A Horizontal Linkage of People and Events. New York: Simon and Schuster Touchstone Books.

Gullemin, Jeanne 1975 Urban Renegades. The Cultural Strategy of American Indians. New York: Columbia University Press. 336pp.

Haas, Mary 1969 The Prehistory of Languages. The Hague: Mouton. 120pp.

Hall, Robert 1977 An Anthropocentric Perspective for Eastern United States Prehistory. AA 42 (4: 499-518.

Hallowell, A. Irving 1926 Bear Ceremonialism in the Northern Hemisphere. AAA 28 (1): 1-175.
    1942 The Role of Conjuring in Salteau Society. Publications of the Philadelphia Anthropological Society II. Brinton Memorial Series. 96pp.
    1957 The Impact of the American Indian on American Culture. AAA 59 (2): 201-217.
    1960 The Beginnings Of Anthropology in America: 1-90. Selected Papers from the American Anthropologist 1888-1920. Frederica de Laguna, ed. AAA Special Publication. 930pp.
    1963 American Indians, White and Black: The Phenomenon of Transculturation. CA 4 (5): 519-531.
    1967 Culture and Experience. New York: Schocken Books. 434pp.

Halpern, A.L. 1953 A Dualism in Pomo Cosmology. Kroeber Anthropological Society Publications 8/9: 151-159.

Harper, Kenn 1989 Give Me My Father's Body. The Life of Minik, The New York Eskimo. Iqaluit (Frobisher Bay): Blacklead Books.

Harper, J. Russell 1971 Paul Kane's Frontier. Fort Worth: University of Texas Press.

Harrington, M.R. 1913 A Preliminary Sketch of Lenape Culture. AAA 15: 208-235.

Harris, Marvin 1968 The Rise of Anthropological Theory (RAT): A History of the Theories of Culture. New York: Thomas Y. Crowell Co. 806pp.

Hassrick, Royal 1964 The Sioux : Life and Customs of a Warrior Society. Norman: University of Oklahoma Press.

Hatt, Gudmond 1916 Moccasins and Their Relation to Arctic Footwear. AMNH-M 3, 149-250.

Hayes, E. Nelson and Tanya 1970 Claude Levi-Strauss: The Anthropologist As Hero. Cambridge: MIT Press. 264pp.

Helm, June, ed. 1966 Pioneers in American Anthropology: The Uses of Biography.

Seattle: University of Washington Press. 247pp.

1981 <u>Subarctic</u>. Handbook of North American Indians. Volume 6. Smithsonian Institution.

Hendry, Jean 1964 Iroquois Masks and Mask-Making At Onondaga. BAE-B 191: 349-409. BAE-AP 74.

Henriksen, Georg 1973 <u>Hunters in the Barrens</u>: The Naskapi on the Edge of the White Man's World. Memorial University of Newfoundland, Institute of Social and Economic Research Studies 12: 1-130.

Herman, Mary 1956 Wampum as Money in Northeastern North America. EH 3 (1): 21-33.

Herzog, George and others. 1934. Some Orthographic Recommendations. AAA 36 (4): 629-31.

Hewitt, J.N.B. 1910, Tuscarora, Handbook of American Indians North of Mexico. Frederick Hodge, ed. Bureau of American Ethnology, Bulletin 30, Volume 2: 842-853

1920 A Constitutional League of Peace in the Stone Age of America: The League of the Iroquois and its Constitution. SI-AR (1918): 527-545.

Hickerson, Harold 1970 <u>The Chippewa and Their Neighbors</u>: A Study in Ethnohistory. New York: Holt, Rinehart and Winston, Studies in Anthropological Method. 133pp.

Hilbert, Violet 1985 <u>Haboo</u>. Seattle: University of Washington Press.

Hill, W.W. 1939 Stability in Culture and Pattern. AAA 41 (2): 258-260.

1944 The Navaho Indians and the Ghost Dance of 1890. AAA 46 (4): 523-27.

Hirchfelder, Arlene 1970 <u>American Indian Authors</u>: A Representative Bibliography. New York: Association of American Indian Affairs. 45pp.

Hittman, Michael 1973 Ghost Dances, Disillusionment and Opiate Addiction: An Ethnohistory of Smith and Mason Valley Paiutes. Ph.D. Dissertation: University of New Mexico.

1973a The 1870 Ghost Dance at the Walker River Reservation: A Reconstruction. EH 20 (3): 247-278.

1990 <u>Wovoka and the Ghost Dance</u>, A Source Book. Yerington, NV: Yerington Paiute Tribe.

Hockett, Charles 1966 What Algonquian is Really Like. IJAL 32 (1): 59-73.

Hodge, Frederick Webb 1907~10 <u>Handbook of American Indians North of Mexico</u>. BAE-B 30, 2 Volumes.

Hoijer, Harry, ed. 1946 <u>Linguistic Structures of Native America</u>. VFPA 6: 1-423.

Holder, Preston 1970 <u>The Hoe and the Horse on the Plains</u>: A Study of Cultural Development Among North American Indians. Lincoln: University of Nebraska Press. 176pp.

Honigmann, John 1976 <u>The Development of Anthropological Ideas</u>. Homewood, Illinois: The Dorsey Press. 434pp.

Howard, James 1957 The Mescal Bean Cult of the Central and Southern Plains: An Ancestor of the Peyote Cult ? AAA 59 (1): 75-87.

1968 <u>The Southeastern Ceremonial Complex and Its Interpretation</u>. Missouri Archaeological Society Memoir 6.

Hudson's Bay Company 1968 A Brief History of the Hudson's Bay Company. Winnipeg: HBC Archives.

Hudson, Travis and Ernest Underhoy 1978 <u>Crystals in the Sky</u> ~ An Intellectual Odyssey Involving Chumash Astronomy, Cosmology, and Rock Art. Ballena Press Anthropological Papers 10: 1-163.

178

Hunter, Helen 1940 The Ethnography of Salt in Aboriginal North America. University of Pennsylvania: Thesis (Ph.D.). 63pp.

Irwin-Williams, Cynthia, Henry Irwin, George Agogino, and C. Vance Haynes 1973 Hell Gap: Paleo-Indian Occupation on the High Plains. PA 18 (59): 40-53.

Jacobs, Melville 1959 Folklore. Anthropology of Franz Boas. AAA 61 (5), Part 2: 119-138.

Jefferson, Thomas 1964 Notes on the State of Virginia. New York: Harper Torchbooks.

Jenness, Diamond 1955 The Faith of a Coast Salish Indian. ABC 3. 92pp.

Jennings, Francis 1975 The Invasion of America: Indians, Colonialism, and the Cant of Conquest. New York: W.W. Norton. 370pp.
1993 Chronology: 412-421. The Founders of America. How Indians Discovered the Land, Pioneered in it, and Created Great Classical Civilizations; How they were plunged into a Dark Age by Invasion and Conquest; and How they are Reviving. New York: WW Norton.

Jewett, John 1987 The Adventures and Sufferings of John R. Jewett, Captive of Maquinna. Annotated and Illustrated by Hilary Stewart. Seattle: University of Washington Press.

Johnson, Elias 1881 Legends, Traditions and Laws of the Iroquois, or Six Nations, and History of the Tuscarora Indians. Lockport, NY: Union Printing and Publishing.

Johnson, Frank 1968 The Tuscaroras: Mythology, Medicine, and Culture (2 Volumes).

Jones, J.A. 1955 Key to the Annual Reports of the United States Commissioner of Indian Affairs. EH 2 (1): 59-64.

Judd, Neil 1967 The Bureau of American Ethnology, A Partial History. Norman: University of Oklahoma Press. 140pp.

Kan, Sergei 1988 The Russian Orthodox Church in Alaska. History of Indian - White Relations. Handbook of North American Indians 4: 506-521.
1989 Symbolic Immortality. The Tlingit Potlatch of the Nineteenth Century. Smithsonian Institution Press.

Kappler, Charles 1904 Indian Affairs: Laws and Treaties. Vol 2: 1778-1883. DC: GPO.

Kardiner, Abram and Edward Preble 1961 They Studied Man. New York: Mentor Books. 255pp.

Kehoe, Alice 1970 The Function of Ceremonial Sexual Intercourse among the Northern Plains Indians. Plains Anthropologist 15: 99-103.

Kinietz, Vernon 1940 Indians of the Western Great Lakes 1615-1760. University of Michigan, Museum of Anthropology, Occasional Contributions 10: 1-427.

Kinkade, M. Dale 1971 Roster of Linguists Studying North American Indian Languages. IJAL 37 (2): 114-121, 38 (3): 201-202.

Kinkade, M. Dale and J.V. Powell 1976 Language and the Prehistory of North America. World Archaeology 8 (1): 83-100.

Knight, Vernon, Jr 1989 Symbolism of Mississippian Mounds: 279-291. Powhatan's Mantle ~ Indians in the Colonial Southeast. Peter Wood, Gregory Waselkov, and M Thomas Hatley, eds. Lincoln: University of Nebraska Press.

Kroeber, Alfred 1925 Handbook of the Indians of California. BAE-B 78: 1-995.
1927 Arrow Release Distributions. UC-PAE 23 (4): 283-296.
1932 Yuki Myths. An 27: 905-940.
1939 Cultural and Natural Areas of Native North America. Berkeley: University of California Press. 240pp. [1963].

Kroeber, Theodora 1961 Ishi in Two Worlds: A Biography of the Last Wild Indian in America. Berkeley: University of California Press.

Kurath, Gertrude 1964 Iroquois Music and Dance. BAE-B 187: 1- 268.
 1970 Music and Dance of the Tewa Pueblos. Santa Fe: Museum of New Mexico Press, Research Records 8. 309pp.

La Barre, Weston 1970 The Peyote Cult. New York: Schocken Books. 260pp.

La Flesche, Francis 1963 The Middle Five: Indian Schoolboys of the Omaha Tribe. Madison: University of Wisconsin Press. 152pp. [1900].

de Laguna, Frederica 1972 Under Mount Saint Elias: The History and Culture of the Yakutat Tlingit. Washington: Smithsonian Contributions to Anthropology. Volume 7: 1-1395 in 3 Parts.

Laird, Carobeth 1975 Encounter with an Angry God. Banning, California: Malki Museum Press. 190pp.
 1976 The Chemehuevis. Banning, California: Malki Museum Press.
 1979 Limbo. San Francisco: Chandler and Sharp.
 1984 Mirror and Pattern: George Laird's World of Chemehuevi Mythology. Banning, California: Malki Museum Press.

Landes, Ruth 1968 Ojibwa Religion and the Midewiwin. Madison: University of Wisconsin Press. 250pp.
 1970 The Prairie Potawatomi: Tradition and Ritual in the Twentieth Century. Madison: University of Wisconsin Press. 420pp.

Landy, David 1958 Tuscarora Tribalism and National Identity. Ethnohistory 5 (2): 250-84.

Lane, Michael 1970 Introduction to Structuralism. New York: Basic Books. 456pp.

Langdon, Margaret 1974 Comparative Hokan-Coahuiltecan Studies: A Survey and Appraisal. The Hague: Mouton. 114pp.

Lantis, Margaret 1947 Alaskan Eskimo Ceremonialism. AES-M 11: 1-127.

Larrabee, Edward 1976 Recurrent Themes and Sequences in North American Indian-European Contacts. APS-T 66 (7): 1-52pp.

Latorre, Felipe and Dolores 1976 The Mexican Kickapoo. Austin: University of Texas Press. 401pp.

Lawson, John 1967 A New Voyage to Carolina. Hugh Talmage Lefler, ed. UNC Press.

Leach, Edmund 1970 Claude Levi-Strauss. New York: Viking Press. 142pp.
 1976 Culture and Communication: The Logic by Which Symbols Are Connected. Cambridge: University Press. 105pp.

Leacock, Eleanor 1954 The Montagnais "Hunting Territory" and the Fur Trade. AAA-M 78: 1- 59.

Leacock, Eleanor Burke and Nancy Oestreich Lurie 1971 North American Indians in Historical Perspective. New York: Random House. 498pp.

Lieber, Michael 1994 More Than a Living. Fishing and the Social Order on a Polynesian Atoll. Conflict and Social Change Series. Boulder, CO: Westview Press.

Leonhardy, Frank and David Price 1970 A Proposed Culture Typology for the Lower Snake River Region, Southeastern Washington. NARN 4 (1): 1-29.

Leon-Portilla, Miguel 1992 The Broken Spears. The Aztec Account of the Conquest of Mexico. Boston: Beacon Press.

Levi-Strauss, Claude 1944 Reciprocity and Hierarchy. AAA 46: 266-268.
 1969 The Raw and the Cooked. Mythologique 1: Introduction to the Science of Mythology. New York: Harper and Row. 390pp. [1964]
 1973 From Honey to Ashes. Mythologique 2. 512pp. [1966].
 1978 Myth and Meaning. New York: Schocken Books. 54pp.

1979 <u>The Origin of Table Manners</u>. Mythologique 3. 551pp. [1968].

1981 <u>The Naked Man</u>. Mythologique 4. 746pp. [1971].

Liberty, Margot, ed. 1976 <u>American Indian Intellectuals</u>. Proceedings of the AES. St. Paul: West Publishing Co. 248pp.

Liljeblad, Sven, and Catherine Fowler 1986 Owens Valley Paiute. <u>Great Basin</u>. Warren D'Azevedo, ed. Handbook of North American Indians 11: 412-34.

Lindsay, Nicholas Vachel 1923 <u>Collected Poems</u>. New York: MacMillan and Co. (Our Mother Pocahantas: 105-8).

Lindquist, G.E.E. 1923 <u>The Red Man in the United States</u> ~ An Intimate Study Of the Social, Economic, and Religious Life of the American Indian. New York: ??

Lips, Julius 1939 Naskapi Trade: A Study in Legal Acculturation. Journal of the Society of Americanists 31: 129-195.

1947 Notes on Montagnais-Naskapi Economy (Lake St John and Lake Mistassini Bands). En 12 (1-2): 1-77.

Lowie, Robert 1963 <u>Indians of the Plains</u>. Garden City: Anchor Books. 258pp. [1954].

1956 <u>The Crow Indians</u>. New York: Holt, Rinehart, and Winston. [1935].

McClellan, Catherine 1975 My Old People Say: An Ethnographic Survey of Southern Yukon Territory. NMM-PE 6 (1): 2 Parts.

MacCannell, Dean 1976 <u>The Tourist</u>: A New Theory of the Leisure Class. New York: Schocken Books. 214pp.

McCoy, Isaac 1840 <u>History of the Baptist Indian Missions</u>: Embracing Remarks on the Former and Present Conditions of the Aboriginal Tribes, Their Settlement within the Indian Territory and Their Future Prospects. Washington: William M. Morrison. 611pp.

McFeat, Tom 1966 <u>Indians of the Northwest Coast</u>. Seattle: University of Washington Press. 270pp.

McGee, Emma 1915 <u>Life of W J McGee</u>. Farley, Iowa. [p78 Powell 52.08 = McGee 49.73 oz]

McNickle, D'Arcy 1973 <u>Native American Tribalism</u>: Indian Survivals and Renewals. London: Oxford University Press. 190pp.

Makarius, Laura 1973 The Crime of Manabozo. AAA 75 (3): 663-675.

Malefijt, Annemarie de Waal 1974 <u>Images of Man</u>. New York: Alfred Knopf. 410pp.

Malinowski, Bronislaw 1954 <u>Magic, Science and Religion</u>. Garden City: Doubleday Anchor Books. 274pp. [1948].

Malouf, Carling 1940 A Study of the Gosiute Indians of Utah. University of Utah: MA Thesis.

1974 The Gosiute Indians. American Indian Ethnohistory: Shoshone, California, and Basin-Plateau Tribes. David Horr, ed. New York: Garland Publishing Co. 172pp.

Malouf, Carling and Elmer Smith 1947 Some Gosiute Mythological Characters and Concepts. <u>Utah Humanities Review</u> 1 (4): 369-377.

Margolin, Malcolm, ed. 1981 <u>The Way We Lived</u>. California Indian Reminiscences, Stories, and Songs. Berkeley: Heyday Books.

Martin, Calvin 1978 <u>Keepers of the Game</u>: Indian-Animal Relations and the Fur Trade. Berkeley: University of California Press. 226pp.

1987 <u>The American Indian and the Problem of History</u>. Oxford University Press. 232pp.

Mason, Otis Tufton 1894 <u>Woman's Share in Primitive Culture</u>. New York: D. Appleton. 295pp.

Mattingly, H, trans. 1948 <u>Tacitus on Britain and Germany</u>. Penguin Classics.

Mead, Margaret and Ruth Bunzel 1960 <u>The Golden Age of American Anthropology</u>. New York: George Braziller. 630pp.

Merriam, Lewis 1928 <u>The Problem of Indian Administration</u>. DC: Brookings Institution.

Michael, Henry 1963a Studies in Siberian Ethnogenesis. Arctic Institute of North America, Anthropology of the North: Translations From Russian Sources 2: 1-313.

　1963b Studies in Siberian Shamanism. Artic Institute of North America, Anthropology of the North: Translations From Russian Sources 4: 1-229.

Miller, Jay 1972 Priority of the Left. M 7 (4): 646-647.

　1974a Why the World Is on the Back of a Turtle. M 9 (2): 306-8.

　1974b The Delaware As Women: A Symbolic Solution. AE 1 (3): 507-14.

　1975a Kʷulakan: The Delaware Side of Their Movement West. PA 45 (4): 45-6.

　1975b Delaware Alternative Classifications. Anthropological Linguistics 17 (9): 434-444.

　1977 Delaware Anatomy: With Linguistic, Social, and Medical Aspects. AL 19 (4): 144-166.

　1979 A 'Struckon' Model Of Delaware Culture And The Positioning Of Mediators. AE 6 (4): 791-802.

　1980a A Structural Study Of The Delaware Big House Rite. <u>Papers in Anthropology</u> 21 (2): 107-133.

　1980b High-Minded High Gods in North America. An 75: 916-19.

　1980c The Matter of the (Thoughtful) Heart: Centrality, Focality, or Overlap. JAR 36 (3): 338-42.

　1982 People, Berdache, and Left-Handed Bears: Human Variation in Native North America. JAR 38 (3): 274-87.

　1983 Numic Religion: An Overview of Power in the Great Basin of Native North America. Anthropos 78: 337-354.

　1984 <u>The Tsimshian and Their Neighbors</u> Of The North Pacific Coast. Jay Miller and Carol Eastman, eds. Seattle: The University of Washington Press. 344pp.

　1988 <u>Shamanic Odyssey</u>: The Lushootseed Salish Journey to the Land of the Dead. A Comparative Study of the Lushootseed (Puget Salish) Ritualized Journey to the Land of the Dead, in terms of Death, Potency, and Cooperating Shamans in North America. Ballena Press Anthropological Papers 32: 1- 215.

　1989a Delaware Traditions From Kansas: Nakoming to Isaac McCoy. Plains Anthropologist 34 (123): 1-6.

　1989b The Early Years Of Watomika (James Bouchard), Delaware and Jesuit. American Indian Quarterly 13 (2): 165-188.

　1989 An Overview of Northwest Coast Mythology. NARN 23 (2): 125-141.

　1990 <u>Mourning Dove</u>, A Salishan Autobiography. Indian Lives Series. Lincoln: University of Nebraska Press. 210pp. [Paperback, 1994]

　1990 Introduction, Notes for <u>Coyote Stories</u> by Mourning Dove. Lincoln: Bison Books, University of Nebraska Press.

　1991a A Kinship of Spirit: 305-337. AMERICA IN 1492 ~ The World of the Indian Peoples Before the Arrival of Columbus. Alvin Josephy, ed. New York: Random House.

　1991b Delaware Masking. Man in the Northeast 41: 105-110.

　1991c Delaware Personhood. Man in the Northeast 42: 17-27 Fall.

　1991d Art, Attitude, and Appropriation. American Woodturner 6 (4): 17.

1992 Earthmaker. Tribal Stories from Native North America. New York: Perigree Books. 176pp.

1994 The 1806 Purge Among the Indiana Delaware: Sorcery, Gender, Boundaries, and Legitimacy. EH 41 (2): 124-266.

1995 Mourning Dove: Editing in All Directions to "Get Real." SAIL (Studies in American Indian Literatures, Series 2) 7 (2): 65-72, Summer.

1996 Changing Moons: A History of Caddo Religion. PA 41 (157): 243-259.

1997a Old Religion Among the Delawares. EH 44(1): 113-134.

1997b Back to Basics: Chiefdoms in Puget Sound. EH 44(2): 375-387.

1997c Tsimshian Culture: A Light Through the Ages. Lincoln: University of Nebraska Press.

ms Keres Culture and Chaco Canyon.

Miller, Virginia 1979 Ukomno'm: The Yuki Indians of Northern California. Ballena Press Anthropological Papers 14: 1-117.

Mooney, James 1928 The Aboriginal Population of America North of Mexico. SMC 80 (7): 1-20. (Pub 2955).

Moore, John 1974 Cheyenne Political History, 1820-1894. EH 21 (4): 329-359.

Moriarity, James 1969 Chinigchinx: An Indigenous California Indian Religion. Los Angeles: Southwest Museum, Frederick Webb Hodge Anniversary Publication Fund, Volume X.

Morgan, Lewis Henry 1959 Indian Journals. Leslie White, ed. Ann Arbor: University of Michigan Press. 229pp.

1963 Ancient Society. Eleanor Leacock, ed. New York: The World Publishing Co. 570pp. [1877].

Muldoon, James 1975 The Indian as Irishman. Essex Insititute Historical Collections 111 (94): 267-289.

Murphy, Robert 1971 The Dialectics of Social Life: Alarms and Excursions in Anthropological Theory. New York: Basic Books. 261pp.

Nabokov, Peter 1967 Two Leggings: The Making of A Crow Warrior. New York: Thomas Y Crowell.

1991 Native American Testimony. A Chronicle of Indian - White Relations from Prophesy to the Present, 1492-1992. New York: Penguin Books.

Needham, Rodney, ed. 1973 Right and Left: Essays on Dual Symbolic Classification. Chicago: University of Chicago Press. 449pp.

Neihardt, John 1961 Black Elk Speaks: Being The Life History of a Holy Man of the Oglala Sioux. Lincoln: University of Nebraska Press. 221pp.

Nettl, Bruno 1954 North American Indian Musical Styles. Philadelphia: American Folklore Society 45: 1-51.

Newcomb, William 1961 The Indians of Texas: From Prehistoric to Modern Times. University of Texas Press. 404pp.

1974 North American Indians: An Anthropological Perspective. Pacific Palisades, Ca: Goodyear Publishing Co.

Nichols, Frances 1954 Index to Schoolcraft's Indian Tribes of the United States. BAE-B 152: 1- 257.

Oliver, Symmes Chadwick 1962 Ecology and Cultural Continuity as Contributing Factors in the Social Organization of Plains Tribes. UC-PAE 48 (1): 1-90.

Olson, Ronald 1933 Clan and Moiety in Native America. UC-PAE 33 (4): 351-422.

Oosten, Jarich Gerlof 1976 The Theoretical Structure of the Religion of the Netsilik and Iglulik. Meppel: Krips Repro. 107pp.

Opler, Morris 1977 The Creek Indian Towns of Oklahoma in 1937. University of Oklahoma, Papers in Anthropology 13.

Ortiz, Alfonso 1969 The Tewa World: Person, Time, Being, and Becoming in a Pueblo Indian Society. Chicago: University Press. 197pp.

Ortner, Sherry 1974 Is Female to Male as Nature Is to Culture: 67-87. Woman, Culture, and Society. Michelle Rosaldo and Louise Lamphere, eds. Sanford: University Press.

Oswalt, Roger, James Deetz, and Anthony Fisher 1967 The North American Indians: A Sourcebook. New York: MacMillan. 752pp.

Pandey, Triloki Nath 1972 Anthropologists at Zuni. APS-P 116 (4): 321-337.

Park, Willard 1937 Paviotso Polyandry. AAA 39 ( ): 366-8.
     1938 Shamanism in Western Native America. Evanston: Northwestern University Press.

Parks, Douglas, and Waldo Wedel 1985 Pawnee Geography, Historical and Sacred. Great Plains Quarterly 5 (Summer): 143-76.

Parks, Douglas 2001 Pawnee. Plains. Raymond De Mallie, ed. DC: Smithsonian Handbook of North American Indians, Volume 13, Part I: 515-547.

Paz, Octavio 1974 Conjunctions and Disjunctions. New York: Viking. 148pp.

Pearson, Bruce 1973 A Grammar of Delaware: Semantics, Morpho-Syntax, Lexicon, Phonology. University of California at Berkeley: Ph.D. Dissertation.

Perrone, Bobette, H. Henrietta Stockel, and Victoria Krueger 1989 Medicine Women, Curanderas, and Women Doctors. Norman: University of Oklahoma Press. 252pp.

Phinney, Archie 1934 Nez Perce Texts. CUCA XXV (25): 1-497.

Piaget, Jean 1970 Structuralism. New York: Basic Books. 153pp.

Pierce, Richard Russian and Soviet Eskimo and Indian Policies. History of Indian - White Relations. Handbook of North American Indians 4: 119-127.

Pope, Saxon 1962 Bows and Arrows. Berkeley: University of California Press. 83pp.

Powell, Jay, and Fred Woodruff 1976 Quileute Dictionary. NARN, Memoir 3.

Powell, Jay and Vickie Jensen 1976 Quileute ~ An Introduction to the Indians of La Push. Seattle: University of Washington Press.

Powers, Marla 1986 Oglala Women: Myth, Ritual, and Reality. University of Chicago Press.

Powers, William 1975 Oglala Religion. Lincoln: University of Nebraska Press. 233pp.

Price, Monroe 1973 Law and the American Indian. Readings, Notes, and Cases. Indianapolis: Bob Merrill. 807pp.

Prince, Dyneley 1912 An Ancient New Jersey Indian Jargon. AAA 14: 508-524.

Prucha, Francis Paul 1975 Documents of United States Indian Policy. Lincoln: University of Nebraska Press. 278pp.
     1984 The Great Father: The United States Government and the American Indians. Lincoln: University of Nebraska Press.

Quimby, George 1979 A Brief History of WPA Archaeology: 110-123. The Uses of Anthropology.

Radin, Paul 1944 The Story of the American Indian. New York: Liveright Publishing Co. 391pp. [1927].

Rasmusen, Knud 1931 The Netsilik Eskimos. Reports of the Fifth Thule Expedition 8.

Ray, Arthur J 1988 The Hudson's Bay Company and Native People. History of Indian -

White Relations. Handbook of North American Indians 4: 335-350.

Ray, Verne   1933   The Sanpoil and Nespelem: Salishan Peoples of Northeastern Washington. UWPA 5: 1-237.

1939   Cultural Relations in the Plateau of Northwestern America.   Los Angeles: Southwest Museum. 154pp.

Rees, Alwyn and Brinley   1961   Celtic Heritage: Ancient Tradition In Ireland and Wales. London: Thames and Hudson. 428pp.

Reichard, Gladys   1934   Understatement or Naivete. American Speech 9 (3): 19x-204.

1951   Navaho Grammar. New York; J.J. Augustin. AES-PXXI (21): 1-393.

Reichel-Dolmatoff, Geraldo   1971   Amazonian Cosmos: The Sexual and Religious Symbolism of the Tukano Indians. University of Chicago Press. 290pp.

Rice, Stuart   1931   Methods in Social Science, A Case Book. University of Chicago Press.

Riddington, Robin   1968   The Medicine Fight: An Instrument of Political Process Among the Beaver Indians. AAA 70 (6): 1152-1160.

1969   Kin Categories Versus Kin Groups: A Two-Section System Without Sections.   E 8 (4): 460-67.

1976   Wechuge and Windigo: A Comparison of Cannibal Belief Among Boreal Forest Athpaskans and Algonkians. Anthropologica 18 (2): 107-129.

1978   Swan People: A Study of the Dunne-Za Prophet Dance. NMM-MS 38: 1-132.

1980   Trails of Meaning.   pp. 265-68 in The World Is Sharp as a Knife.   An Anthropolgy in Honor of Wilson Duff.   Donald Abbott, ed.   Victoria, BC: British Columbia Provincial Museum.

1988   Trail to Heaven.   Knowledge and Narrative in a Northern Native Community. Ames: University of Iowa Press. 301pp.

1990   Little Bit Know Something.   Stories in a Language of Anthropology.   Ames: University of Iowa Press. 281pp.

Ritzenthaler, Robert and Pat   1970   The Woodland Indians of the Western Great Lakes. Garden City: Anchor Books. 178pp.

Roe, Peter   1982   The Cosmic Zygote.   Cosmology in the Amazon Basin.   New Brunswick: Rutgers University Press.

Rohner, Ronald   1966   Franz Boas, Ethnographer on the Northwest Coast.   Pioneers in American Anthropology, The Uses of Biography.   June Helm, ed.   Seattle: University of Washington Press. AES-M 43: 150-247.

Romero, Javier   1970   Dental Mutilation, Trephination, and Cranial Deformation (in Middle America).   Handbook of South American Indians.   T.D. Steward, ed.   Volume 9: 50-67. Austin: University of Texas Press.

Romney, A Kimball   1957   The Genetic Model and The Uto-Aztecan Time Perspective. Davidson Journal of Anthropology 3: 35-41.

Rooth, Anna Birgetta   1957   The Creation Myths of the North American Indians.   Anthropos 52: 497-508.

Rosman, Abraham and Paula Rubel   1971   Feasting with Mine Enemy.   New York: Columbia University Press.

Rossi, Ino, ed. 1974   The Unconscious in Culture: The Structuralism Of Claude Levi-Strauss in Perspective. New York: E.P. Dutton.

Rossman, Douglas   1988   Where Legends Live.   A Pictorial Guide to Cherokee Mythic Places. Cherokee, NC: Cherokee Publications. 48pp.

Rostlund, Erhard   1952   Freshwater Fish and Fishing in Native North America.   Berkeley:

University of California Publications in Geography 9: 1-313.

Royce, Charles 1899 Indian Land Cessions. BAE-AR 18 (2).

Rudes, Blair, and Dorothy Crouse 1987 The Tuscarora Legacy of JNB Hewitt. NMC: 2 Volumes.

Sabo III, George 1992 Paths of Our Children: Historic Indians of Arkansas. Arkansas Archaeological Survey, Popular Series 3. 144pp.

Sapir, Edward. 1915. Abnormal Types of Speech in Nootka. Ottawa: Canada Department of Mines, Anthropology Series 62 (5): 1-21.

1916 Time Perspective in Aboriginal American Culture: A Study in Method. Ottawa: Canada Department of Mines, Geological Survey Memoir 90, Anthropology Series 13: 1-87.

1929 Central and North American Languages. Encyclopedia Britannica 5: 138-141.

1949 Language. New York: Harcourt, Brace and World. 242pp. [1921].

Schaeffer, Claude 1949 Wolf and Two-Pointed Buck: A Lower Kutenai Tale of the Supernatural World. PM 22 (1/2): 1-22.

1965 The Kutenai Female Berdache: Courier, Guide, Prophetess, and Warrior. EH 12 (3): 193-236.

1966 Bear Ceremonialism of the Kutenai Indians. Browning: Museum of the Plains Indian, Studies in Plains Anthropology and History 4: 1-54.

1969 Blackfoot Shaking Tent. Calgary: Glenbow-Alberta Institute Occasional Paper 5: 1-38.

Schele, Linda, and David Freidel 1990 A Forest of Kings: 26-33. The Untold Story of the Ancient Maya. New York: William Morrow.

Scherman, Katharine 1981 The Flowering of Ireland. Saints, Scholars, and Kings. Boston: Little, Brown and Co.

Schoenberg, Wilfred 1962 A Chronical of Catholic History of the Pacific Northwest: 1743-160. Portland: Catholic Sentinel Printing. 570pp.

Schmidt, Fr Wilhelm 1933 High Gods in North America. Oxford University Press. 149pp.

Sebeok, Thomas, ed. 1976 Native Languages of the Americas. New York: Plenum Press. Volume I. 630pp.

Shapiro, Warren 1970 The Ethnography of Two-Section Systems. E 9 (4): 380-388.

Shafer, Robert 1952 Athapaskan and Sino-Tibetan. IJAL 18 (): 12-19.

Sharp, Henry 1976 Man:Wolf::Woman:Dog. Arctic Anthropology 13 (1): 25-34.

Sheehan, Bernard 1973 Seeds of Extinction: Jeffersonian Philanthropy and the American Indian. Chapel Hill: University of North Carolina Press.

Shelford, Victor 1963 The Ecolocy of North America. Urbana: University of Illinois Press. 610pp.

Siebert, Frank 1967 The Original Home of the Proto-Algonquian Languages. Contributions To Anthropology: Linguistics I (Algonquian). NMM-AS 78 (Bulletin 214): 13-47. 162pp.

Simmons, Leo 1969 Sun Chief: The Autobiography of a Hopi Indian. New Haven: Yale University Press. 460pp. [1942].

Sinclair, A.T. 1909 Tattooing of the North American Indians. AAA 11 ( ): 362-400.

Slotkin, J.S. 1965 Readings in Early Anthropology. Chicago: Aldine. 530pp.

Smith, Marian 1940 The Puyallup-Nisqually. CUCA 32: 1-336.

Snellgrove, David, and Hugh Richardson 1968 A Cultural History of Tibet. New York: Frederick A Praeger.

Speck, Frank 1909 Ethnology of the Yuchi Indians. University of Pennsylvania Museum 1 (1): 1-154.

1915a The Family Hunting Band as the Basis of Algonkian Social Organization. American Anthropologist 17: 289-305.

1915b The Eastern Algonkian Wabanaki Confederacy. American Anthropologist 17: 492-508.

1917 Game Totems Among the Northeastern Algonkians. American Anthropologist 19: 9-18.

1928 Native Tribes and Dialects of Connecticut. BAE-AR 43: 205-287.

1933 Notes on the Life of John Wilson, the Revealer of Peyote, as Recalled by His Nephew, George Anderson. The General Magazine and Historical Chronicle 35: 539-556.

1935 Naskapi, The Savage Hunters of the Labrador Peninsula. Norman: University of Oklahoma Press.

1945 The Iroquois: A Study in Cultural Evolution. Cranbrook Institute of Science. Bulletin 23: 1-84.

Spencer, Robert, Jesse Jennings, and others 1977 The Native Americans: Ethnology and Backgrounds of the North American Indians. New York: Harper and Row. 584pp. [1965].

Spier, Leslie 1921 The Sun Dance of the Plains Indians: Its Development and Diffusion. AMNH-AP 16 (7): 453-529.

Spier, Leslie, Irving Hallowell, and Stanley Newman, eds. 1960 Language, Culture, and Personality: Essays in Memory of Edward Sapir. Salt Lake City: University of Utah Press. [1941].

Spindler, George and Louise 1957 American Indian Personality Types and Their Sociocultural Roots. The Annals of the American Academy of Political and Social Science: 147-156.

Spiro, Melford, ed. 1965 Context and Meaning in Cultural Anthropology: in Honor of A. Irving Hallowell. New York: The Free Press. 442pp.

Spitzka, Edward Anthony 1903 A Study of the Brain of the Late Major J.W. Powell. AAA 5 (4): 583-643.

Spuhler, James 1951 Some Genetic Variations in American Indians. Physical Anthropology of the American Indian: 172-202.

Staden, Hans 1557 The True History of His Captivity. Marburg, Germany. Republished 1929. The Argonaut Series. Malcolm Letts, trans. and ed. New York: Robert M. McBride and Company.

Standing Bear, Luther 1978 Land of the Spotted Eagle. Lincoln: University of Nebraska Press. 259pp. [1933].

Stemple, Ruth 1963 Author - Subject Index to Articles in Smithsonian Annual Reports 1849-1961. SI #4503: 1-200.

Steward, Julian 1931 The Ceremonial Buffoon of the American Indian. Papers of the Michigan Academy of Science, Arts, and Letters. 14: 187-207.

1938 Basin - Plateau Aboriginal Sociopolitical Groups. BAE-B 120: 1-346.

Stewart, T.D. 1973 The People of America. New York: Charles Scribner's Sons. 262pp.

Stewart, T.D. and Marshall Newman 1951 A Historical Resume of the Concept of Differences in Indian Types. AAA 53 (1): 19-36.

Stocking, George 1974 The Boas Plan for the Study of American Indian Languages: 454-

484. <u>Tradition and Paradigms</u>: Studies in the History of Linguistics. Dell Hymes, ed. Bloomington: University of Indiana Press.

Straus, Anne S 1975 Northern Cheyenne Ethnopsychology. <u>Ethnos</u> 5 (3): 326-57.

1978 The Meaning of Death in Northern Cheyenne Culture. <u>Plains Anthropologist</u> 23 (79): 1-6.

Stonechild, Blair, and Bill Waiser 1997 <u>Loyal till Death, Indians and the North-West Rebellion</u>. Calgary: Fifth House Publishers.

Strong, William Duncan 1927 An Analysis of Southwestern Society. AAA 29 (1): 1-61.

Sullivan, Lawrence E 1989 <u>Native American Religions</u>: North America. New York: MacMillan Publishing Co. 220pp.

Susman, Amelia 1976 The Round Valley Indians of California. An Unpublished Chapter in <u>Acculturation in Seven (or Eight) American Indian Tribes</u>. Contributions of the University of California, Archaeological Research Facility 31: 1-120.

Suttles, Wayne 1977 The 'Coast Salish' of the Georgia - Puget Basin – Another Look. Puget Soundings. April.

1987 <u>Coast Salish Essays</u>. Seattle: University of Washington Press. 320pp.

Suttles, Wayne, ed. 1990 <u>Northwest Coast</u>. Handbook of North American Indians. Volume 7. Smithsonian Institution.

Svensson, Frances 1973 <u>The Ethnics in American Politics</u>: American Indians. Minneapolis: Burgess Publishing Co. 53pp.

Swan, James 1870 The Indians of Cape Flattery, At the Entrance to the Straight of Fuca, Washington Territory. Smithsonian Contributions to Knowledge 16 (#220): 1-108.

Swanson, Earl, ed. 1970 <u>Languages and Cultures of Western North America</u>: Essays in Honor of Sven Liljeblad. Pocatello: The Idaho State University Press. 288pp.

Swanton, John 1928 Social Organization and Social Usages of the Indians of the Creek Confederacy. BAE-AR 42: 25-472.

1928a Religious Beliefs and Medical Practices of the Creek Indians. BAE-AR 42: 473-672.

1928b Aboriginal Culture of the Southeast. BAE-AR 42: 673-726.

Tantaquidgeon, Gladys 1972 <u>Folk Medicines of the Delaware and Related Algonkian Indians</u>. Harrisburg: The Pennsylvania Historical and Museum Commission, Anthropological Series 3: 1-145. [1942].

Tedlock, Dennis 1985 <u>Popul Vuh</u>. The Mayan Book of the Dawn of Life. New York: Simon and Schuster Touchstone Books.

Thompson, Stith 1966 <u>Tales of the North American Indians</u>. Bloomington: Indiana University Press. 386pp. [1929].

Toelken, Barre 1979 <u>The Dynamics of Folklore</u>. Boston: Houghton Mifflin. 395pp.

Tooker, Elizabeth 1970 <u>The Iroquois Ceremonial of Midwinter</u>. Syracuse: University Press. 189pp.

Trigger, Bruce 1978 Northeast . Smithsonian Handbook of North American Indians, Volume 15.

Trowbridge, Charles Christopher 1939 Shawnee Traditions. Vernon Kinietz and Erminie W. Voegelin, eds. University of Michigan, Museum of Anthropology, Occasional Contributions 9. 71pp.

Turney-High, Harry Holbert 1941 Ethnography of the Kutenai. AAA-M 56: 1-202.

Umiker-Sebeok, D Jean and Thomas A Sebeok 1978 <u>Aboriginal Sign Language of the Americas and Australia</u>. Volume 2: The Americas and Australia. New York: Plenum

188

Press.

Underhill, Ruth 1938 A Papago Calendar Record. UNM-AS 2 (5): 1-66.
  1939 Social Organization of the Papago Indians. CUCA 30: 1-280.
  1946 Papago Indian Religion. CUCA 33: 1-359.
  1965 Red Man's Religion. Chicago: University Press.

Vanstone, James 1965 The Changing Culture of the Snowdrift Chipewyan. NMC-B 208 (-AS 74): 1-131.
  1974 Athapaskan Adaptations: Hunters and Fishermen of the Subarctic Forests. Chicago: Aldine. 145pp.

Varenne, Herve 1977 Americans Together: Structural Diversity in a Midwestern Town. New York: Teacher's College Press. 242pp.

Voegelin, Charles 1952 The Boas Plan for the Presentation of American Indian Languages. APS-P 96 (4): 439-451.

Wagner, Gunter 1931 Yuchi Tales. AES-P 8: 1-357.

Walker, Deward 1970 Systems of North American Witchcraft and Sorcery. University of Idaho, Anthropological Monographs 1. 295pp.
  1972 The Emergent Native Americans: A Reader in Culture Contact. Boston: Little and Brown. 818pp.

Walker, Willard 1969 Notes on Native Writing Systems and the Design of Native Literacy Programs. AL 11 (5): 148-166.
  1975 The Proto-Algonquians: 633-647. Linguistics and Anthropology: In Honor of C.F. Voegelin. M. Dale Kinkade, Kenneth Hale, and Oswald Werner, eds. Lisse: The Peter de Ridder Press. 720pp.

Wallace, Anthony F.C. 1952 The Modal Personality Structure of the Tuscarora Indians, As Revealed by the Rorschach Tests. BAE-B 150: 1-120.
  1969 The Death and Rebirth of the Seneca. New York: Vintage Books. 395pp.
  2012 Tuscarora ~ A History. Albany: State University of New York Press.

Walsh, Jane MacLaren 1976 John Peabody Harrington: The Man and His California Indian Fieldnotes. Ballena Press: Anthropology Series 6: 1-58.

Ward, Martha C. 1989 Nest in the Wind. Adventures in Anthropology on a Tropical Island. Prospect Heights, IL: Waveland Press

Warren, William 1885 History of the Ojibways, Based Upon Traditions and Oral Statements. Collections of the Minnesota Historical Society 5: 1-527.

Washburn, Wilcomb, ed. 1964 The Indian and the White Man. Garden City: Anchor Books. 480pp.
  1988 History of Indian - White Relations. Handbook of North American Indians #4. Smithsonian Institution.

Weinman, Paul 1969 A Bibliography of the Iroquoian Literature. New York State Museum and Science Service Bulletin 411: 1-254.

Weltfish, Gene 1971 The Lost Universe: The Way of Life of the Pawnee. New York: Ballantine Books. 617pp. [1965].

White, Leslie 1966 The Social Organization of Ethnological Theory. Rice University Studies 52 (4): 1-66.

White, Raymond 1963 Luiseño Social Organization. UC-PAE 48 (2): 91-194.

White, Richard 1980 Land Use, Environment, and Social Change. The Shaping of Island County, Washington. Seattle: University of Washington Press.
  1991 "It's Your Misfortune and None of My Own." A New History of the American

West. Norman: University of Oklahoma Press.

Widmer, Randolph J. 1988 The Evolution of the Calusa. A Nonagricultural Chiefdom on the Southwest Florida Coast. Tuscaloosa: University of Alabama Press.

Wildschut, William 1975 Crow Indian Medicine Bundles. John Ewers, ed. Contributions from the Museum of the American Indian, Heye Foundation, 17: 1-178, 68 plates.

Willey, Gordon 1966 An Introduction to American Archaeology. Volume I: North and Middle America. Englewood Cliffs: Prentice-Hall. 526pp.

Ted Williams 1976, The Reservation. Syracuse U Press.

Winter, George 1948 The Journals and Indian Paintings of George Winter, 1837-1839. Indianapolis: Indiana Historical Society.

Wissler, Clark 1917 The American Indian. New York: MacMillan.
1926 The Relation of Nature to Man in Aboriginal America. New York: Oxford University Press. 248pp.

Witherspoon, Gary 1975 Navaho Kinship and Marriage. University of Chicago Press. 137pp.
1977 Language and Art in the Navajo Universe. Ann Arbor: University of Michigan Press.

Witthoft, John 1949 Green Corn Ceremonialism in the Eastern Woodlands. UM-AP 13: 1-91.

Wolff, Hans 1951 Yuchi Text With Analysis. IJAL 17: 48-53.

Woodman, David Unravelling the Franklin Mystery: Inuit Testimony. Montreal: McGill-Queen's University Press.

Wright, Muriel 1977 A Guide to the Indian Tribes of Oklahoma. Norman: University of Oklahoma Press. 300pp.

Yanovsky, Elias 1936 Food Plants of the North American Indians. United States Department of Agriculture, Miscellaneous Publication 237: 1-83.

Zeisberger, David 1910 History of the North American Indian. Archer Butler Hulbert and Rev. William Nathaniel Schwarze, eds. Columbus: Ohio Archaeological and Historical Quarterly 19 (1-2): 1-189.

Important general sources are the Handbook of American Indians North of Mexico (BAE-B 30) and the Handbook of North American Indians (20 volumes, already published are 4 Indian – White Relations, 5 Arctic, 6 Subractic, 7 Northwest Coast, 8 California, 9 Southwest (Pueblo), 10 Southwest (others), 11 Great Basin, 12 Plateau, 13 Plains, 15 Northeast, and 17 Languages).

ACKNOWLEDGEMENTS

Throughout, my families of Millers, Toulouses, Dunns, Liebers, and Chesnins. More individually, Florence Hawley Ellis, Cynthia Irwin Williams, Philip Bock, Nibs Hill, Stanley Newman, Mary Elizabeth Smith, John, Peggy, Stella, Luceen Latorre Dunn, Michael Hittman, Bruce Rigsby, Alfonso Ortiz, Robin Fox, Margaret Bacon, Yehudi Cohen, Warren Shapiro, Mark Leone, Esther Goldfrank, Karl Wittfogel, Raymond Fogelson, Sam Stanley, William Fenton, Fred & Joan Eggan, Alice Kehoe, Don & Catherine Fowler, Sven & Astrid Liljeblad, Terry Strauss, Colin Calloway, Raymond De Mallie, Douglas Parks, Harvey

Markovitz, Ruth Hamilton, Violet Brown, Donald Fixico, Fred Hoxie, LaVonne Brown Ruoff, Dick Shiels, Jackie Royster, Brad Lepper, Joe Saunders, Jay Johnson.

Ernie, Lynne Jodi, Cameron Hill, John & Helen Clifton, Oliver & Kristi Clifton, Marjorie Halpin, Viola Garfield, Erna Gunther, Wayne Suttles, Dale Kinkade, JV & Vickie Powell, Dell and Virginia Hymes, Warren Snyder, Patrick Twohy SJ, Michael Fitzpatrick SJ, Ray Bucko SJ, Vi & Don Hilbert, Robert Rudine & Janet Yoder, Pam Amoss, Christopher Roth, Pam Cahn, Ed Davis, Lawrence Webster, Isadore & Jackie Tom.

Gladys Tantaquidgeon, Nora Thompson Dean, Lucy Blalock, Lillie Whitehorn, Isabel Arcasa, Adeline & Larry Fredin, Jim Rementer, Linda Poolaw, TB & Pearl Charlie, Christine Sam, Fred Bruner, Barney Leader, Alfred Berryhill, Agnes Wagosh, Frances Ashanany, Christine & Charles Quintasket, Juliann Timentwa, Herman Friedlander, Sue Matt, Jerome & Mary Miller, Shirley Palmer, Lucy Covington, Emily Peone, Richard & Nora Dauenhauer, Marilyn Richen, Tammt Jackson, Ann Schuh, Joanne Miller & Joe Kfouri, Donna Steinburn, Andy & Nancy Core, Glenn Williams & Dottie Heck, Roland Wildman, Gerald Eck, Diana Riesky, Gerry DeLay, Larry & Michiko Epstein, Hiroko Roe, and, as always, Monday Nite.

Index

#f = entries scattered before & after this specified page number
#0f = entries scattered for ten pages after this specified page number: 10f, 20f ... 120f

Help defeat typo-gnomes

Proof reading has no mercy

Please report all offenders

Sold @ Amazon.com

Index

ACCULTURATING AMELIA ~ Round Valley 1937 California
ALASKA EDGE ISLAND ~ Siberian Yupiks of St Lawrence Island
ALLIED MOUNDS ~ Touching the Earth, Modeling the World, Reaching the Sky
ANIMAL PEOPLE ADVENTURES ~ Native North American Tribal Stories
AT BAY ~ Cultures Converging through Southwest Washington   > 5
BALLARD BULWARK ~
CHACO ECHOES ~ Pervasive Keresan Priesthoods
CHACOKIA ~ Chaco, Cahokia, Cities & Ceremonies ~ Bundles & Blood Lines Centuries Ago
CHINOOK CONCERNS ~ Emma Millett Luscier, Isabella Bertrand, Verne Ray
CIRCLING FOUR CORNERS ~ Re-Viewing Native American Indiens   > 10
CROSSING ~ LINES: An Educational Memoir of Native North America
DEL-AWARE ~ Lenape Legacies
DELAWARE INTEGRITY ~ Rituals, Removals, Reforms by Lenape Indiens
DISCLAIMING TREATIES I ~ Puget Tribes 1927 Testimonies
DISCLAIMING TREATIES II ~ Puget Tribes 1927 Testimonies   > 15
ELDERS' DIALOG ~ Ed Davis & Vi Hilbert Discuss Native Puget Sound Language, Culture, & Heritage
EVERGREEN ETHNOGRAPHIES ~ Hoh, Chehalis, Suquamish, and Snoqualmi of Western Washington
FEDERAL FISH FILES ~ Swindell 1942 Treaty Rights Report
GEORGE GIBBS NORTHWEST ARRAY ~ Full Reports, Place Names, Word List, Artifact Names, and Guide
GRASSROOTS JANET ~ Advancing Salish and Traditional Cultures   > 20
HERMAN HAEBERLIN REGAINED ~ Anthropology and Artifacts of Puget Sound 1916-17
HERSTORY NW ~ Women Upholding Native Traditions
INDIEN ~ ETHNOGRAPHY: Cultural Traditions of Native North America
INDIEN ~ ETHNOLOGY: Grounded, Gendered, Meaningful Cultural Traditions
LESCHI IN LOVE ~ A Novel of Native Puget Sound > x2   > 25
MARCO MUCK MASKS ~ Frank Cushing on Marshes and Mounds
MINTER BAY ~ Land, Lore, Loss, and Lucre in the South Salish Sea
NATIVE MET HOW ~ Improving Posterity
OLD LUKH ~ A Novel of Native Puget Sound Daily Life, Places, and Stories
OVER THE FALLS ~ Sdoqwalbixw Survivance Surrounding Seattle   > 30
PACIFIC PLATEAU PORTRAYALS ~ People Places Ponderings
RAY'S ARRAY ~ Raymond D Fogelson's Works
RIGHTING NATIVE PLACES ~ Adventures in Northwest Geography
SAHAPTINS STUDIES ~ Columbia River Plateau, Cora Du Bois, Homer Garner Barnett, Gerald Raymond Desmond
SDOQWALBIXW   > 35
SOUND SALISH STRAITS ~ Central Salish Sea Cultures
UNSETTLING SEATTLE ~ Arresting Local Talent and Academic Illiteracy
WRITING WORDS IN WARY WORLDS ~ World Wide Improved Spellings of Native America Languages

JONA Memoirs

RESCUES, RANTS, & RESEARCHES ~ A Re-View of Jay Miller's Writings on Northwest Indien Cultures ~ #9
TRIBAL TRIO of the Northwest Coast by Kenneth D Tollefson ~ #10   > 40
INTERWEAVING COAST SALISH CULTURAL SYSTEMS ~ Collected Works of Pamela Thorsen Amoss ~ #14

University of Nebraska Press

ANCESTRAL MOUNDS ~ Vitality and Volatility Crossing Native North America 2015
HONNE ~ The Spirit of the Chehalis 2015

Jay Miller's books & E-books @ Amazon.com